Inventing Eleanor

Inventing Eleanor

The Medieval and Post-Medieval Image of Eleanor of Aquitaine

Michael R. Evans

Bloomsbury Academic
An imprint of Bloomsbury Publishing Plc

B L O O M S B U R Y
LONDON · OXFORD · NEW YORK · NEW DELHI · SYDNEY

Bloomsbury Academic

An imprint of Bloomsbury Publishing Plc

50 Bedford Square
London
WC1B 3DP
UK

1385 Broadway
New York
NY 10018
USA

www.bloomsbury.com

Bloomsbury is a registered trade mark of Bloomsbury Publishing Plc

First published 2014
Paperback edition first published 2016

British Library Cataloguing-in-Publication Data
A catalogue record for this book is available from the British Library.

ISBN: HB: 978-1-4411-6900-6
PB: 978-1-4742-7918-5
ePDF: 978-1-4411-4135-4
ePub: 978-1-4411-4603-8

Library of Congress Cataloging-in-Publication Data
Evans, Michael R., 1967-
Inventing Eleanor : the medieval and post-medieval image of
Eleanor of Aquitaine / Michael R. Evans.
pages cm
Includes bibliographical references and index.
ISBN 978-1-4411-6900-6 – ISBN 978-1-4411-4135-4 (ePDF) – ISBN 978-1-4411-4603-8 (ePub)
1. Eleanor, of Aquitaine, Queen, consort of Henry II, King of England, 1122?-1204.
2. Great Britain–History–Henry II, 1154-1189–Biography. 3. Louis VII, King of France,
approximately 1120-1180–Marriage. 4. Henry II, King of England, 1133-1189–Marriage.
5. France–History–Louis VII, 1137-1180–Biography. 6. Queens–Great Britain–Biography.
7. Queens–France–Biography. I. Title.
DA209.E6E93 2014
942.03'1092–dc23
2014004171

Typeset by Integra Software Services Pvt. Ltd.
Printed and bound in Great Britain

Contents

Acknowledgements

Like the best Hollywood historical epic, this book was years in the making and has a cast of thousands. It began ten years ago with a twenty-minute paper on Niketas Choniates and Eleanor's role in the Second Crusade, a small portion of which made its way into the final version of this book. Thomas Asbridge and Susan Edgington encouraged me to work on turning some of the ideas in that paper into a book-length work on how Eleanor's image has been created and interpreted. My former colleague Nicholas Vincent was very helpful in pointing me towards readings, including his own work on Eleanor's charters. Katrin Thier played a more valuable role than she probably realizes, as someone to bounce ideas off at that early stage. Alan Murray helped both my research and my wallet by steering review copies of new works on Eleanor and the Plantagenets in my direction. The number of people who helped me simply by suggesting sources or allowing me to talk through my ideas is too large for me to list (or even remember). The collective wisdom of members of the listservs Medfem-L and H-France was an invaluable source of knowledge and suggestions. RáGena DeAragon and Lois Huneycutt both discussed ideas with me, but many others also helped by answering my questions. The International Conference on Medievalism proved an ideal venue for me to venture off my home turf of medieval history and address the post-medieval development of Eleanor's image. Karl Fugelso in particular deserves thanks for encouraging me to publish my preliminary thoughts on the historiography of Eleanor, as does Alicia Montoya for discussing eighteenth-century French medievalism with me and helping me obtain funding to attend the 2010 conference in the Netherlands. Lorraine Stock was a great help in discussing cinematic and televisual representations of Eleanor. Mark Herman and Ronnie Apter helped answer my questions about opera and Occitan. Several people assisted me by providing me with their unpublished material or discussing their work with me, including Kinoko Craft, Mary Jo Lanphear, Mary Ann Capiello and David Scaer. Aviva Kakar kindly agreed to be 'paid in books' in return for checking and reworking my translated quotations from the French; time constraints prevented me from incorporating all her suggested changes, so any infelicities of style in the English versions are entirely my own. The inter-library loan staff at Central Michigan University and the Michigan Electronic Library were, of course, of vital assistance.

The passage of time and conglomeration within the publishing industry meant that this project passed through the hands of three different publishers, and my thanks go out to all of them: Tony Morris and Martin Sheppard at Hambledon, Michael Greenwood at Continuum and Frances Arnold, Ian Buck, Emily Drewe, Emma Goode and Rhodri Mogford at Bloomsbury, as well as Balaji Kasirajan at Integra.

In the course of writing this book, I got married, acquired a new family and became a cat-owner and a resident of the United States – four changes of status that are connected. I therefore dedicate this book to Kenlea, Ben and Emma, for their love and encouragement.

Introduction: Eleanorian Exceptionalism

'An incomparable woman'?

Eleanor of Aquitaine is one of the most famous women in medieval history, yet also one of the most inaccessible, '[f]amiliar and elusive, well-known and yet ultimately unknowable', in the words of Theresa Earenfight.[1] RáGena DeAragon has posed the question, 'do we know what we think we know about Eleanor?'[2] We possess comparatively little evidence of her life from twelfth-century historians. Georges Duby reckoned that we have only nine sources for her life history,[3] while John Parsons and Bonnie Wheeler remark that '[r]arely in the course of historical endeavor has so much been written, over so many centuries, about one woman of whom we know so little'.[4] The frequent appearance of lengthy biographies of Eleanor would suggest an abundance of evidence for an account of her life, yet many of these works have at their core the same sparse chronicle and literary references, a flimsy foundation on which a large edifice of speculation has often been erected. Richard Barber argues that 'to print all the records and chronicle entries about Eleanor would take less than a hundred pages'.[5] In the absence of hard evidence, these biographies have often been fleshed out by speculation and the creation or perpetuation of myths.

The attraction of Eleanor of Aquitaine to post-medieval historians, novelists and artists is obvious. Heiress in her own right to Aquitaine, one of the wealthiest fiefs in Europe, she became in turn queen of France by marriage to Louis VII (1137–52) and of England by marriage to Henry II (1154–89). She was the mother of two of England's most celebrated (or notorious) kings, Richard I and John, and played an important role in the politics of both their reigns. She was a powerful woman in an age assumed (not entirely correctly) to be dominated by men. She was associated with some of the great events and movements of her age: the crusades (she participated in the Second Crusade, and organized the ransom payments to free Richard I from the imprisonment that he suffered returning from the Third); the development of vernacular literature and the idea of courtly love (as granddaughter of the 'first troubadour' William IX of Aquitaine, she was also a patron of some of the earliest Arthurian literature in French, and featured in one of the foundational works on courtly love); and the Plantagenet–Capetian conflict that foreshadowed centuries of struggle between England and France (her divorce from Louis VII and marriage to Henry II took Aquitaine out of the Capetian orbit, and created the 'Angevin Empire'). She enjoyed a long life (she was about eighty years old at the time of her death in 1204) and produced nine children who lived to adulthood. The marriages of her offspring linked her (and the Plantagenet and Capetian dynasties) to the royal houses of Castile, Sicily and Navarre, and to the great noble lines of Brittany and Blois-Champagne in France and the Welfs in Germany. A sense of both the geographical and temporal extent of Eleanor's world can be appreciated when we consider an example from the crusades. Eleanor accompanied her husband Louis VII on the Second Crusade in 1147–9; when Louis IX went on crusade over a hundred years later, he left France in the care of Blanche of Castile, a Spanish princess and Eleanor's granddaughter, whose marriage to Louis's father had been arranged by Eleanor. Just this single example shows her direct influence spanning a century, two crusades and three kingdoms.

Eleanor's life story also comes down to us accompanied by a whiff of scandal. A 'Black Legend'[6] was formed within her own lifetime and in the decades immediately after her death by clerical chroniclers who viewed her with suspicion as a powerful and independent woman. Incidents from her life such as her rumoured incest with her uncle, Raymond, Prince of Antioch, or her dressing as a man to flee from her husband Henry II following a failed rebellion that she supposedly instigated, were framed by these chroniclers to paint her as a licentious and rebellious woman. The Black Legend was inflated by posthumous exaggeration or invention, so that as early as the mid-thirteenth century her rumoured affair with Prince Raymond was transformed into a dalliance with Saladin. The later Middle Ages and early-modern period added further calumnies, notably the legend that she murdered Rosamond de Clifford, her rival for the affections of Henry II.

If the medieval and early-modern image of Eleanor was a largely negative one, the twentieth century saw a backlash – inspired to a great extent by Second-Wave Feminism – which sought to restore the image of Eleanor, with a few added embellishments. A 'more flattering kind of character distortion' developed that created 'an idealized picture of her as a romantic figure'.[7] For authors such as Amy Kelly, Régine Pernoud and Marion Meade, Eleanor became a feminist heroine, political thinker and activist, patron of the troubadours, judge of the 'Courts of Love' and bearer of the enlightened culture of the *Midi* to a gloomy and priest-ridden north. While providing a useful corrective to the Black Legend, the twentieth-century backlash threatened to create a counter-mythology as powerful as the one it sought to overturn. In the words of Jacques Le Goff, she is as much a figure of romance as of history, and 'has been both the victim of a black legend and the beneficiary of an embellished [or golden] myth'.[8]

A central element of the myth of Eleanor is that of her exceptionalism. Historians and Eleanor biographers have tended to take literally Richard of Devizes's conventional panegyric of her as 'an incomparable woman'.[9] She is assumed to be a woman out of her time – unique among women in an age which is assumed to be benighted and misogynistic. Among popular writers on Eleanor, a fascination with her seems to reflect an amazement at discovering that the Middle Ages could be anything more than (in the words of children's fiction author E. L. Konigsburg) a 'thousand years without a bath', and furthermore that a woman – '[w]hat a woman!' – could play a powerful and independent role in such an age.[10] Even the more sceptical academic historians such as Jean Flori declare her to have possessed an 'exceptional character'.[11] Amazement at Eleanor's power and independence is born from a presentism that assumes generally that the Middle Ages were a backward age, and specifically that medieval women were all downtrodden and marginalized. Eleanor's career can, from such a perspective, only be explained by assuming that she was an exception who rose by sheer force of personality above the restrictions placed upon twelfth-century women. Viewed through this perspective, a pseudo-Eleanor of historiography has been created, owing little to the historical record, as writers have felt free to 'pile conjecture upon conjecture'[12]:

> Eleanor … has inspired some of the very worst historical writing devoted to the European Middle Ages … The Eleanor of history has been overshadowed by an Eleanor of wishful thinking and make-believe.[13]

This has often led to a focus on Eleanor's personality and psychology. Martin Aurell criticizes such 'Freudian' approaches,[14] which are impossible to prove one way or the other, based as they are on medieval chronicles that aimed to illustrate not the interior motives of individuals but the unfolding of divine providence 'so that the invisible things of God may be clearly seen by the things that are done, and men may by examples of reward or punishment be made more zealous …'[15]

The idea of Eleanor's exceptionalism runs through the popular image of her like letters through a stick of rock. Douglas Boyd, in his popular biography of 2004, calls Eleanor '[c]harismatic, beautiful, highly intelligent and literate, but also impulsive and proud'. She 'did not conform to preconceptions of medieval European womanhood',[16] and was an 'extraordinary woman' who 'lived a remarkable life'.[17] For Alison Weir (writing in 1999), Eleanor was 'remarkable in a period when females were invariably relegated to a servile role ... an incomparable woman'.[18] The 1993 work *Queen Consorts of England* by Petronelle Cook states that '[i]f a prize were given for England's liveliest queen, Eleanor of Aquitaine would undoubtedly win'.[19] Marion Meade, writing in 1977, asserts that 'although Eleanor of Aquitaine ... lived at a time when women as individuals had few significant rights, she was nevertheless *the* [my emphasis] key political figure of the twelfth century'.[20] Amy Kelly's 1950 biography was 'offered as a study of individuals who set their stamp on events of their time, rather than as a study of developing systems of politics, economics, or jurisprudence'.[21]

The context of medieval queenship

From Boyd to the more sober reflections of Kelly, there is a consensus that Eleanor was a remarkable individual, who shone despite the limits placed on women of her time. As such, she has become for many 'the first heroine of the feminist movement or even of Occitanian independence' in the words of Georges Duby.[22] Yet the idea of Eleanor's exceptionalism rests on an assumption that women of her age were powerless. On the contrary, in Western Europe before the twelfth century there were 'no really effective barriers to the capacity of women to exercise power; they appear as military leaders, judges, castellans, controllers of property'.[23] There is a danger that focusing on (supposedly) exceptional women, especially those from the elites, can distort our view of medieval women as a whole. In the words of Janna Bianchini, writing about Eleanor's granddaughter Berenguela of Castile:

> Her exceptionalism threatens to relegate her to the dustbin of 'women worthies', those exemplars whose enormous distance from the experience of most women makes them seem, at best, irrelevant to history. At worst, they can be seen as falsifications of women's lived experience – their success seems to elide the misogyny or oppression suffered by their contemporaries.[24]

This is certainly true of Eleanor, as she overshadows even her fellow queens, to the extent that Berenguela '[c]ompared to her grandmother Eleanor of Aquitaine or her sister Blanche of Castile ... is at best an obscure figure in the already shadowy ranks of medieval queens'.[25]

Until relatively recently, the academic study of queens was neglected, for reasons which will be outlined in Chapter 2. Between 1900 and 1990, only three scholars in the academy devoted full-length biographies to Eleanor – Amy Kelly and Curtis Walker in 1950, and Régine Pernoud in 1965.[26] These biographies did little to challenge the myth-making process; indeed, Kelly was the chief popularizer of the modern concept of Eleanor as patron of the Courts of Love, which has subsequently come under sustained assault by literary scholars and historians alike.[27] Since 1990, however, there has been something of a turn towards Eleanor among scholars, marked by the appearance of D. D. R. Owen's work in 1993, which was in any case not a true biography.[28] Owen, a literary scholar, focused on the literary and legendary accounts of Eleanor, tracing the development of her image through these texts.

The last two decades have seen the rise, particularly among US historians, of the serious study of queenship; of the role not merely of individual, exceptional queens, but of the function of queenship as an office, of queens both as rulers (in their own right and as regents) and as co-rulers with their husbands or sons.[29] The old view of the queen as a passive victim of diplomatic marriages and brood-mare of future kings has been replaced by a view of her as an active partner in royal authority. Recent historians have come to argue that 'monarchy (despite its name) was a collaborative and potentially multigendered phenomenon, not an institution that depended on the single, male, person of the king. In doing so, they have called into question the idea that powerful queens were exceptions to a strictly masculine norm.'[30]

As well as providing a more rounded view of medieval queenship, recent scholarship has also challenged the idea that female power was in decline during Eleanor's twelfth century. Georges Duby regarded the rise of a new territorially based aristocracy and patrilineal inheritance in the eleventh and twelfth centuries, alongside church reform that tended to reinforce patriarchal marriage practices, as marking an eclipse of female aristocratic power. The rise of bureaucratic administrations staffed by educated male clerks also tended to exclude women from the public world of politics and restrict them to the domestic sphere.[31] Marion Facinger, in an important 1968 study of Capetian queens, including Eleanor, detected a rise and subsequent decline in the power of French queens, peaking with Adelaide of Maurienne, Eleanor's mother-in-law.[32]

The charter evidence supports the picture of female marginalization to some extent; for example, the term *domina* – which could be translated as 'lady' but has a more specific meaning of a woman with authority, a female 'lord' – occurs less frequently in charters from the period 1120–1220 than previously. In Poitiers in the thirteenth century, the percentage of women named in charters as donors to the Abbey of St-Hilaire was half of what it had been in the tenth.[33] However, it is difficult to make any generalizations, and the careers of Eleanor and her contemporaries should warn us against assuming that female authority was in decline. Recent research has pushed the life-span of the age of female administrators and war-leaders well into the twelfth century and beyond, and challenged Facinger's pessimistic verdict on twelfth-century queenship,[34] emphasizing that, even though the formal, public role of queens may have declined, their private, familial role as wife and consort of the King made them 'often their husbands' equals in a wide range of issues that span the public-private continuum that encompasses governance, religion, art, culture and family'.[35] Seen through this perspective, Eleanor, far from being Amy Kelly's proto-modern, proto-feminist figure, represents a medieval world of powerful royal and aristocratic women.

Eleanor in the roles of queenship

'A queen was more than just a ruler or a mother, so much so that she needed an adjective to clarify precisely who she was and what she did.' A regnant queen might govern in her own right, but '[s]he was a queen-consort when she married a king, a queen-mother when she bore his children, a queen-regent when she governed for or with her husband and possessed female sovereignty. When her husband died she was queen-dowager'.[36] Eleanor fulfilled most of these roles in her lifetime. She was never a queen regnant, but she did hold Aquitaine in her own right, and governed it even during her marriage to Henry II between 1168 and 1173, and Henry's later attempts to endow his sons with her duchy required Eleanor's nominal approval.[37] She was queen-consort twice, alongside Louis VII of France from 1137 to 1152, and Henry II of England from 1154 to 1189. Eleanor was effectively regent during some of Henry's absences in the 1150s and '60s, and again during the absence of her son Richard I, and while he was held captive in Germany.[38] As queen mother, she played a crucial role in political life during the reigns of her sons Richard I and John, including securing the succession for the latter in 1199. A brief overview of Eleanor in the various roles of a twelfth-century queen can give a sense of whether she was remarkable or typical in relation to the office of queenship.

Eleanor as queen of France

Marion Facinger, in an article on Capetian queenship originally published in 1968, did much to shape the idea that the power of queens was in decline in the twelfth century. When it came to Eleanor:

> A dispassionate examination of the documentation for the first ten years of Eleanor's career as queen of France … reveals almost no information about either her activities or her influence. Her presence in the royal *curia* is unnoted, her name rarely appears on Louis's charters, and no sources support the historical view of Eleanor as bold, precocious, and responsible for Louis VII's behavior.[39]

As discussed elsewhere, more recent scholarship has tended to challenge the idea of the decline of queenship,[40] but even some more recent scholars agree in seeing Eleanor as a minor player in the politics of Louis VII's France. Theresa Earenfight argues that '[i]n terms of queenship, Eleanor was a very conventional queen during the fifteen years she was married to Louis, doing everything that was expected of a queen'.[41] Marie Hivergneaux's study of Eleanor's charters shows that only three of Eleanor's twenty charters from the time of her marriage to Louis were issued in her capacity as queen of France, with the remaining seventeen relating to her role as Duchess of Aquitaine. Even here, she played a secondary role to Louis, who took the title 'Dux Aquitanorum' (Duke of Aquitainians) and appointed his own officials to the government of the duchy. Of Eleanor's seventeen 'Aquitanian' charters, only four appear to have been initiated by the duchess herself. In Hivergneaux's words 'she is therefore far from acting alone even in this duchy to which she is the heiress'.[42] After her divorce from Louis, she on occasion reissued deeds from her time as queen of France, as if her authority in the duchy had been compromised by having been subsumed into that of her royal husband.[43] This has not prevented historians from speculating on Eleanor's role. Ralph Turner claims – referring to the work of Marcel Pacaut, but without citing a primary source – that Louis 'readily allowed her to take a part in political decision-making', despite the fact that the charters suggest otherwise, and discusses Eleanor's role in the sidelining of her mother-in-law, Adelaide of Maurienne, without citing any sources at all.[44] Jean Flori is among historians who suggest a rivalry between Eleanor and Suger, abbot of Saint Denis, who had been Louis VI's chief minister and advisor, but admits that '[t]here is nothing to prove it, but it is not impossible …'.[45] This period in her life, about which we know comparatively little, offers perhaps the most fertile ground for conjecture and myth-making. There is a tendency to assume that because Eleanor was 'remarkable', her personality must have manifested itself in her early years. To cite Facinger again, 'because her later career was extraordinary, there has been a tendency to fabricate an early queen consonant with the later one'.[46]

Eleanor as queen of England

What role did Eleanor play in her northern kingdom? Eleanor is often associated with the south of France, and this identification has been used to portray her as an exotic alien in England, or to romanticize her as an exile in a cold, uncultured north. Yet Eleanor lived for fifty-two years after her marriage to Henry II; she spent half of these in England.[47] It was in England that she gave birth to two future kings of that land (Richard and John), and a king who might have been (Henry, the Young King). Events such as her support for the Young King's revolt in 1173–4, and her subsequent imprisonment in Salisbury, have been portrayed as examples of her political alienation from Henry II. Amy Kelly saw Eleanor's imprisonment as an act of oppression by a patriarchal feudal order against the enlightened, feminine, culture of the future:

> For the moment the feudal system triumphed. Sedition looked out from barred windows upon a world of havoc. But ideas had gone forth from the high place in Poitiers which survived to shed a brightness in the world when rods had fallen from the hands of feudal kings and bolts had rusted in the Tower of Salisbury.[48]

Eleanor's role in England has been marginalized not only by those who portray her as a victim, but by historians who view her as largely irrelevant to its government. This reflects the heavy reliance made by Eleanor's biographers until recently upon narrative chronicle sources. W. L. Warren, biographer of Henry II, asserts that 'to judge from the chroniclers, the most striking fact about Eleanor is her utter insignificance in Henry II's reign'.[49] Referring to Roger of Howden's chronicles, Richard Barber writes that 'Eleanor, as far as they are concerned, is merely part of the king's entourage … From her marriage until 1173, Eleanor barely figures in Howden's chronicles.'[50] Chronicles of course do not tell the full story, and recent work on charters corrects the perspective of Eleanor as an inactive queen a little, but Eleanor's near absence from the narrative record is significant nonetheless. Popular historians such as Kelly and Pernoud have read into this a marginalization of Eleanor during the years in which Becket was in favour, but there is no evidence to support this assumption.

and accounts of a queen's intercession dominate many sources on queenship.' It was a means by which a queen could, either pre-emptively or retroactively, temper royal power by requesting an act of mercy. In some ways it reflects the limitations on queenly authority as she sought to mitigate royal power, but also reflects the queen's positive authority, as it 'was accepted as part of queenship as office'. Her role as intercessor mirrored biblical models such as the Virgin Mary (Queen of the Heavens) and Esther (Queen of the Persians).[70]

The most celebrated instance of queenly intercession was the case of Philippa of Hainault (Edward III's queen) intervening on behalf of the Burghers of Calais in 1347, when she successfully had Edward's death sentence upon the unfortunate *bourgeois* rescinded. Philippa's role as intercessor has been seen as symbolic of the decline of queenly authority in the later Middle Ages: 'checked in the exercise of power, queens were showered with symbolic recognition...queenly influence was *petitionary*, in the sense that it cast the queen as one seeking redress rather than one able to institute redress in her own right, and *intercessory*, in that it limited its objectives to the modification of a previously determined male resolve'.[71] Yet we see Eleanor displaying a similar intercessory role 200 years previously; given the argument that the twelfth century marks a turning-point towards the decline of female authority, can we see in Eleanor's intercession the actions of an authoritative early-medieval queen, or of a late-medieval queen whose authority has become subsumed into that of a male sovereign?

Philippa appealed to Edward as a wife heavily pregnant with a future royal child (although her advanced pregnancy as described in the chronicles does not match the chronology of her children's births, and was clearly exaggerated to play up the pathos of her maternal role).[72] Eleanor's position was, however, very different. In 1192, while visiting some of her dower lands in the Cambridgeshire, she was accosted by villagers who complained of the effects of an interdict upon the diocese of Ely:

> Human bodies lay unburied here and there in the fields, because their bishop had deprived them of burial. When she learned of the cause of such suffering, the queen took pity on the misery of the living because of the dead, for she was very merciful. Immediately dropping her own affairs and looking after the concerns of others, she went to London. She requested, indeed commanded, the archbishop of Rouen [Walter of Coutances] that the confiscated revenues of the bishop [of Ely, William Longchamp] be repaid to the bishop, and that the same bishop ... be proclaimed as freed from the excommunication that had been pronounced upon him ... Thus through the queen's mediation the open enmity between the two parties was laid to rest ...[73]

We may note the differences between Philippa's and Eleanor's intercessions. Philippa was a pregnant woman married to the king; Eleanor a widow long past child-bearing age, a queen-mother, and playing a quasi-monarchical role in her son's absence on crusade. Philippa sought mercy from her husband the king; Eleanor, acting in Richard's absence, had no king to whom she need appeal, enacting mercy under her own authority when she 'requested, indeed commanded' Walter of Coutances to reverse the excommunication of Longchamp. Richard of Devizes may present her as mediating a dispute,[74] but Eleanor does so under her vice-regal authority. Her attempt to settle a conflict between two leading clerics (and rivals for power within the administration established in Richard's absence) was a highly political one, not a symbolic display of womanly mercy. In Jane Martindale's words, her action was 'entirely typical of Angevin methods of government: it might have been employed by Henry or Richard'.[75]

How exceptional was Eleanor?

In an important article published in 1992, Jane Martindale sought to locate Eleanor in context, stripping away much of the conjecture that had grown up around her, and returning to primary sources, including her charters.[76] Martindale also demonstrated how Eleanor was not out of the ordinary for a twelfth-century queen either in the extent of her power or in the criticisms levelled against her. Even she, however, concluded that 'it is Richard of Devizes' phrase which stays in the memory: Eleanor of Aquitaine was the *femina incomporabilis* – "a woman without compare"'.[77] In Theresa Earenfight's words, however, Eleanor 'sits in the middle of the spectrum of queenship … [f]or all her fame, she had less official political authority than her mother-in-law, Matilda'.[78] Her role in Henry's government in the late 1150s and early 1160s was limited, probably due to her frequent pregnancies (eight in thirteen years).[79]

A brief survey of royal or aristocratic women of Eleanor's world shows that powerful women were far from unusual. We can point to a number of examples of regnant queens in Western Europe in the twelfth and early thirteenth centuries, including Mélisende of Jerusalem, Urraca of León and Berenguela of Castile (Eleanor's granddaughter).[80] Medieval Spain alone, where there was a tradition of female co-rulership, has become a focus for recent scholarship by authors such as Theresa Earenfight, Miriam Shadis and Janna Bianchini, which has helped to redefine our understanding of the important and active office of queenship.[81]

Berenguela of Castile acted as consort of her husband (the king of León) and as co-ruler with her son (Fernando III of Aragon), while her sister Blanche (also, of course, a granddaughter of Eleanor) was regent of France during the minority of her son, Louis IX. While Norman-Angevin England did not see a regnant queen, Eleanor's mother-in-law, the Empress Matilda, was engaged in a long and bitter struggle for the English crown, and was briefly *de facto* queen bearing the title 'lady [*domina*] of the English'.[82]

If we look at Eleanor's predecessors as Anglo-Norman queens of England, we find many examples of women wielding political power.[83] Matilda of Flanders (wife of William the Conqueror) acted as regent in Normandy during his frequent absences in England following the Conquest,[84] and the two wives of Henry I (Matilda of Scotland[85] and Adeliza of Louvain) all played some role in governing England during their husbands' absences, while during the civil war of Stephen's reign Matilda of Boulogne led the fight for a time on behalf of her royal husband, who had been captured by the forces of the empress.[86] And if we wish to seek a rebel woman, we need look no further than Juliana, illegitimate daughter of Henry I, who attempted to assassinate him with a crossbow,[87] or Adèle of Champagne, the third wife of Louis VII, who '[a]t he moment when Henry II held Eleanor of Aquitaine in jail for her revolt ... led a revolt with her brothers against her son, Philip II'.[88]

Eleanor is, therefore, less the exception than the rule – albeit an extreme example of that rule. This can be illustrated by comparing her with a twelfth-century woman who has attracted less literary and historical attention. Adela of Blois died in 1137, the year of Eleanor's marriage to Louis VII. Her career and that of Eleanor touch, albeit indirectly; she was the mother of King Stephen, who contested the crown of England with Henry II's mother, Empress Matilda; mother of Count Thibaud IV, against whom Louis VII fought a war while married to Eleanor; and grandmother of Count Thibaud IV and of Count Henry I of Champagne, who each married one of Eleanor's daughters by Louis.

The chronicle and charter evidence reveals Adela to have 'legitimately exercised the powers of comital lordship' in the domains of Blois-Champagne, both in consort with her husband and alone during his absence on crusade and after his death.[89] Before Stephen of Blois' departure on the First Crusade, he and Adela witnessed charters jointly, with Adela 'an active and acknowledged participant in comital lordship'.[90] After her husband's death, Adela retained that authority even after their sons attained adulthood.[91] There was, however, nothing atypical about the nature of Adela's power. In the words of her biographer Kimberley LoPrete, 'while the extent of Adela's powers and the political impact of her actions were exceptional for a woman of her day (and indeed for most men), the sources of her powers and the activities she engaged in were not fundamentally different from those of other women of lordly rank'. These words could equally apply to Eleanor; the extent of her power, as heiress to the richest lordship in France, wife of two kings and mother of two or three more, was remarkable, but the nature of her power was not exceptional. Other noble or royal women governed, arranged marriages and alliances, and were patrons of the church. Eleanor represents one end of a continuum, not an isolated outlier.

Eleanor of Aquitaine was the only twelfth-century queen of England or France to take part in a crusade. However, the exceptionalism of her role as a crusader queen can be overplayed. She was neither the only English queen to go on crusade (her great-granddaughter Eleanor of Castile accompanied the future Edward I on crusade in 1270–2),[92] nor was she unusual as a royal woman crusader; the Provençal sisters Marguerite (queen of Louis IX of France) and Béatrice (wife of Louis' brother Charles of Anjou, future king of Sicily) both accompanied their husbands on crusade in the 1250s, and both gave birth while on the expedition.[93] Louis IX's mother, Blanche of Castile, even went through the same experience as Eleanor of having to deal with the problem of an absent royal son taken captive on crusade. Nor was Eleanor alone in being a warrior woman (and there is no evidence of her playing a role in any fighting in the crusade or during the revolt of the Young King). One of Eleanor's ancestors, Agnes of Burgundy, wife of Duke William V, was the effective ruler of Aquitaine after her husband's death and led the duchy's forces against rebellious vassals in 1044–5.[94]

Another attribute that is offered as proof of Eleanor's exceptionalism is her position as a uniquely educated woman, and as an outstanding patron of literature and the arts. Brought up at the cultured court of the Dukes of Aquitaine, a granddaughter of William IX 'the First Troubadour', Eleanor is supposed to be remarkable in having been an educated woman. One obvious objection to this alleged uniqueness is that Eleanor was a younger contemporary of Héloïse of the Paraclete and Hildegard of Bingen, two of the most celebrated educated women of the Middle Ages, whose reputations are known to popular as well as academic readers. Popular historians have tended to exaggerate the extent of Eleanor's learning; Amy Kelly has her 'using dialectic' in her arguments with figures such as Bernard of Clairvaux. 'It seems certain that she mastered the rudiments of dialectic and examined the structure of the syllogism, for she was able later on her own behalf to cite Scripture, chapter and verse, even to popes and cardinals, and to employ the syllogism with good effect in Rome and Tusculum.'[95] This ignores the fact that Eleanor's letters would have been composed by learned amanuenses such as Peter of Blois.

Even those cultural historians who have developed a scepticism about the extent of Eleanor's patronage tend to accept the idea of her exceptionalism. For example, June Hall McCash accepts the assumption that 'Eleanor was certainly extraordinary in many respects, and ... she spawned an entire generation of literary patrons', before citing, approvingly, Margaret Schauss and Susan Mosher Stuard's view that 'powerful women like Eleanor of Aquitaine ... were often treated as anomalies whose achievements could reveal nothing about female agency and influence in general ...'.[96]

Eleanor was far from unique as an educated woman from the secular nobility. Referring to Adela of Blois, LoPrete writes about the typical education of a twelfth-century French woman from the upper aristocracy:

> Her education would have included elementary training in the liberal arts based on standard textbooks and both poetical and historical works commonly used when teaching those disciplines in her day. Adela's mother [Matilda of Flanders] came from a family with a generations-old tradition of Latin literacy and several of Adela's siblings are known to have received at least the rudiments of a literary education.[97]

It is often assumed that Eleanor was especially well educated, or spoke many languages, but evidence for either is lacking. It seems reasonable to assume that she received an education at her father's court. There is an intriguing story from St Albans Abbey, recorded by Matthew Paris, that Eleanor had given a ring to one Richard Animal, a companion and fellow-scholar from her childhood, which Richard had in turn given to the abbey.[98] She almost certainly did not speak English; when, as described by Richard of Devizes, the people of the diocese of Ely appealed to Eleanor against the interdict, '[t]here was no need for an interpreter ... they spoke through their tears',[99] implying of course that an interpreter would have been required for Eleanor to converse with her English subjects. This may be contrasted with Henry II's reputation for being able to speak every language as far as the Jordan.[100]

The questions of Eleanor's role as a patron will be discussed in detail in Chapter 3, but again, we cannot view her cultural patronage as out of the ordinary for a high-status woman of her era. Her contemporary Ermengarde, viscountess of Narbonne,[101] was named alongside Eleanor and Marie de Champagne as holding court by Andreas Capellanus, but until recently had received considerably less attention than the other two ladies. Whereas Eleanor was only referred to once for certain in troubadour literature, we can find five such references to Ermengarde, whose fame was so widespread that she was mentioned in the Icelandic *Orkneyingasaga*.[102] Other twelfth-century queens such as Matilda of Scotland were important as patrons and as conveyers of cultural influences from their homelands to their adopted countries.[103]

Eleanor was, however, a patron in another sense that was central to the role of a medieval queen, if less appealing to modern interpretations that stress her exceptionalism: patron of religious institutions. She was associated particularly with Fontevraud, a house to which she would retire in her last years and where she would be buried along with Henry II and Richard I. The abbey had close ties to both her family and the Angevins, and was the beneficiary of many charters issued by Eleanor.[104]

Inventing Eleanor

Clearly, therefore, Eleanor of Aquitaine was far from unique among twelfth-century royal and noble women. So, how then did she acquire her reputation for exceptionalism? In this book I intend to investigate that question. It is not a biography of Eleanor – there are plenty of those available, both popular and scholarly – and I am assuming a certain amount of prior knowledge of Eleanor's life and career on the part of the reader. It is, rather, an attempt to understand how and why the received image of Eleanor has grown so far beyond – and at times at variance with – what we know from the medieval sources. In so far as it is a biography, it is of a legendary Eleanor, tracing how both the Black Legend and the 'Golden Myth' developed, first from the often scandalized reports of medieval chronicles, via late-medieval and early-modern legends, to the modern portrayals of Eleanor in both history and the arts. How, for example, did an ambiguous reference in a Byzantine chronicle develop into Eleanor 'riding bare-breasted half-way to Damascus' in a twentieth-century play and film? Why is a woman whose power-base lay in the north-west of France celebrated as a heroine of regionalism in parts of southern France over which she never ruled? How has a queen of both France and England, who belonged entirely to neither, been treated in the historiographical narrative of each of those nations? What does the continual reshaping of Eleanor's image in both history and culture tell us about the evolution of attitudes towards women, power and the medieval past? The approach is selective; so much has been written about Eleanor that it is not possible to do justice to all the interpretations of her life or all the historical controversies that surround her. Instead, I have chosen at points to focus on specific issues or authors to illustrate how the image of Eleanor has been shaped.

In the process of tracing the evolution of Eleanor's legend, we can also see the evolution of larger questions in historiography, such as the treatment of women's history, uses of the medieval past, the development of national (and nationalist) histories in Britain and France and of a regional history of southern France. But Eleanor is not simply a figure of history; she has appeared so prominently in fiction, drama, film, television and the visual arts that we can also trace the development of a second Eleanor – we might even say a meta-Eleanor – whose myth has been so powerful as to shape the perceptions of the historical queen. Just as Eleanor's image has been reshaped by successive developments in historiography, so too has meta-Eleanor been presented through a series of new genres and media, from early-modern ballads to twenty-first-century social media. Indeed, there is scarcely a medium in which she has not featured: novels, plays, films, television and radio series, the visual arts, the internet and even the names of streets and institutions, all reveal our continued fascination with this twelfth-century queen. The development of the image of Eleanor of Aquitaine has therefore been one of constant (re)invention over eight centuries. Each reinvention reflects contemporary social concerns about gender, power, nationalism and sex. They also reveal how we stigmatize the medieval past as part of a modern desire to make ourselves feel more comfortable about our own age by exaggerating the ignorance and poverty of earlier eras, as expressed in the words put into Eleanor's mouth by James Goldman in *The Lion in Winter*: 'It's 1183 and we're barbarians!'

Chapter 1 traces the origins of the Black Legend to its medieval sources. I have chosen to focus on two incidents that framed the reputation of Eleanor for centuries. The first is the claim that she committed adultery with her uncle, Raymond, prince of Antioch, on the Second Crusade. Of all the accusations laid at Eleanor's door, this is the one that has the earliest origin, and is one of the few parts of the Black Legend which dates back to Eleanor's own lifetime. The second incident covered in this chapter is Eleanor's reputation as a warrior queen for her role in the rebellion of her sons against Henry II. The chapter then traces the subsequent development of the Black Legend in later-medieval and early-modern literature, before considering as a 'case-study' the stories of Eleanor's supposedly dressing as an Amazon during the Second Crusade.

Chapter 2 introduces the historians who arguably have been as responsible as anyone for myth-making about Eleanor. This chapter follows the development of her image in both French and Anglophone histories, demonstrating how

Eleanor has been reassessed by different generations in the light of contemporary concerns, from the Enlightenment via the nationalist histories of the nineteenth century to late twentieth-century intellectual influences such as feminism and New Age religion.

Chapter 3 sees the focus shift from national to regional historiographies – in this case the concept of a 'southern' Eleanor who was a queen of the troubadours. In this chapter, I critically assess the concept of Eleanor as a southern or Occitan figure and the influence of this concept on contemporary Occitan identity and culture.

The rest of the book is devoted to the posthumous 'history' of Eleanor in artistic representations. Chapters 4 and 5 address her portrayal in drama, on the stage before 1900, and on stage and screen in the twentieth century. These portrayals reflect the historical reassessment of Eleanor, as Shakespeare's 'canker'd grandam' was transformed into the imperious queen portrayed by Katharine Hepburn in *The Lion in Winter*.

In Chapter 6, I address the portrayal of Eleanor in fiction from the late eighteenth century to the present. In this chapter I have also raised questions of the interaction between the Eleanor of popular culture and audience perceptions of history. How far is the public's view of Eleanor shaped by popular culture portrayals rather than by academic history? And does it matter?

Chapter 7 looks briefly at Eleanor in the visual arts, from medieval tombs, paintings, church windows and seal matrices to modern paintings and popular fiction book covers, addressing the desire to 'know' the appearance of a queen who left no true portraits, and what it tells us about the cultural, political or even sexual agenda of artists and viewers. A conclusion assesses the state of Eleanor historiography in the early twenty-first century, and considers where Eleanor's image stands in the modern world, and why – despite the exponential expansion of scholarship on medieval queenship in the last two decades – she continues to fascinate more than her fellow medieval queens.

Creating the Black Legend:
The Origins and Development of
Eleanor's Scandalous Reputation

One of the key arguments of this work is that the continuing fascination with Eleanor is based in part on a negative image of her that is rooted in early-modern or modern myth-making. However, some of the more serious accusations against her – that she was everything from an adulteress to a murderer and even a demon – have their roots in later medieval legend or even, in the case of her alleged adultery, in contemporary or near-contemporary chronicle accounts. These were later embroidered in late-medieval romance and the culture of early-modern popular ballads. By the sixteenth and seventeenth centuries, antiquarians attempted to challenge the image of a murderous, adulterous, demonic queen, but paradoxically helped perpetuate the negative mythology about her by giving credence to some of the legends, now given the imprimatur of scholarship. By the nineteenth century, when both modern academic history and the modern historical novel were maturing, she may no longer have been regarded as the demonic mother of Richard the Lionheart, but she remained for many the murderer of Rosamond de Clifford and the lover of Saladin.

In many senses, we can view Eleanor (or, at least, Eleanor as viewed by her critics) as a type that occurs frequently in medieval literature and chronicles: the scandalous, adulterous queen. We have seen how Eleanor was far from unique as a medieval woman who wielded effective power; such women might be praised as loyal and effective rulers if they successfully exercised power in a manner deemed appropriate on behalf of their husband or son. For example, John of Salisbury argued in his *Policraticus* that women were unsuited to rule, yet in his *Historia pontificalis* expressed support for the Empress Matilda (the mother of the current king, Henry II), who he regarded as the legitimate ruler.[1] However, if their exercise of power was viewed as flawed or excessive, women were often denigrated by means of attacking their personal and moral conduct.

If medieval chroniclers were critical of the conduct of queens, such criticism was often magnified by later historians. Both medieval and post-medieval historians tended to ignore queens unless their lives were scandalous and sensational: 'lustful queens, adulterous queens, queens who gave bad counsel, poisoned relatives and enemies, or instigated civil war'.[2] In a study of the fifteenth-century French Queen Isabeau of Bavaria, Rachel Gibbons argues that 'the most accessible weapons for an historian to use against a woman were criticism of her looks and her sexual conduct, an ugly, adulterous woman who also neglects her children thus being totally beyond redemption'.[3] Other medieval queens were stigmatized by posterity as 'she-wolves', such as Isabella of France and Margaret of Anjou.[4]

Adultery was an especially serious accusation to make against a queen, as her sexual probity was so closely tied to her role as wife of the king and mother of future kings. According to Kantorowicz's theory of the 'king's two bodies', the public royal body – the institution of kingship – transcends the mortal body of the king: 'le roi est mort, vive le roi'. However, the queen's body is constrained by her mortal flesh, specifically her ability to produce a legitimate male heir.

> The queen's sexual role was of central importance to the realm in an age when the marital debt was understood as a cultural imperative in a patriarchal society. Royal maternity was the matrix of future kings, and a pregnant queen was seen as a guarantor of the realm's survival and integrity, and so of peace and control … The rumor of sexual infidelity established a link between a queen's influence and bad government.[5]

Furthermore, the motif of the adulterous queen, 'a distressingly common storyline in medieval literature',[6] was developing in the romance literature of the twelfth and thirteenth centuries, represented by figures such as Guinevere and Iseult. The relation of cause and effect between the historical Eleanor and these queens of literature is problematic: did the stories circulating about Eleanor following the Second Crusade inspire these literary depictions, or were they inspired by them?[7] It seems unlikely that authors such as Wace or Benoît de Sainte-Maure, who received patronage from Henry and Eleanor's court,[8] would seek to draw attention to the queen's alleged indiscretions on crusade. Nevertheless, the adulterous queen motif remained one of the negative stereotypes against which medieval female rulers' reputations would be measured.

The Second Crusade and Eleanor as adulteress

The role of Eleanor of Aquitaine on the Second Crusade has been the cause of much debate, and many misapprehensions. She has been accused, both by contemporaries and later generations, and with varying degrees of fairness and credibility, of being responsible for the French crusader army's defeat at Mount Cadmos; of dressing herself and her ladies as Queen Penthesilea and the Amazons; and even of sleeping with Saladin. The above accusations are (with the possible exception of the claims that she dressed as an Amazon) the creation of late-medieval romancers and post-medieval historians, and have been largely refuted by academic historians – although this does not prevent the less obviously ludicrous legends from living on through the medium of popular history. Perhaps the most serious accusation against her – which is also the one to be recorded by near-contemporary chroniclers – was that while in Syria she conducted an incestuous affair with her uncle.

These events have often been interpreted, even by academic historians, in terms of received images of a lively and feckless Eleanor confronted with a dull, pious Louis. For example, the English translators of William of Tyre's chronicle wrote that Louis and Eleanor

> were of incompatible temperament, socially active and pleasure-loving Eleanor contrasting with the pious, almost puritanical Louis. Eleanor was thrilled by the elaborate social life of the East, both at Constantinople and at Antioch. Whether her indiscretions involved any more than overindulgence in this social life may be questioned.[9]

The outline of events is as follows, based on the testimonies of our two most reliable sources, John of Salisbury and William of Tyre. When in Antioch in the spring of 1148, Eleanor had a relationship – 'if not sexual, at least political' in the words of Georges Duby[10] – with her uncle Raymond, prince of Antioch. This led to a breach with her husband Louis VII of France, who forcibly removed her from Raymond's company as the French army marched south to Palestine. On the return journey to France, Louis and Eleanor met Pope Eugenius III, who forbade them to divorce and even oversaw a formal 'bedding' of the royal couple.

Much attention – arguably too much – has been devoted to whether Eleanor *really* committed incest with her uncle. I would argue, however, that we should focus less on the unverifiable truth of these accusations, and more on the ideas expressed by the chroniclers who made them, specifically, the use of imagery of incest and sexuality. Bull and Léglu express amazement that historians are still debating the issue 'whereas the true significance of the scandal is what it reveals about the manner in which a fascinated fear of female sexuality readily surfaced when male warriors were casting around for scapegoats'.[11]

The anti-Eleanor sentiment has been blamed on French writers; William of Tyre's translators attribute this to the chronicler employing French sources.[12] According to Richard Barber, 'there is a very good case to be made that most, if not all, of the gossip about her stems from the French court after her divorce, an attempt by those loyal to Louis to justify the incredible political folly of his actions'.[13] This is hard to prove, as many of the more explicit accusations are made not by French writers but by later historians writing in Angevin England either side of the year 1200, namely Walter Map and his associate and fellow Welshman Gerald of Wales. However, these English (or rather, Anglo-Norman-Welsh) writers, despite their ties to the Angevin court, had a deep affection for the Capetian dynasty and strong ties to France through their education in the schools of Paris.[14] Their accounts of Eleanor's adultery should therefore be viewed as 'part of English [sic] writers' anti-Angevin sentiments',[15] projecting their criticisms of Henry II's queen backwards to portray her as sullying the Capetian Louis VII's crusade.

Suggestions of incest were common to many clerical critiques not only of Eleanor herself but of the Angevin dynasty in general. An echo of the claims made against Eleanor and Raymond can be found in a letter from Jean Bellesmains, bishop of Poitiers, to Thomas Becket in 1165.[16] He complains about Eleanor's reliance upon her uncle, Raoul de Faye (who was disliked by the clergy for his oppression of religious houses in Poitou and the Saintonge), and hints at rumours about her conduct.

> But we wish you to know that you [Becket] can expect no help from the queen, especially since she relies entirely on Ralph de Faie, who is persecuting us no less than before. Every day many tendencies come to light which make it possible to believe that there is truth in the dishonourable tale we remember mentioning elsewhere.

If the 'dishonourable tale' related to her conduct on crusade, then the stories about Eleanor and Raymond were apparently circulating even in her native Poitou in the mid-1160s.[17] It is possible that rumours of Eleanor's adultery with Raymond had become attached to a different uncle, Raoul. If this is so, the rumours may have had a common root to those about her and Raymond; namely, disapproving clerics attributing sexual motives for a woman's political actions. Raoul, Eleanor's maternal uncle, was one of her most consistent lieutenants, and acted as Eleanor's seneschal of Poitou from 1168 to 1173, before she fell from grace following her role in the revolt of 1173–4.[18]

Walter Map's *De Nugis Curialium* was probably written mostly in the 1180s, at the time of Eleanor's imprisonment.[19] It has been described by its modern editors as a satire or parody, 'shot through with errors' that may even be deliberate.[20] In contrast to his favourable view of Louis VII, who was 'remarkable for wisdom in act and simpleness in speech',[21] Map views Eleanor's match with Henry with disfavour. In describing Eleanor's marriage to Henry, he claims that 'she was secretly reputed to have shared the couch of Louis with his [Henry's] father Geoffrey'. This made Eleanor guilty of the double sin of adultery and incest (by having sex with both father and son). Writing with the retrospective knowledge of the rebellion of Henry and Eleanor's sons against their father, Walter was unsurprised that such a marriage produced 'offspring, tainted at the source, [that] came to naught'.[22] Map seems to view Eleanor's match with Henry as a seduction on her part, as she turned her 'unchaste eyes' upon the young Angevin. In view of the accusations of incest, Walter's choice of the words 'oculos incestos' may be revealing. *Incestus* can have the general meaning of unchaste, but could also specifically mean incest.

Walter's associate Gerald of Wales made direct reference to Eleanor's supposed incest with her uncle in his *De Principis Instructione*. Gerald, writing sometime before 1216, blamed Eleanor for the Plantagenets' misfortunes. He repeats Map's story of Eleanor's adultery with Geoffrey of Anjou, and like Walter, blames her subsequent incestuous match with Henry for the fact that 'her sons…died without bearing fruit'. Gerald added details of Henry II's and Eleanor's dubious ancestries, including the legend of their descent from the devil, to add to the sense of a family punished for their and their progenitors' sins.[23]

The notion of Henry's family as tainted by the sin of incest is shared by Richard of Devizes, writing during the reign of Richard I. Richard's view of the Angevins is more ambivalent: he was highly favourable to Richard I, and produced a couple of flattering accounts of Eleanor. Elsewhere, however, he alludes cryptically to the queen's behavior at Antioch. In the introduction to his chronicle, he compares the family of Henry II to the 'confused house of Oedipus'.[24] This may be a generic reference to the rebellion of Henry's sons against him, but it is hard to avoid the implication of incest contained in it. Henry also faced attacks on his legitimacy; a story circulated that the Empress Matilda's first husband, the Emperor Henry V, was not dead but had instead become a hermit. If true, this would have rendered her second marriage to Geoffrey of Anjou bigamous, and Henry II a bastard.[25] Ralph Niger employed this argument while criticizing Henry for his imprisonment of Eleanor. Ralph's criticism of Henry is highly sexualized; in the same passage he calls the king a 'corrupter of modesty' and a 'satyr' who married Eleanor for lust, and now wishes to put her aside so that he can indulge his sexual appetites.[26]

What of earlier and possibly more reliable sources? The Englishman John of Salisbury was well placed to comment on Eleanor and Louis's crusade, as he was with the papal court when the Capetian couple visited Pope Eugenius III on their return journey. John was, however, even more closely linked to France than were Gerald or Walter Map. He was educated in Paris, shared Becket's exile in France, and was bishop of Chartres from 1176 to his death in 1180.[27] John's *Historia pontificalis* was written sometime between 1164 and 1180, with its modern editor favouring an earlier date.[28] It was therefore written after Becket's breach with Henry in 1164, and possibly after Eleanor's imprisonment in 1174; so John may also be engaging in anti-Angevin invectives, although his tone in describing Eleanor's behaviour at Antioch is more measured than that of later writers. John's sympathies with Louis are reflected in his emphasis that Eleanor and Raymond's primary fault was their disloyalty to the French king: Raymond 'owed the king loyalty, affection, and respect for many reasons…'[29] The earliest reference, however, comes from German theologian Gerhoh of Reichersberg's *De investigatione Antichristi*, written around 1158–61. Offering a moralizing interpretation of the failure of the crusade, Gerhoh records that Eleanor was taken away by Raymond, but managed to escape. Gerhoh believed that she had not broken her marriage vows, but reports that Louis did not believe her.[30] There is no reason to believe that Gerhoh was better informed than, say, William of Tyre, but it is noteworthy that the story of Eleanor and Raymond was in circulation in Germany at this time, but that Gerhoh interpreted it in terms more favourable to Eleanor.

The Franco-Syrian historian William of Tyre was likewise writing some years after the event, in 1170 at the earliest, with the knowledge of Eleanor's divorce and remarriage to Henry, the death of Becket and probably the rebellion of Henry and Eleanor's sons. Furthermore, despite his physical distance from the Plantagenet–Capetian struggle, William can in some ways be seen as a 'French' writer. He was educated in Paris and was in the West from around 1146 to 1165, and was therefore not in Syria at the time of the Second Crusade. He seems to have intended his *History* for a French readership, to encourage aid for Outremer.[31] William's account of Eleanor's presence in Antioch may therefore be based as much on rumours circulating in the West as on any special access to Eastern sources. It also depends on hindsight for its image of Eleanor, demonstrated in the comment that '[h]er conduct before and after this time showed her to be … far from circumspect'.[32] The idea, implied by John of Salisbury, that Raymond's behaviour was repugnant because it was an act of *lèse majesté* is developed further in William's account, which Jean Flori sees as a 'political' interpretation, with Raymond as the prime mover. Angered by Louis snubbing him, Raymond 'openly plotted against him and took means to do him injury'.

The accusations of incest, while far from absent in the accounts of John and William, therefore should be viewed as judgements made in hindsight by hostile commentators in the light of Eleanor's later career. Hugh of Poitiers and Richard le Poitevin, writing before 1172, make no reference to anything untoward happening between Eleanor and Raymond. These chroniclers might, of course, have kept quiet because of their Poitevin sympathies. Likewise, the silence of Louis's chaplain Odo of Deuil, who accompanied the king on crusade, on any of the latter part of the crusade may equally be motivated by a desire not to sully the Capetian's reputation. However, the judgement of contemporaries was that the Second Crusade had failed because of the general sins of the crusaders, not the specific sin of the queen of France.[33] Bernard of Clairvaux used this argument to deflect criticisms of the wisdom of preaching the crusade. He had been critical of Louis before the latter took the cross, and popular historians would have us believe that he disliked Eleanor, yet he made no attempt to blame the queen in his *apologia* for the crusade.[34] William of Newburgh refers to Louis's decision to have Eleanor accompany him, and blames the presence of women on the crusade for its failure, but does not single out the queen for blame:

> The King, whose love for his young wife was a jealous one, thought he should not leave her behind and decided to take her to war. Many other nobles did likewise and brought their wives along. And as the wives could not do without their serving women, a whole host of women found their way into that Christian camp where chastity should have reigned. And this was an occasion for sin in our army …[35]

Note that there is no explicit accusation of adultery, still less of incest; the presence of women (even the crusaders' wives) *per se* was an 'occasion for sin', as crusaders were supposed to remain chaste until they had fulfilled their vows. William elsewhere refers to sexual sin within the army, which he refers to as 'defiled and unclean'. He punningly contrasts the chasteness that should exist within the camp (*castra*) with the lack of chastity that existed within the army.[36] Alluding to the biblical story of the army of Joshua, which was punished for the sin of one of its members, William writes of how 'a most numerous army of the

Lord was defiled by the secret crime of one man, and deprived of divine favour, that those troops became powerless and listless'. Is he referring to Raymond and Eleanor's alleged sin? This seems unlikely, as elsewhere he praised Raymond as 'the stoutest champion of Christianity in the east ... [through whose] claims to outstanding achievements he had transferred to himself the glory of Maccabee of old'.[37] Not all accounts, however, comfortably fit the 'anti-Plantagenet propaganda' model. For example, Richard of Devizes, writing in the 1190s, was an enthusiast of Richard I, and fiercely anti-French.[38] Yet he alluded cautiously to the supposed Antioch incident in a marginal note stating that 'many know what I would that none of us knew. This same queen, during the time of her first husband, was at Jerusalem. Let no one say any more about it. I know it well. Keep silent!'[39] Richard's contemporary and fellow Englishman, Gervase of Canterbury, wrote that something 'perhaps better not spoken of' occurred in Syria.[40]

Even if we cannot be sure of the truth, we can perhaps shed some light on why the sexual accusations were specifically raised. All these accounts date from after the annulment of Eleanor's marriage to Louis VII. No contemporary accounts name adultery as a reason for this annulment; the earliest such reference comes from antiquarian sources in the sixteenth century. The question of consanguinity was the stated reason for the annulment. The author of the *Historia gloriosi Ludovici regis* claimed that Louis sought an annulment after learning that his marriage to Eleanor was within the prohibited degrees and he 'did not wish to keep his wife any longer against Catholic law'.[41] The story of Louis suddenly discovering his pious scruples is a little improbable, given that both St Bernard and Eleanor had previously complained about this very issue.[42] William of Newburgh identified Eleanor as the moving spirit behind seeking a divorce, on the grounds that she 'longed to be wed to the duke of Normandy [Henry] as one more congenial to her character' and subsequently 'with unlawful license [she] soon set off for her new partner'[43] Gervase of Canterbury reported that 'people said that it was she who had cleverly brought about that contrived repudiation'.[44] John of Salisbury's account of events at Antioch is important here. He claimed that when Louis insisted on Eleanor leaving with him for Jerusalem, it was she who first raised the question of their consanguinity:

> And when the king made haste to tear her away, she mentioned their kinship, saying that it was not lawful for them to remain together as man and wife, since they were related in the fourth and fifth degrees.[45]

The failure of Eleanor to produce male heirs is often cited as a reason for the annulment. Ralph Turner even calls it the 'decisive factor',[46] and Jacques

Le Goff argues that to the clergy who pronounced the annulment this was of greater concern than any supposed misdeeds of Eleanor.[47] It appears as a reason for the divorce in subsequent imaginative portrayals of Eleanor, from the Ménestral de Reims writing c. 1260 to *The Lion in Winter*, 700 years later. While there is little contemporary evidence of Louis's thinking on this matter, it is difficult to imagine Louis seeking an annulment had Eleanor produced a male heir.

Regardless of the motives and stated reason for the annulment, it is not hard to see how speculation on the 'real' reason for the breach between Louis and Eleanor could be projected back to an alleged act of adultery during the crusade. Claims that Eleanor was the one seeking the annulment, thereby threatening male authority within marriage; that she was eager to marry Henry; that her complaints against Louis had originated in the Antioch incident; and that incest (albeit the technical incest of marrying within the prohibited degrees) had been committed could coalesce into the accusation of adulterous incest committed on the Second Crusade.

We might also look for literary influences or parallels to the accusations. Peggy McCracken, in her analysis of the chronicle accounts of Eleanor, points to the topos of the 'Seductress Queen' derived from the *Roman des sept sages de Rome*.[48] In this romance, an empress attempts to seduce her stepson, and, upon being rejected, accuses him in turn of rape. This is an ancient topos, with precedents in the story of Phaedra and Hyppolitos. This incest (or attempted incest) with an in-law (incest 'of the second kind') is also present in Arthurian romances, in the relationship between Tristan and Iseult, and between Mordred and Guinevere.

There are, however, few obvious literary models for the idea of uncle–niece incest.[49] Nor does the seductress queen always comfortably fit the accusations against Eleanor. The nearest we come to a Phaedra scenario is the claim that she slept with Henry's father before her second marriage, but this is a poor parallel, as Geoffrey was neither the king nor Eleanor's husband. Furthermore, William of Tyre's version of the events at Antioch has Raymond, not Eleanor, as the active party in the affair. Having clashed with Louis over the conduct of the crusade, Raymond 'began to hate the king's ways; he openly plotted against him and took means to do him injury. He resolved also to deprive him of his wife, either by force or by secret intrigue.'[50] In this version, it is Raymond who is the principal transgressor: he is closer to Mordred or Tristan, seducing the wife of the man to whom, in the words of John of Salisbury, he 'owed … loyalty, affection, and respect …'

Finally, can we view the accusations against Eleanor as part of a more general misogynist critique, independent of – or at least larger than – specific allegations of incest, or criticisms of the Angevins? Flori argues persuasively that the criticisms of Eleanor are political in nature, based on a fierce disagreement between her and Raymond on the one hand, and Louis on the other, over the conduct of the crusade. 'Eleanor (a woman!) had dared to take a political decision on the basis of her own feelings, to behave like a fully paid-up human being...'[51] There is not the space here to pursue the 'political' argument, and the idea that it was so unusual for a twelfth-century queen to play an active political role should be questioned. The notion that there is an anti-feminist element in the criticism of Eleanor is unsurprising to the point of obviousness. There are, however, interesting gendered elements in the representation of Eleanor and Louis, with Louis's manhood challenged by Eleanor's assertion of her sovereignty.

In his account, John of Salisbury emphasizes the role of Thierry Galeran, a knight and secretary of Louis. He was 'a eunuch whom the queen had always hated and mocked'. Thierry persuaded the king to remove Eleanor from Antioch to avoid the 'shame' of being 'deserted by his wife, or robbed of her'. The king was reluctant to lose Eleanor, whom he loved 'almost beyond reason'.[52] In this passage, it is Louis who is unmanned. He allows his reason to be overruled by his feelings, a stereotypically female attribute according to medieval ideas about the two sexes. It is the unmanly eunuch Galeran who stiffens Louis's resolve and makes him act like a man, regaining control of the situation and reasserting his authority over his wife. John returns to the theme of Louis's helpless love for his wife when he describes Pope Eugenius's attempt to reconcile the couple at Tusculum (Frascati) on their return journey. He tells us that the king 'loved the queen passionately, in an almost childish way'.[53] Once again, Louis is portrayed as less than manly, reduced to a childlike state by his excessive uxorious love. For the chronicler Lambert of Waterlos, a monk of Cambrai who perhaps reflected the anti-French sentiment of the towns of the Low Countries, Louis was a weak figure, who was easily swayed and who picked a 'childish' (*puerilis*) quarrel with his wife. Finally, William of Newburgh describes Louis as 'enslaved' by Eleanor's beauty to the extent that out of jealousy he dared not leave her behind when he departed on crusade.[54]

The idea that the allegations about Eleanor's behaviour about Antioch were motivated by anti-Plantagenet propaganda or by anti-feminism is broadly sound. However, a closer reading of the sources should warn us against any one simple interpretation. Notions of incest or gender raised in the chronicle accounts raise wider issues that cannot be made to fit a single explanation of the events that may have occurred at Antioch in 1148.

Eleanor as a cross-dresser

In 1174, Eleanor of Aquitaine attempted to flee to the court of her former husband, Louis VII of France, following the collapse of the rebellion of her son Henry, the Young King. According to Gervase of Canterbury, writing at the end of the twelfth century, '[a]s the Queen was in flight, having put off women's dress, she was captured and placed in custody. For it was said that all this [i.e., the rebellion] had been fomented by her machinations and at her prompting. For she was a very shrewd woman, nobly born, but fickle.'[55]

Cross-dressing could be viewed as transgressive or praiseworthy in medieval clerical writing, depending upon the context. Vern Bullough, in a discussion of medieval attitudes to cross-dressing,[56] argues that for women, cross-dressing was a means to attain a 'higher' state, reflecting not only social and religious views of gender status, but also Aristotelian ideas that women were 'incomplete' men. Female saints, for example, might dress as men to avoid seduction or rape. Such behaviour was condoned or even praised by hagiographers. '[I]t seems clear that the reason female crossing of the gender barriers was tolerated in the medieval period, even encouraged, was because it was assumed such women were striving to be more male-like and therefore better persons.'[57] In Eleanor's case, however, it was a symbol of her 'unnatural' action of rebelling against her husband and overlord, Henry II. By becoming male in her dress, she was defeminized, as was fitting (in the eyes of the clerical chroniclers) for a woman who had set aside her 'natural' role as wife and mother, and her aspiration to the 'higher' status of a man is symbolic of her threat to the established order. For Gervase of Canterbury, Eleanor's behaviour was symptomatic both of her rebellion (taking on a male role) and of her fickleness (changing her dress and therefore her gender role). In the words of Jean Flori, this 'could only discredit her further in the eyes of her contemporaries by reinforcing her image as a woman who behaved like a man ...'.[58] Gervase's view of her as an instigator of rebellion fits with his other references to her taking the lead in intrigue, as when he describes her divorce from Louis as a 'contrived repudiation' brought about by Eleanor to facilitate her marriage to Henry of Anjou.[59]

There was also a strong association between hermaphroditism and monstrosity in the medieval imagination. Among the races who were believed to inhabit the farthest reaches of the world were the *Androgini*, who were said to possess both male and female genitalia, bearded women, and *Gorgades* – hairy women.[60] While in pre-Christian sources these races might be viewed as curiosities of the distant East, in the medieval Christian worldview, monstrosity was the mark of

Cain, who was believed to be the ancestor of such deviant forms of humanity.[61] A more positive – or at least ambiguous – model for androgynous women among the peoples of the East could be found in the figure of the Amazon, who provided medieval writers with an archetype of the warrior woman.

Eleanor's behaviour can also be viewed in terms of chroniclers' accounts of martial women. Although Gervase does not accuse Eleanor of taking up arms, by her involvement in the revolt she is, in a sense, taking on the 'male' role of military leader. This phenomenon invariably created problems of definition for clerical chroniclers, who felt torn between praising the woman concerned for rising 'above' her sex and disdaining her for acting in an unnatural manner. For example, William of Tyre, describing the capture of Jerusalem by the forces of the First Crusade, wrote that 'even women, regardless of sex and natural weakness, dared to assume arms and fight manfully, far beyond their strength'.[62] In contrast, a woman fighting in a cause judged less honourable by a clerical author was criticized for her presumptions to masculinity. Eleanor's mother-in-law, the Empress Matilda, was described as a 'virago' by William of Malmesbury,[63] and was accused by Henry of Huntingdon of displaying 'womanly rage' when she imprisoned King Stephen.[64] So Matilda was condemned both when she assumed male behaviour and when she acted as stereotypically female.

Chroniclers of the twelfth century had therefore created the basis for the Black Legend, a queen who was not only an adulteress but who usurped male sovereignty by demanding an annulment of her first marriage, choosing her second husband on her own authority and later instigating her sons into rebellion against him. Later medieval romance would develop the legend further, to the extent that Eleanor became a lover of Saladin and a demonic figure.

Late-medieval legends

By the thirteenth century, the original allegations against Eleanor were being augmented by additional material appearing in chronicles and vernacular verse. Daniel Power has studied the development of her reputation in Normandy in the thirteenth century:[65] an early- to mid-century Norman vernacular chronicle represents one of the first appearances of the diabolical Eleanor of legend. Accused of being a devil by her lords, Eleanor disrobes to prove that she is in fact a beautiful woman.[66] On the face of it, the account exonerates Eleanor, and reflects the medieval belief that beauty is an expression of godliness. However, the disrobing surely also hints at her reputation as an adulteress. In the vernacular rhymed chronicle of Philippe Mousket, written sometime after 1242, the disrobing scene is expanded, and Eleanor is presented as a descendant of a devilish ancestor of the counts of Poitou.[67] Legends of a diabolical ancestor were common in north-west France in this period; the Angevins were supposed to have been descended from the devil, hence the famous remark attributed by Gerald of Wales to St Bernard upon meeting the future Henry II that 'from the devil they came, and to the devil they shall go!'[68] The most famous serpent-woman of legend, Mélusine, was the supposed ancestor of the counts of Lusignan. By the late thirteenth century, Eleanor herself has been replaced as Richard I's mother by the demonic Cassodorien in the Middle-English romance *Richard Coeur de Lion*.[69]

The *Récits d'un Ménestral de Reims* c. 1260 combines the claims of Eleanor's adultery with the notion of her diabolical nature. In the words of its modern editor, the *Récit* is '[u]nreliable, entertaining, and difficult to classify … many of its incidents and all of the direct discourse are fictional'.[70] The Ménestral's agenda was 'to praise the Capetians … [and] to castigate enemies of the Capetians', hence the anti-Plantagenet tone. The section covering the Second Crusade has Louis anachronistically fighting Saladin. It recounts the story of Eleanor's adultery, but this time it is Saladin with whom she seeks to run away. Louis is able to prevent her from absconding just in time:

> When the king heard this, he jumped up, got dressed, went out and ordered his entourage to arm themselves, and he went off to the harbor. There he found the queen, with one foot in the galley, and he took her by the hand, and brought her back to her room. The king's entourage captured the galley and its crew, for they were too surprised to defend themselves.
>
> The king asked the queen why she wanted to do this and she replied: 'In the name of God, because you are not worth much. I heard so much about Saladin that I love him better than I love you. Be sure that you understand that you will never hold me.' The king quickly departed, leaving her heavily guarded, and decided to return to France, for his money was running out, and in the East he had acquired only dishonor.[71]

This episode is the first recorded version of the legend that Eleanor had committed adultery (or at least intended to do so) with Saladin, a claim that would continue to appear in popular fiction up until the nineteenth century. Saladin and Eleanor's relationship is, perhaps surprisingly, portrayed in chivalrous terms, with the two would-be lovers exchanging letters. Eleanor is attracted to Saladin by his reputation as 'she heard men speak of the goodness and strength and understanding and generosity of Saladin', while the Saracen ruler 'was very pleased, for he knew that she was the most aristocratic and wealthiest lady in Christendom'.[72] Saladin is portrayed as 'a noble pagan, like Rainouart or Wolfram von Eschenbach's Feirefiz'.[73] Nevertheless, it is hard to avoid an implication that Eleanor's diabolical nature is reflected in her dalliance with the leader of the Muslim enemies of the faith; this might explain why the identity of her lover had evolved from the crusader-prince Raymond to the infidel Saladin.

Despite its strange mutation, with the identity and even religion of Eleanor's would-be lover switched, the Ménestral's story is recognizably based on the allegations of Eleanor's adultery with Raymond. Familiar elements are there, such as Eleanor's disgust at 'the king's weakness'[74] and Louis's seizure of Eleanor (although in this case, Louis prevents her from leaving with his rival, rather than taking her away from him).

The sequel of Eleanor and Louis's divorce, however, owes more to the legends of the diabolical queen. We are told at the beginning of the account that 'Eleanor... was a very evil woman...'.[75] On returning to France, Louis is told by his barons that he should divorce her

> 'since she is the devil, and we fear that, if you keep her any longer, she will have you killed. In addition she has given you no child'. The king foolishly agreed, and carried out this plan; he should have cloistered her, so that his land would have remained great all his life, and the disasters of which you are about to hear would not have taken place.[76]

Divorced, Eleanor is now free to marry Henry of Anjou. The incident of the devilish Eleanor is therefore the origin story for Capetian–Plantagenet conflict in the *Récit* author's schema of history, reflecting perhaps the chroniclers' claims that the strife among Henry II's sons was a reflection of their dubious ancestry.

By the mid-thirteenth century, even chronicle accounts were beginning to incorporate claims about Eleanor's diabolical nature and her dalliance with the infidel, suggesting a complex, two-way relationship between history and romance (and indeed, a blurring between the two). Matthew Paris accused her of adultery with 'an infidel prince'[77]; writing about her divorce and subsequent marriage to Henry, he described Eleanor as possessing 'diabolical craftiness'.[78] John Carmi Parsons compares the criticism of Eleanor in the twelfth- and early thirteenth-century chronicles to that of other foreign queens, citing Matthew Paris's criticism of Henry III's queen, Eleanor of Provence.[79] It is possible that Paris's opinion of Queen Eleanor of his own time, and of the king's Poitevin relatives, coloured his opinion of the Poitevin Eleanor of Aquitaine.

By c. 1300, the idea of the diabolical Eleanor had entered Middle-English romance in the poem *Richard Coeur de Lion*. Richard's devilish mother is, however, not named Eleanor, but Cassodorien. It is problematic as to whether Cassodorien really *is* Eleanor, as the queen appears elsewhere in the romance under her real name. She seems to be based on the legend of the Angevins' demonic female ancestor, who flew out of the roof when confronted with the consecrated host. Stories of Richard's otherworldly ancestress and the Ménestral's story of a devilish Eleanor therefore seem to have become conflated.[80] The fact that Cassodorien is described as daughter of the king of Antioch may also be an allusion to the tales of Eleanor's adultery with Prince Raymond. Curiously, however, this ancestry did not diminish Richard in the eyes of the romancer; he also attributed to the king descent from Alexander, Charlemagne, Arthur and Gawain, and Richard possessed the ability to triumph over the evil spells cast by Saladin. Richard's diabolical ancestry, like that of Merlin, is a source of strength rather than of evil.[81]

The motif of female monstrosity in medieval literature carries with it important implications for views of female sovereignty. Perhaps the most celebrated redaction of the monstrous woman motif was the later medieval story of Mélusine, which first appeared in written form in the work of Jean d'Arras c. 1380, and which is associated with Eleanor's house, the counts of Poitou. Rémond, a nephew of the count of Poitiers, marries Mélusine, who appears as a serpent from the navel downwards on Saturdays. This secret is discovered by her husband when he spies on her while bathing, a breach of trust that arises from sexual jealousy after his brother has convinced him that Mélusine has taken a lover. However, this is merely the most celebrated element of a complex story. Mélusine and her sisters are themselves the result of a liaison between a mortal man and a supernatural mother, and they went into exile along with their mother after their father had broken his promise not to observe their mother as she gave birth to or bathed her children. Mélusine's partly serpentine form is a punishment imposed on her by her mother after she and her sisters imprisoned their father in a mountain as revenge for his broken promise to their mother. The legend therefore has heavy overtones of female authority, and of broken trust, themes that are familiar to us from Eleanor's life. In the words of Gerhild Scholz Williams, '[s]tories of Mélusine and women like her...show that it is unacceptable for such creatures to govern, unchecked by males, over their realm and their people'.[82] Representations of Eleanor as a monstrous woman therefore tapped into a tradition that was suspicious of female power. So deeply engrained was this image of Eleanor that by the nineteenth century Jules Michelet could write: '[t]he real Mellusine, imbued with contradictory natures, mother and daughter of diabolical conception, *is in fact Eleanor of Guyenne* [my emphasis]'.[83]

As the Ménestral's account shows, the transformation of Eleanor into a devilish figure was linked to her portrayal as an adulteress. A rather more innocent legend of Eleanor's adultery is that of her relationship with the troubadour Bernart de Ventadorn. The claim that the two were lovers has become so entrenched in Eleanor mythology that it was still appearing in fiction and drama at the end of the twentieth century.[84] It derives from the *Vida* of Bernart by Uc de St-Cerc:

> And he left and went to the Duchess of Normandy, who was young and of great merit, and she understood worth and honor and fine words of praise. And very pleasing to her were the songs and verses of Sir Bernart, and she received him and welcomed him very heartily. He stayed in her court for a long time, and he fell in love with her, and she with him, and he made very good songs about her. And during his stay with her, King Henry of England took her to England. Sir Bernart remained here, sad and grieving…[85]

This passage, along with the dedication of one of Bernart's poems to 'the Norman Queen',[86] should not lead us to believe that Eleanor and Bernart were lovers (and even if they were, the *Vida* does not suggest their love was consummated sexually). The *Vida* was written perhaps as late as 1253,[87] and should not be taken too literally; *vidas* of troubadours tended to be formulaic: 'And the troubadour Sir X fell in love with the lady Y, wife of his lord, and she with him out of all measure, etc.'[88]

A variation of the legend of Eleanor's lascivious nature occurs in the *Anecdotes* of Stephen of Bourbon, written sometime between 1250 and 1261. Stephen claimed that the 'queen of France' attempted to seduce the pious scholar Gilbert de la Porée, who was the bishop of Poitiers from 1142 to 1154.[89] This incident was supposed to have occurred at the Council of Sens in 1140, which would make Eleanor the queen of France at the time.[90] Eleanor's reputation for adultery, which clerical writers had helped to promote, was recast as a direct threat to clerical celibacy.

The thirteenth-century development of the Black Legend is therefore somewhat contradictory. The *Richard Coeur de Lion*'s presentation of 'Cassodorien' as an exotic but not wholly negative figure, and the *Vida* of Bernart's *fin'amor* interpretation of the troubadour's love for the queen, counter-balanced the more openly hostile representations of Eleanor. On the other hand, the story of her alleged adultery with Raymond of Antioch is transformed into even more transgressive approaches to the infidel Saladin or the saintly bishop of Poitiers. In the account of the Ménestral, the adulterous and diabolical queen are even combined. The legend continued to reflect unease over female authority, including perhaps criticism of contemporary queens such as Eleanor of Provence. In later legend, however, Eleanor was accused of a further transgression: murder.

Fair Rosamond

Gerald of Wales described Henry II's mistress Rosamond de Clifford in a famous pun as a 'rosa immundi' (unclean rose), not as a *rosa mundi* (rose of the world). He implied that Henry planned to imprison Eleanor in order to spend more time with his mistress, and that after his victory over the rebellion of 1173–4 he, like Pharaoh, relapsed into vice.[91] Roger of Howden records that, following Rosamond's death and burial at Godstow Abbey in Oxfordshire, the bishop of Lincoln had her reburied outside the abbey grounds 'for she was a harlot'.[92] Yet from this unflattering beginning developed a legend in which Rosamond was transformed into an innocent heroine, she and Henry into star-crossed lovers, and Eleanor – the wronged party – into a murderess.

A key element of the legend is that Henry hid Rosamond deep within a bower at Woodstock to protect her from the queen's vengeance. This first appears in Ranulph Higden's early fourteenth-century *Polychronicon*, which passed into English through John Trevisa's translation later in the century.[93] Higden made no mention of Eleanor having killed Rosamond, the queen being in prison at the time of her death. The bower with its maze is at this point merely a wonderfully crafted chamber. Rosamond was buried at Godstow, where her grave bore the inscription

> Hic jacet in tumba Rosa mundi non sed rosa munda,
> Non redolet sed olet redolere solet.

Trevisa translated this as

> Here lieth in tombe the rose of the world, nought a clean rose; it smelleth nought swete, but it stinketh, that was wont to smelle ful swete.[94]

The epitaph is clearly a development of Gerald of Wales's judgement, but with an added element of *memento mori*.

The first claims that Eleanor was a murderer come from secular chronicles of the city of London. The mid-fourteenth-century *French Chronicle of London* confuses Eleanor with her namesake, Eleanor of Provence, the wife of Henry III, who was deeply unpopular with the people of London. The author has Eleanor bleed Rosamond to death, and, in a peculiar twist, has an old woman place toads upon the dying girl's breasts.[95] The toad is a symbol of death, poison, and decomposition.[96] Fabyan's Chronicle, an English chronicle of London from the turn of the sixteenth century, adds another element that became a key part of the Rosamond legend, the claim that Eleanor found her rival within the maze with the aid of a ball of silk or thread.[97] The late sixteenth-century ballad *Fair Rosamund* by Thomas Delony[98] develops the themes further, with the addition of a 'trusty knight' who provides Eleanor with the silken thread. Eleanor kills Rosamond with poison, despite the young woman pleading for her life – two more elements that would be repeated in later retellings of the legend. The story also entered antiquarian histories in Raphael Holinshed's chronicle.[99] John Stowe in the 1601 edition of his *Annales of England* describes Eleanor poisoning Rosamond, probably reflecting the developing ballad tradition.[100]

The later Fair Rosamond story had therefore developed a long way from the first chronicle references; Rosamond had evolved from whore to wronged heroine. This may reflect the increasingly negative reputation of Eleanor through the thirteenth century: the demonic queen was now capable of increasingly evil actions. It may also result from confusion between the historical Eleanor of Aquitaine and her namesake Eleanor of Provence. As we have seen, the London chronicle made Eleanor of Provence the evil queen of the legend, reflecting her unpopularity among thirteenth-century Londoners, who attacked her barge in 1263.[101] The Fair Rosamond tale also includes familiar mythological and folklore motifs. The bower and golden thread are clearly derived from the Theseus myth, which was well known in the Middle Ages, as was the concept of the labyrinth, which served as a metaphor for many purposes: 'amusement, entrapment, protection, penitence, allegory' (for example, of the path of human life, as a person seeks to avoid the entrapments of sin and emerge successfully into salvation), and was frequently represented in art, including on the walls or floors of churches.[102] The twelfth-century writer Lambert of Ardres claimed that an inventive Frenchman had built 'a nearly inextricable labyrinth …'[103] This need not be taken literally but indicates that the idea of constructing a labyrinth existed in Eleanor's time, while the fact that it was envisaged as a building rather than a bower recalls the chamber which was the form that Rosamond's legendary bower took in Higden's early version of the tale. The other element of the tale – the jealous older queen who poisons her rival – recalls folk-tales such as Snow White (Aarne-Thompson-Uther type 709).[104]

Early-modern developments of the Black Legend continued the tradition of Eleanor's adultery. In the ballad 'Queen Eleanor's Confession' (Child No. 156),[105] Eleanor, thinking that she is at death's door, summons two confessors, who are actually Henry II and William Marshal in disguise. The 'priests' hear Eleanor admit to adultery with Marshal. The ballad was first printed in 1685, but probably composed much earlier, perhaps in Elizabethan times.[106] This is the only tradition that suggests an affair between Eleanor and William Marshal, although we know that Marshal served Eleanor in Poitou, and she was viewed favourably in the Anglo-Norman poem that celebrated his life, the *Histoire de Guillaume le Maréchal*.[107] It is possible that the story was originally attached to a queen other than Eleanor. The *Histoire* records rumours aimed at blackening Marshal's reputation that claimed an affair between him and Marguerite, the wife of Henry, the Young King.[108] As Eleanor became notorious through the development of the Fair Rosamond legend, scandalous accusations against other queens began to attach themselves to her, as we have previously seen in the confusion between her and Eleanor of Provence, or the subsuming of the diabolical ancestors of the Angevins into the character of Cassodorien, mother of Richard the Lionheart. Famous legendary or pseudo-historical figures tend to act like magnets, drawing stories towards them based on the power of their legend. In much the same way as Celtic warrior-legends coalesced around Arthur,[109] in a negative example of the same process evil-queen legends coalesced around the pseudo-historical figure of meta-Eleanor.

Eleanor and the antiquarians

By c. 1600, therefore, key elements of the Black Legend in English popular culture had developed. The later evolution of these on the eighteenth- and nineteenth-century stage is traced in Chapter 4. However, in the sixteenth and seventeenth centuries the legend, while continuing and indeed developing further in popular literature, coexisted with more serious historical studies that gave a more nuanced view of Eleanor. Didier le Fur has argued that the early sixteenth century was an era when chroniclers were favourable to the idea of female power, as this was an age of female regents, such as Anne of France, who acted on behalf of Charles VIII. However, Eleanor's problematic reputation led these chroniclers to treat her with ambivalence. For example, Robert Gaguin in the *Mer des chroniques*, while not making any mention of Eleanor committing adultery with Raymond of Antioch, did describe her as 'lubrique' (lecherous).[110]

In 1524, the French poet and historian Jean Bouchet published his *Annales d'Aquitaine*.[111] Poitiers-born Bouchet initiated a more positive view of Eleanor, perhaps because of his origins in Eleanor's home region.[112] Bouchet attempted to 'restore a more honorable memory of its [Aquitaine's] former duchess', a need that confirms the extent to which the Black Legend of the ballads had taken hold.[113] Bouchet was writing as part of a trend for regional histories and assessed Eleanor in the context of the history of Poitou or Aquitaine. While remaining perfectly loyal to the kings of France, Bouchet expresses a certain regionalist sentiment, referring, for example, to how 'le Royaume d'Aquitaine' was suppressed by the French kings in the early Middle Ages.[114]

Bouchet's approach can be seen in the way he addresses the controversial issue of Eleanor's relations with Raymond of Antioch. His account seems to be based on William of Tyre, and is sober and fair-minded up to a point, as Bouchet leaves out William's claims that Raymond sought to deprive Louis of his wife and that Eleanor agreed to this. However, he then introduces the legend from the Ménestral de Reims that Eleanor had considered running away with Saladin; Bouchet combines this with the accusations made against Raymond by claiming that Eleanor's uncle had conspired with Saladin to marry Eleanor to him, by which arrangement Raymond would have gained some territory from the Sultan.[115] Bouchet states that the Bishop of Langres raised the issue of Eleanor's adultery as grounds for divorce, a claim that is not to be found in any surviving medieval sources, but which has made its way into some modern histories.[116] Nevertheless, he portrays Eleanor as the innocent party, victim of machinations against her at a council from which she is absent.[117]

Jean Besly (1572–1644), whose *Histoire des comtes de Poictou et ducs de Guyenne* was published posthumously in 1647,[118] has been described as 'the first historian of Poitou'.[119] He made reference to 'an immense quantity' of original sources,[120] some of which were transcribed in a long appendix to his work.[121] Like Bouchet, he refers to the allegations of Eleanor's adultery, but disputes them. His version of what transpired between Eleanor and Raymond at Antioch is heavily influenced by the accounts of William of Tyre and John of Salisbury. Raymond at first welcomes Louis and entertains him liberally, but becomes contemptuous toward the king when he refuses to listen to Raymond's strategic advice.[122] Not only did the Poitevin Besly not draw attention to Eleanor's adulterous reputation, he actively defended her. He mentions the story of her flirtation with Saladin, but specifically to refute it, condemning 'the deceits that have been invented and written about this divorce [from Louis VII] to the prejudice of this illustrious princess …'[123] Furthermore, he challenges those historians who blamed Eleanor for the loss of Aquitaine, pointing out that she held it in her own right, and it was therefore hers to dispose of as she saw fit,[124] opinions that hint at Poitevin regional pride on Besly's part.

The work of Besly in challenging the early-modern version of the Black Legend was set back somewhat by the work of another Poitevin historian, Isaac de Larrey. Larrey was a Protestant, who was living in exile in the Netherlands following the revocation of the Edict of Nantes when his *Histoire d'Éléonor de Guienne* was published in 1691.[125] In his introduction, De Larrey set out how he would take pleasure in challenging the myths that were growing up around Eleanor, including that of her affair with Saladin (or 'a Turkish soldier'). 'To the accounts of historians which are hardly in her favour, storytellers have merely added fictions that are even more disparaging… There is pleasure in defending injured innocence …'[126] His position as a Huguenot exile may explain his defence of Eleanor against pro-Capetian and Catholic chroniclers who had been responsible for her bad reputation. Like Besly, he exonerates Eleanor of wrongdoing at Antioch, claiming that Louis's suspicions were 'unfounded (*mal fondés)*'.[127]

However, De Larrey made his own contributions towards mythologizing Eleanor. The story that she and her ladies dressed as Amazons at Vézelay seems to have originated with his history,[128] although, as we will see, it is ultimately based on a (mis)reading of a single reference by the Byzantine historian Nicetas Choniates.

> The women themselves, not wishing to exempt themselves from this holy militia, formed squadrons, reenacting the story of the Amazons: and Queen Eleanor for her part wanted to go on the journey, believing she would find further amusements…[129]

Thus was born another myth that continues to surface in the historical fiction and popular history of the early twenty-first century – that Eleanor light-heartedly set off on crusade in fancy dress in search of adventure.

The history of a legend: Eleanor as Amazon-queen

The next chapter will trace the history of Eleanor's reinvention in the light of modern history – both popular and academic – in the eighteenth, nineteenth and twentieth centuries. That process was not, however, an uncomplicated one of replacing the Black Legend with historical 'truth'. So before moving on, let us consider a case study of a legend of Eleanor that began with an imprecise medieval chronicle reference, and grew into a fully fledged romantic myth, through early-modern antiquarian history into the modern age. The story of how Eleanor was reinvented as an Amazon Queen on the Second Crusade allows us to see how the mythmaking process develops, illustrating how the Black Legend often owes as much to nineteenth- and twentieth-century historians as to pre-modern lore.

In the *Historia* written by the Byzantine courtier Niketas Choniates, a remarkable woman is described among the crusader army that passed through Constantinople in 1147:

> A cloud of enemies, a dreadful and death-dealing pestilence, fell upon the Roman borders: I speak of the campaign of the Germans, joined by other kindred nations. Females were numbered among them, riding horseback in the manner of men, not on coverlets sidesaddle but unashamedly astride, and bearing lances and weapons as men do; dressed in masculine garb, they conveyed a wholly martial appearance, more mannish than the Amazons. One stood out from the rest as another Penthesilea and from the embroidered gold which ran around the hem and fringes of her garment was called Goldfoot [Chrysópous].[130]

It is worth remarking firstly what Niketas did *not* say; the woman was not named Eleanor, nor was she referred to as a queen. She and her companions were said to have dressed in a masculine fashion, carrying arms, and were compared to Penthesilea and her Amazons, but were not said to have deliberately dressed in such a way as to imitate these mythological figures. Nor did Niketas call them French: he used the term *Alemanoi*, which applies to the German people of the western Empire.[131] Furthermore, he was writing more than half a century after Louis and Eleanor's visit to Constantinople in 1147, which occurred several years before his own birth. From these bare bones, many have concluded that this Amazonian woman was Eleanor, and historians have subsequently cited one another in circular fashion to support this identification. For example, Harry Magoulias, the modern editor and English translator of Choniates, refers the reader to Steven Runciman for the identification of 'Goldfoot' with Eleanor, warning the reader that 'Runciman, however, does not cite his sources.'[132] Runciman in turn refers to 'a remark by Nicetas … that the German army contained a number of fully armed women.'[133] Van Dieten, in his edition of Niketas' chronicle published in 1975, identified *Chrysópous* as 'Eleanora Franciae regina' without citing a source.[134] Amy Kelly's 1950 biography called the Amazonian incident 'a legend' but went on to say that '[t]he tale is in character, and later allusions to Amazons en route, found in Greek historians, give substance to it'.[135] The Greek 'historians [*sic*]' is of course Niketas. Kelly accepted a second level to the legend, that Eleanor and her ladies had previously dressed as Amazons at Vézelay when Louis's crusade was launched, before repeating the performance in Constantinople.[136] Roy Owen, in his 1992 biography of Eleanor, acknowledged that Eleanor's Amazonian performance was a legend, but then asserted that Niketas 'surely had Eleanor herself in mind when he described the arrival of the crusaders at Constantinople'.[137] Alison Weir, in her popular biography of Eleanor in 1997, which is heavily dependent on Kelly's at this point, argues that '[m]ost historians dismiss the tale as pure legend, because there are no contemporary accounts of it, but it is in keeping with what we know of Eleanor's character... The tale may have originated from the eye-witness account of a Greek observer ....'[138] The Greek 'eye-witness' is of course Niketas, who was not a contemporary.

Jean Flori cautions us to be wary of the accounts of Eleanor during the crusade, reminding us, for example, that the reference to her taking the cross in 1146 was written by the continuator of Suger some thirty years after the event.[139] He urges prudence in assessing tales of Eleanor's Amazonian behaviour, arguing that a combination of Niketas's account and medieval Amazon literature such as Benoît de Sainte-Maure's *Roman de Troie*, 'excited the imagination of many historians, who are rather too quick to link them to the chroniclers who tended to conclude that the Second Crusade failed due to the presence of too many women among the Christian armies'.[140] He credits de Larrey and Gervaise with the creation of Eleanor's Amazonian myth, before pointedly reminding us that 'even in the twentieth century, certain authors still give credence to this romanticized version'.[141] Even he, however, writes that 'the queen to whom he [Niketas] alludes would seem to be Eleanor, whose presence obviously did not go unnoticed'.[142] Historians have apparently reinforced one another by citing the identification of Chrysópous with Eleanor without backing up the assertion with a careful reading of the evidence. In the words of F. M. Chambers, the legend has thereby 'gained a certain respectability from the company it has kept'.[143]

From where, then, did the idea of the Amazonian Eleanor originate? The identification in the modern imagination – in the English-speaking world, at least – would seem to be based not on any medieval account but on the nineteenth-century presentation of Eleanor by Agnes Strickland and her sister Elizabeth, the biographers of England's queens (whose work is discussed at greater length in the next chapter). The Stricklands took up the theme of Eleanor's masculine behaviour which was so clearly contrary to the Victorian view of how a decent woman should behave. In Elizabeth's biography of Eleanor, published in 1840, the queen's fancy-dress appearance as Penthesilea occurred when Louis and his lords took the cross at Vézelay in 1147:

> When queen Eleanora received the cross…she directly put on the dress of the Amazons; and her ladies, all actuated by the same frenzy, mounted on horseback, and forming a light squadron, surrounded the queen when she appeared in public, calling themselves queen Eleanora's bodyguard. They practised Amazonian exercises, and performed a thousand follies in public, to animate their zeal as practical crusaders. By the suggestion of their young queen, this ban of mad-women sent their useless distaffs, as presents, to all the knights and nobles who had the good sense to keep out of the crusading expedition.[144]

The reference that Elizabeth Strickland cites for Eleanor's Amazonian performance is post-medieval, although in the first edition she refers – erroneously – to Suger and 'contemporary historians'. In the 1889 condensed edition, she refers the reader to *La Vie de Suger*, an eighteenth-century history written by M. d'Aubigny in 1739.[145] Suger himself did not record the events of the Second Crusade. His successor as the chronicler (and later abbot) of St Denis, Odo of Deuil, makes no mention of Eleanor behaving in this manner, and presents Louis's crusading exploits in flattering terms. However, by the nineteenth century, Eleanor's scandalous reputation was so firmly implanted that even 'objective' historians' opinions of her were coloured by the legend.

In fairness to the Stricklands, it must be noted that their account of Eleanor's Amazonian exploits was shared by the pioneering crusade historian Joseph Michaud. In his *Histoire des Croisades* of 1829, he stated that '[a] great number of women, attracted by the example of Eleanor of Guienne, took up the cross, and armed themselves with sword and lance…History relates that distaffs and spindles were sent to those who would not take up arms, as an appropriate reproach for their cowardice'.[146] The distaff incident seems to be based on an account of such behaviour by the author of the *Itinerarium* of Richard I on the Third Crusade, and in this instance it was men who sent distaffs to one another.[147] Michaud's account was dependent upon those of seventeenth- and eighteenth-century historians. De Larrey's *Histoire d'Eléonor d'Aquitaine* of 1691 seems to mark the earliest appearance of the story that Eleanor and her ladies dressed as Amazons at Vézelay.[148] The tale was repeated in Dom François Armand Gervaise's *Histoire de Suger* of 1721,[149] and thence by d'Aubigny in his *Vie de Suger* cited by the Stricklands.

Curtis Walker deconstructs the history of a related accusation against Eleanor on the Second Crusade.[150] The defeat of the French crusader army at Mount

Cadmos was widely blamed by later historians on Eleanor, who supposedly took command of part of the army and interfered with the tactics of Louis and his generals. Inappropriate female behaviour was therefore held responsible for military disaster, as Eleanor, like Niketas's 'Goldfoot', scandalously usurped the male prerogative of making war. Walker cites how Victorian historians such as Bishop Stubbs were influenced by the Eleanor myth, decrying how 'her undisguised flirtations had spread confusion and dismay and discord in the noblest host that ever went to the East'.[151] To this we can add the Stricklands again, who railed against 'the freaks of queen Eleanor and her female warriors [who] were the cause of all the misfortunes that befell king Louis and his army, especially the defeat at Laodicea'.[152] She interfered with Louis's strategy for no better reason than that she wished to make camp 'in a lovely romantic valley, full of verdant grass and gushing fountains', while the army was encumbered by having to carry the outlandish 'array of the lady warriors'. Walker points out that the accounts of Odo of Deuil (who accompanied the army) and of William of Tyre make no mention of Eleanor having a role in the battle. The notion that Eleanor intervened in the battle 'riding at the head of a column' emerged in the work of the French historian Alfred Richard, writing in 1903, and (like the Vézelay story) is dependent on a seventeenth-century source, the historian Maimbourg.[153] Odo and William's accounts blamed the defeat on the rash actions of Geoffrey of Rancon, a leading Poitevin vassal, but later accounts shifted the blame on to Eleanor.[154] Comments such as Stubbs's 'noblest army', betray the emotional engagement of many nineteenth- and early twentieth-century historians with crusades. They identified with the crusaders, lamented their defeats and looked for someone to blame, with Eleanor proving a useful scapegoat. Conversely, the Stricklands did not identify with the crusade, and regarded it as a ridiculous exercise. In their view, it was therefore wholly appropriate that it should be sabotaged by Eleanor's outrageous behaviour.

The Black Legend of Eleanor was therefore many centuries in the making, and included elements as diverse as chronicle references from Eleanor's own lifetime, later-medieval romances, early-modern ballads and antiquarian histories. It reflected a general unease about female authority alongside specific criticisms of Eleanor by her contemporaries, as well as political concerns, with anti-Plantagenet or anti-Capetian opinions often colouring verdicts on Eleanor. As the last case-study demonstrates, it was a process that continued even with the emergence of supposedly more critical approaches to historiography in the Enlightenment and the nineteenth and twentieth centuries.

'A Realistic Image of Eleanor of Aquitaine'? Eleanor in Historiography

The Black Legend of Eleanor has competed with, existed alongside and – on occasions – been reinforced by the 'historical' Eleanor of both academic and popular histories. Nineteenth- and twentieth-century historians sometimes challenged meta-Eleanor, but at other times added new elements to the myth, or reinvigorated older ones. Historians may have striven to create (in the words of Edmond-René Labande) 'a realistic image of Eleanor of Aquitaine', but that image has struggled to replace that of the more colourful meta-Eleanor in the public consciousness. Hence an online author in 2013 is still able to write of Eleanor in stereotypical terms that would have been familiar to a mid-nineteenth century readership of popular history, focusing on personality and emotion: 'Although Louis adored Eleanor and gave her everything she asked for, their marriage was stormy, mostly due to Eleanor's high spirits and interference in political and religious matters'.[1]

The problems in establishing an objective, realistic image of Eleanor reflect her position at the intersection of questions of ideology, gender, nationalism and academic versus popular history. For many authors of the Enlightenment and French revolutionary eras, medieval queens were suspected to be representatives of the clerical, feudal and monarchical past. For both eighteenth-century *philosophes* and nineteenth-century academic historians, queens (and women in general) belonged to the private sphere, largely invisible in the official, public documents that were the raw materials for a new academic, empirical discipline of history. The history of women was therefore frequently relegated (or delegated) to the world of popular history, often written by women who were denied access to the resources of the academy, and for a female audience. Nineteenth-century academic history, despite its claims to objectivity and historicism, often served the needs of a growing nationalism. In this context, Eleanor's reputation also suffered: being an alien figure to both England and a Parisian-centred modern France, she was unable to fit comfortably into discourses of either French nationalism or English constitutionalism. Finally, in the late twentieth century, the Second-Wave Feminist movement gave birth to a new interest in Eleanor of Aquitaine as a female hero, but often at the expense of exaggerating her deeds and influence, and reinforcing the myth of her exceptionalism.

Enlightenment, revolution and the denigration of female authority

The Enlightenment did not treat Eleanor, or the medieval queen in general, kindly. While the evolution of more sceptical and scientific attitudes towards history might have cleared away some of the mythology of the Black Legend, this was offset by a set of negative assumptions about the medieval period and women. The Middle Ages were viewed by Enlightenment *philosophes* as an age of priests, kings and nobles, when the Catholic Church maintained its control over an ignorant, superstitious peasantry. Voltaire condemned the Middle Ages as 'barbarous' (*barbare*) and 'coarse' (*grossier*), and the period suffered from 'the disdainful indifference of the *philosophes*...'[2] Moreover, women were seen as creatures who should remain in the domestic sphere to which nature and reason had consigned them – as the bearers and nurses of children. In the writings of Rousseau, traditional views of the separate spheres for the sexes were reinforced by a 'scientific' belief that woman's biology consigned her 'naturally' to the role of breeder and nurse of children. 'Women received stereotypical criticisms' from eighteenth-century historians 'just as the church and religion did'.[3] Medieval women were therefore all the more likely to be described in misogynist terms, as we see in David Hume's verdict: 'Queen Eleanor, who had disgusted her first husband by her gallantries, was no less offensive to her second by her jealousy; and after this manner carried to extremity, in different periods of her life, every circumstance of female weakness.'[4]

The French Revolution, with its rejection of monarchy and the Catholic, medieval past, dealt Eleanor's reputation a further blow. In 1791, a work with the unambiguously anti-monarchical title *Les Crimes des reines de France, depuis le commencement de la monarchie jusqu'à Marie Antoinette* was published in Paris, written by Louise Keralio Robert.[5] The year of the Flight to Varennes, 1791 was arguably the high point of anti-monarchist sentiment, with Marie Antoinette in particular identified as a scapegoat for royal misdeeds. John Carmi Parsons has argued persuasively for the parallels between the accusations made against Eleanor and those against Marie Antoinette, including incest and adultery.[6] Keralio Robert's invective against the 'crimes' of French queens was coloured by anti-feminism as well as anti-monarchism. 'Any queen pursuing a forceful role against royal father, husband, or son ... became in her history a perpetrator of heinous crimes against the French people.'[7] The sins of women, she argued, were worse than those of men, because women led men astray. Queen consorts were viewed with suspicion because they hid behind their husband's power, allowing them to perform acts of mischief that they would not otherwise have dared do: 'like one of the mistresses of Jupiter, a queen jealously wishes to throw lightning bolts herself, even at the risk of being consumed by them herself'. But reigning queens were equally bad: 'A woman who has the power to do anything is capable of anything; a woman who becomes queen, changes her sex, believes anything is possible, and doubts nothing...'[8]

Unsurprisingly, Keralio Robert also displayed the anti-clerical revolutionary's disdain for the role of the Catholic Church during the Middle Ages. Eleanor and Louis's involvement in 'la folie des Croisades'[9] at the prompting of the 'fanatical' preaching of Bernard of Clairvaux is represented as a wasteful enterprise in which the lives and taxes of the common people of France are squandered in a struggle against innocent Muslims who were living under the tyranny of kings and priests of their own.[10] The familiar stories are told about Eleanor's misbehaviour on crusade. She took with her an excessively opulent entourage 'of poets and players' (*de poëtes et d'histrions*); she enjoyed 'incestuous relations' (*un commmerce incestueux*) with Raymond of Antioch, had a dalliance with Saladin and conducted herself overall 'like a true prostitute' (*en véritable prostituée*).[11] When Eleanor finally divorces Louis and marries Henry II, the author blames her – and the institution of monarchy in general – for the centuries of conflict that were to come between Britain and France:

> When the British Isles attain liberty like us, when, like us, they recognize that kings never exist in free countries, when they wish to know the crimes of their crowned heads, Eleanor of Guyenne will figure in this tableau, and she alone, among all the princesses of France, will have fulfilled the fatal destiny of bringing the torch of discord and the germ of civil wars to two nations, and of carefully fomenting a long and unrelenting conflict between the land that she left and that which she entered.[12]

Male history: Michelet and academic history in the nineteenth century

The early-to-mid nineteenth century was the founding era of history as an academic discipline. The gentleman or clerical antiquarian of the seventeenth and

eighteenth centuries was being replaced by the professional historian attached to
a university faculty. Leopold von Ranke was appointed to the University of Berlin
in 1825, Jules Michelet was made chair of history at the Collège de France in 1838
and William (later Bishop) Stubbs was elected a fellow of Trinity College, Oxford,
in 1850. The new academic history tended, however, towards the exclusion of
women. 'With the advent of … "scientific" history, women were dropped from the
historical texts with bewildering speed' as historians focused on 'public, verifiable'
sources that tended to privilege male actors.[13] '[A] queen who was not active in
public action and did not leave a paper trail of official documents, who focused
her attentions on her more private role as a king's wife or daughter or mother, fared
worse in modern historical study.'[14] Hard sources such as charters and archives
replaced a reliance on 'gossip mongering' chroniclers, and a focus on the evolution
of institutions replaced an interest in personalities. Charles Petit-Dutaillis in the
late nineteenth century 'dealt with queenship and women as little as possible. His
institutional history concerned instead the evolution of administrative agency
and the course of public history … most … accounts of historically prominent
women survived only in popular literature. Ranke, who had inspired the new
thinking, fastidiously avoided legend and popular embellishment in history'.[15] In
early nineteenth-century French historiography, women, where they appeared at
all, tended to be paired with men and were frequently employed as exemplars
of virtues or vices. 'The Romantic historian never found it necessary to treat
medieval women as autonomous persons who controlled events. This pairing
had a profound impact upon French historiography and upon the public's
imagination. Eleanor of Aquitaine was paired with Louis VII or Henry II…'.[16] As
a result of such attitudes, there was an almost complete absence of serious studies
of queens and queenship (a term still not recognized by the version of Microsoft
Word used to type this manuscript); in the words of Theresa Earenfight in a
recent work on medieval queenship, '[u]ntil the 1980s, professional scholars did
not consider queens worthy of serious study … scholars put kings at the center
of the history of medieval Europe and ignored most queens, dismissing them as
unimportant, forgetting their actions and obscuring their lives'.[17]

    Jules Michelet was the pivotal figure in the formation of a national, academic
history for a nineteenth-century France caught between a monarchical past
and a revolutionary republican modernity. A committed republican, Michelet's
view of the Middle Ages was shaped by his hostility towards the crown,
the aristocracy and the Catholic Church.[18] He 'dedicated his life to "People,
Revolution, France"'.[19] His career at times reflected the revolutionary tumults of
his age; his republican opinions cost him his position at the Collège de France

in the months preceding the 1848 revolution and his position at the Records Office after Louis Napoleon's rise to power, when he refused to take the oath of allegiance to the new emperor. Michelet saw French history as the victory of *le peuple*, of republicanism over monarchy, of reason over the backwardness of the Catholic Church and of the French nation over the forces that stood in the way of its unity. The revolution marked the culmination of a process whereby the French people had overcome sectional divisions in order to create a French nation. Michelet's French Revolution possessed, in the words of Robert Gildea, a 'profoundly pacific, benevolent character…'[20]

In such a framework, the medieval past and the medieval Catholic Church in particular were part of the old world that stood in the way of justice, the people and the nation. Michelet viewed 'the religion of the Middle Ages' as '[a] sombre doctrine… which… for a thousand years veiled the face of eternal justice'.[21] The 'study of the Middle Ages' was a 'dismal' pursuit.[22] The cruelty of the revolutionary terror could not be compared to that of the Inquisition, which 'would have good cause to laugh' at such a comparison.[23]

When Michelet treated medieval women, it was within the context of male–female pairings; he 'viewed Joan the Maid as a national heroine because she found her energies directed at furthering the Dauphin's cause'.[24] Despite his claims to create an objective history,

> [e]ven Michelet was not above moralizing. In his early years he had served as a tutor to the royal daughters of Louis XVIII, and he did not entirely resist the temptation to instill lessons about the abuses of intimacy and personal access to the monarch by reference to France's increasingly notorious medieval queens… men's roles often bore the weight of the new historicity, whereas women's roles still provided moral lessons and appealed to the popular audience.[25]

We see this in the relatively sympathetic treatment of Eleanor's first husband, Louis VII, who was viewed as an historically progressive figure, despite his personal weakness:

> There was in this pale and mediocre figure an immense will developing. This king of the church and of the bourgeoisie, the king of the people and of the law… His personality is feeble; he is less a man than an idea; an impersonal being, he lives in the universal (*l'universalité*), in the people, and in the church, daughter of the people…[26]

The weak figure of Louis was but a vehicle for the historical processes that would lead to France's future development as a nation state. In such a Hegelian conception of history, where Great Men embody vast historical forces, there could be no role for queens, driven as they were by the petty emotions that afflicted women. Referring to her controversial role on the Second Crusade, Michelet describes 'the proud and forceful Eleanor' (*la fière et violente Eléonore*),[27] and refers to the rumours that she was having an affair with Raymond of Antioch, or even 'a handsome Saracen slave' (*un bel esclave sarrasin*).

Paradoxically, however, Michelet viewed the twelfth century – generally approvingly – as a period of female power:

> Woman [i.e. the Virgin Mary] reigned in heaven, and reigned on earth ... Bertrade de Monfort governed both her first husband Fulk of Anjou, and her second Philip I, king of France ... Louis VII dated his acts from the coronation of his wife Adèle [in 1164]. Women, natural judges of combat and poetry and the courts of love, also sat as judges, equal to their husbands, in serious affairs.[28]

Women had previously been excluded from power by 'feudal barbarism' (*la barbarie féodale*) but the 'rapid extinction of males [through warfare], the softening of manners, and the progress of equity, reopened inheritances for women'.[29] Eleanor, however, did not figure among those Capetian queens of whom Michelet approved. Rather, she remained the diabolical witch of late-medieval legend: 'the true Mellusine',[30] 'proud and vindictive'. The idea of Eleanor as a vindictive woman became commonplace in mid-nineteenth century French historiography. Guizot, for example, blamed the rebellion of Henry II's sons on 'their mother, the *vindictive* [my emphasis] Eleanor, to whom Henry II had always been a good husband'.[31] Indeed, the adjective *vindictive* was something of a commonplace among French historians of Michelet's time when describing the conduct of wicked queens. For example, Augustin Thierry in 1833 described how the Merovingian queen 'Brunhild possessed in the highest degree that vindictive and relentless character whose archetype is personified by the old Germanic poets in a woman bearing the same name'.[32]

Why did Michelet's view of Eleanor contradict his more sympathetic treatment of other twelfth-century women? We find some clues in a work in which he crossed the divide between academic and popular history. His 1862 book on witchcraft, *La Sorcière*, was essentially a potboiler: '[i]t was dashed off in a couple of months and was intended to be a populist and sensationalist work ... [research] for the medieval section was virtually non-existent'.[33] Michelet paired witches and the peasantry as two groups who were oppressed and excluded by the feudal order.[34] 'To Michelet, the witch was an archetypal figure, representing spiritual freedom, and the rights of women and the working classes ... [He] portray[ed] witchcraft as a surviving pagan religion which had kept the spirit of liberty alive through the "thousand long, dreary, terrible years" of the Middle Ages ...'[35]

The polar opposite figure to Michelet's peasant village sorceress was the aristocratic woman, the Chatelaine. Insofar as she kept the old, Pagan religion alive, it was only in a degenerate form. These women were, for Michelet, 'bold-faced Jezebels'. In the words of Ronald Hutton, 'Michelet's respect for women evaporated as soon as they ceased to fit his preferred political models.'[36] In *La Sorciére* Eleanor is presented as one of these 'Jezebels', holding sinister power over men at her court:

> The proud 'heiress of broad lands,' who brings a dowry, a throne, or a rich fief, an Eleanor of Guyenne, will maintain under her husband's nose, her court of lovers, and will do very much what she pleases ...
>
> By what the romances tell us, the lady Châtelaine would seem to have delighted in collecting round her a court of pretty girls; but history and our own common sense say just the contrary. Queen Eleanor was not so silly as to set the Fair Rosamund as a counterfoil to her own beauty ... The high-born dame's power over men, we repeat, depended on her being alone and without rivals ... The Sorceress enjoys the fine sport in rousing her to abuse this divinity of hers, to make mock of this herd of besotted and submissive males.[37]

The aristocratic woman thus represented a perverted, diabolical form of the old religion: '[t]he effrontery of the feudal dame comes out in a devilish fashion in the two-horned headdress of state occasions ...'[38] For Michelet, then, Eleanor symbolized not the progressive twelfth century in which women were attaining a degree of equality but the repressive feudal order, the last vestiges of which post-revolutionary France was struggling to erase.

Women historians and women's history in the nineteenth century

The academic world of the mid-nineteenth century was therefore one in which 'serious' history, with its focus on the public sphere, was increasingly disdainful of the history of women. It was also a world from which women themselves were largely excluded. The history of queens was therefore taken up outside or on the margins of academia, often by women authors for an audience which hungered for a history that was thoroughly researched and reliable, but which addressed the private sphere largely ignored by academic historians.

This is why, from at least the nineteenth century, most of what was known about queens in the Middle Ages came from biographies of famous heroic queens written by gentlewomen for gentle readers. Because women were not seen as suitable subjects for serious historical study, queens were portrayed as sentimental, passionate and often ill-fated Great Women married to Great Men, or doing unexpected things.[39]

The Bourbon Restoration brought with it a return to respectability for the queens of French history, and a number of popular histories of these queens by women authors appeared during the years of the *Restauration* and the July Monarchy. Heta Aali has argued that these works tended to favour queens as models for saintly, passive behaviour and that after the installation of the 'bourgeois' Orléanist monarchy in 1830, they presented queens as models for middle-class respectability. Louis-Philippe's wife Marie-Amélie was the first queen-consort France had known since Marie Antoinette, reviving interest in the history of the country's queens, and providing a role model of bourgeois domesticity.[40]

A portrait of Marie-Amélie appears as the frontispiece of Laure Prus's *Histoire des reines de France*, published in 1846.[41] Prus and her family were supporters of the July Monarchy, and she and her brother settled in France's colony of Algeria in 1848 after they were 'ruined by the consequences of the revolution of 1848...'[42] The events of Eleanor's life in Prus's book essentially follow what had become the standard version of the Eleanor legend: her leading the court's ladies on crusade as Amazons; her conduct at Antioch, which Prus interprets as Raymond attempting to arrange her marriage to Nur ad-Din (although she believed the legend of Eleanor's relationship with a Saracen leader, Prus at least historicized it by connecting her to the correct sultan at that time, not to Saladin); and her poisoning of the Fair Rosamond.[43] Although Prus presents Eleanor as a vain and frivolous young queen, she also allows her some political intelligence. She attributes Eleanor's decision to go on crusade to her unwillingness to remain in France under Suger's rule, and sees her differences with Louis at Antioch as being based on a clash of wills, not on Eleanor's supposed adultery.[44] She presents Eleanor as a strong-willed and vain young woman who matured into a senior stateswoman through the experience of her captivity at the hands of Henry II.[45]

Across the English Channel, Agnes Strickland and her sister Elizabeth's twelve-volume *Lives of the Queens of England*, published in the 1840s, became a bestseller.[46] Their biography of 'Eleanora of Aquitaine' helped popularize the view of Eleanor as an outstanding figure: 'As a sovereign, she ranks among the first of female rulers.'[47] The work was credited jointly to the two sisters; in fact Agnes, the more lionized of the two, worked principally on the early-modern and modern queens, while Elizabeth wrote the biographies of medieval queens, including that of Eleanor. The Stricklands' work should warn us against drawing too definitive a line between 'male/academic' and 'female/popular' history, as the sisters viewed themselves as serious historians. While excluded by their sex from academia, they approached their research in a spirit of serious scholarship, making use of available archives, and expressing a belief in writing (in Agnes's words) 'facts, not opinions.'[48]

Nevertheless, the Stricklands' portrait of Eleanor was highly opinionated and often misleading. They shared Prus's view of Eleanor as a flighty young girl who grew into a mature ruler: she was 'among the very few women who atoned for an ill-spent youth by a wise and benevolent old age.'[49] They described, and went some way towards popularizing, the claim that Eleanor and her ladies put in a fancy-dress appearance on crusade as Penthesilea and her Amazons,[50] and repeated the myth that Eleanor had an affair with Saladin.[51]

The Stricklands' view of Eleanor can be viewed as a product of their Victorian morality and conservatism. Agnes, the more celebrated of the sisters, was anti-Catholic, a great supporter of the Anglican establishment, and she refused to lend her support to a petition for women's property rights.[52] They enjoyed the support of Queen Victoria, to whom they dedicated their work, and who requested Agnes's autograph for her collection.[53] Thus their mildly feminist admiration for Eleanor as a female ruler was tempered by their horror at her 'ill-spent youth'. Eleanor the crusader, taking on a male role, was a 'freak' compared to the older, wiser Eleanor, spending her 'benevolent old age' looking after the interests of her sons. Their ambivalent attitude to Eleanor reflected their own ambiguous position in relation to the establishment. Agnes may have been a supporter of the status quo, but she and her sister also suffered from the restrictions set upon women. The State Paper Office, which housed many of the archives to which they needed access, was effectively barred to women. However, they were able to count upon friends in high places, and gained access to the archives when Lord Melbourne, a friend and confidant of the queen, became Home Secretary.[54] The independent women writers might therefore view Eleanor as a role model while the conservatives who were fêted by the establishment might disapprove of her alleged high spirits and independence. The older, sober, Eleanor matched more closely the character of their own royal benefactress.

Neither French nor English: Eleanor in nationalist history

As Patrick Geary succinctly puts it, 'Modern history was born in the nineteenth century, conceived and developed as an instrument of European nationalism.'[55] New nation states such as Belgium, the Kingdom of Italy and the Wilhelmine German Empire were being born, but longer established nations were also redefining themselves, including England (developing an ambiguous new identity as part of a United Kingdom of Great Britain and Ireland) and France (struggling to reinvent itself as a constitutional monarchy or a democratic republic). The palaces, parliaments and public places of Europe's capitals were being decorated with the images of kings and heroes from the medieval past. The nation states of Europe looked back to the medieval past for real or imagined ancestries – a search that affected the interpretation of medieval history even among academic historians.[56]

Eleanor occupies a problematic position in the framing of French and English national identity; belonging to both nations' histories, she could not be wholeheartedly embraced by either. Her marriage to Henry II deprived the French crown of Aquitaine and created an entity that was so ambiguous in its nature that modern historians have struggled to even agree upon a name for it: Angevin Empire? Plantagenet Empire? *Espace Plantagenêt?*[57]

> It is only necessary to call to mind the lengthy diatribes against the Plantagenet Empire by Jules Michelet and William Stubbs to appreciate the unanimous condemnation that it gave rise to on both sides of the Channel in the age of nationalism. Partisans of 'eternal France' and admirers of the superiority of the British constitution and splendid isolation, these historians deplored, around 1850, the ambition of Henry II and his advisors.[58]

Eleanor in French history

In France she could be viewed as a traitor, as the woman who divorced a Capetian king and married a king of England, taking the vast lands of Aquitaine with her. Such actions could only be possible under a feudal system, based on ties of personal loyalty that appeared absurd in an age of nation states. Jules Michelet viewed Eleanor and Louis's divorce as a rupturing of the French nation: 'And so the south of France was once again isolated from the north. A woman was about to carry off the bulk of the West [of France] to whomsoever she chose.'[59] The conglomeration of lands that resulted from Eleanor's subsequent marriage to Henry of Anjou was regarded by Michelet as an 'English Empire', standing in the way of France's national ambitions.[60] Furthermore, by joining Aquitaine to the English crown Eleanor perpetuated the division of the French nation and initiated a conflict between England and France that would lead to the Hundred Years' War.

Michelet had decided views on the role of regionalism in French history. Parisian centralism was seen as a progressive force: 'The Parisian spirit [*génie*] is the most complex and at the same time the highest manifestation of France.'[61] Volume two of his *Histoire de France* commences with an entertaining overview of the regions of France: for example, Nantes, a cosmopolitan port located between the conservative bastions of Brittany and the Vendée, was described as 'civilized between two barbarisms' (*[c]ivilisé entre deux barbaries*). The Touraine was 'the land of laughter and indolence' (*le pays du rire et du rien faire*).[62] For Michelet, the French nation had evolved through its people's shared historical experiences. It was a nation 'of will' (*de volonté*).[63] The 'Gallic genius' would overcome these regional differences to form a nation,[64] the frontier would give way to the centre, and nature to civilization.[65] Michelet – who was a student of nature as well as of history – had an almost organic view of national development, describing nations as organisms, some of which were more highly evolved than others.[66]

In this context, Eleanor became a fiery southerner, 'the jealous Eleanor, passionate and vindictive like a woman of the South...'[67] She is a reflection of her regional identity, with its mixed northern and southern influences: 'Poitou is the battle of north and south... Poitou is itself like its Mellusine, an assemblage of diverse natures, half woman and half serpent.'[68] The revolt of her son, Henry the Young King, in which Eleanor played a key role, was viewed by Michelet as a struggle of regional separatism, of the 'diverse races' of France against the 'English Empire' (*empire anglais*) of Henry II.[69] So, while southerners might have a sense of identity, even of patriotism, of their own, it was not legitimate in the sense that the French *génie* was. It was based on a love of conflict and 'vain pleasure' (*vain plaisir*), while that of France was part of an historical mission.

The beginning of the twentieth century saw something of a return to the regional histories of Bouchet and Besly in Alfred Richard's *Histoire des comtes de Poitou, 778–1204* of 1903.[70] Richard was a Poitevin, born in St-Maixent in the Vendée. He was an archivist for the departments of Creuse and Vienne in the Limousin and Poitou.[71] As such he was a serious historian in the spirit of his age, whose work was based on primary evidence. Most of the second of the two volumes was devoted to Eleanor, and could arguably be viewed as the first truly scholarly work devoted to her life and actions as a ruler. In many ways a scholarly scepticism shows through, as he challenges received ideas and the romanticized approaches to his subject. He dismisses Bouchet's version of the divorce proceedings at Beaugency as 'pure invention' and sees 'more calculation than sentiment' (*plus de calcul que de sentiment*) in the motives of Henry II in marrying Eleanor.[72] As a regional historian, Richard showed some sympathy for Eleanor's Aquitanian or 'southern' identity. Describing the Young King's rebellion in 1173–4, Richard saw Eleanor asserting her culture, but in an anti-English context, against the 'English crudeness' (*la rudesse anglaise*).

Yet even Richard tended to fill with speculation the voids left by the lack of hard evidence. The negative influence of Eleanor over Louis before and during the Second Crusade is assumed.[73] There are no Amazons, but Eleanor and her women are accused of taking the challenge of the crusade light-heartedly:

> The journey to Constantinople was no more than a pleasure party, during which Eleanor, taken away from the jealous surveillance of her husband and the vigilant eye of Suger, surrounded by ladies of Aquitaine who were initiated into the mysteries of the game of gallantry with troubadours as well as the debates of the courts of love, felt the blood of la Maubergeonne and of William VII [i.e. her grandfather the troubadour William IX and his lover, Eleanor's maternal grandmother] stir within her.[74]

He even gives some credence to the possibility that she committed adultery while at Antioch with her uncle Raymond or with 'a captive Saracen leader', blaming such indiscretions on the atmosphere of decadence and courtly love at her uncle's court.[75] Richard indulged in some crude and misogynistic examples of what would later be known as psycho-history. He opines that she was attracted to the 'rough' (*rude*) Henry of Anjou over the effeminate Louis because 'she wanted to be dominated, and as people said rather coarsely, she was one of those women who like to be beaten'.[76]

In the twentieth century, Eleanor's role in French history was viewed alongside emerging regional and pan-European identities. For Jacques Chaban-Delmas, mayor of Eleanor's putative birthplace of Bordeaux, she 'betrayed France for England'.[77] However, he qualified his complaint by underlining the ambiguities of her identity:

> Become French (or should that be Frankish?) by her marriage, she ceased to be upon her divorce. Become English (or should that be Anglo-Norman?) by her remarriage, she conducted herself as queen as she had done alongside Louis VII but without ever … ceasing to feel and to act firstly as mistress of Aquitaine.[78]

So, at one level Eleanor could be understood as a predominantly Aquitainian figure; yet for the *ancien résistant* Chaban and the Gaullist politician Chaban-Delmas, Eleanor had a modern parallel in De Gaulle: the *raison d'être* was 'for Eleanor, to safeguard her ancestors' inheritance ... for Charles de Gaulle, to liberate the *Patrie*, then elevate France and save the Republic ...' Eleanor was – 'like de Gaulle' – and like a certain little Gaulish village? – 'indomitable'.[79] Eleanor may have fought for a different cause, but she shared de Gaulle's strength and single-mindedness. Chaban-Delmas also saw her as serving France in other ways, such as bringing southern culture to Paris through her marriage to Louis VII,[80] while her mission to bring her granddaughter Blanche of Castile to the French court to marry the future Louis VIII was part of a process that would allow the 'absorption of Aquitaine' into France without any 'allergic reactions'.[81]

Chaban-Delmas reconciled the apparent paradox between Eleanor as both an Aquitainian and a French figure by placing her in a context that transcended both – as an early advocate of European unity, just as he was a pioneer of European unity at an inter-regional level. His Eleanor understood that Aquitaine was too weak to stand on its own, and could only survive as part of a union between the English and French crowns – a union that was to be facilitated by the marriage of the future Louis VIII to Eleanor and Henry's granddaughter Blanche of Castile.[82] This vision matched Chaban-Delmas's view of Bordeaux and Aquitaine as part of a 'Europe of the Regions'.

Eleanor in English/British history

For English historians, Eleanor was a founder of a problematic, binational 'Angevin Empire', to which they had an ambivalence in their attitude, disagreeing as to whether it was a glorious appendage to the English crown – 'a big blob of red on the maps of textbooks'[83] – or a continental encumbrance that had to be discarded before Englishmen could apply themselves to their historical destiny as shapers of their nation's constitution. In the latter viewpoint, the 'Loss of Normandy' (and of Anjou, Poitou, etc.) was no loss at all. For Thomas Macauley, England 'owed her escape from such calamities' as the loss of its language and the draining of its resources to finance the king's French possessions 'to an event which her historians have generally represented as disastrous'. For Bishop William Stubbs, 'the fortunate incapacity of John' enabled England 'to cut herself free from Normandy'.[84]

The English historian Kate Norgate, writing towards the end of the nineteenth century, rejected this narrowly English emphasis on the Angevin monarchy, and coined the term 'Angevin empire', albeit with a lower-case 'e'.[85] However, she retained much of the institutional focus of English constitutionalist historiography, viewing the marriage of Eleanor to Louis VII as a moment that brought Aquitaine from southern backwardness into the world of more advanced northern institutions, 'suddenly dragged out of her isolation and brought into contact with the general system of northern Europe, somewhat as England had been by its association with Normandy'.[86] The period of the Angevin kings remained for Norgate a key phase in the evolution of an English nation and monarchy: 'it was as "Kings of the English" that their successors were to stand there still, when the Angevin empire had crumbled into dust'. A 'new spirit of patriotism' embodied by Layamon's *Brut* was evident 'ten years and more before the signing of the Great Charter ...'.[87]

Not only was the 'Angevin Empire' treated as suspiciously un-English, the focus of much of English historiography on the development of administration, law and the constitution also tended to underplay the role of queens, including Eleanor. William Stubbs, one of the founders of the constitutionalist approach to English history, had little to say about Eleanor in his three-volume *Constitutional History of England*, despite dedicating an entire chapter to 'Henry II *and his sons* [my emphasis]'.[88] Her importance as a 'counsellor' to Henry and John is acknowledged,[89] and she is even described as 'head of the administration' during Richard's captivity,[90] but otherwise her role is downplayed in a history that is more concerned with formal offices and (male) office-holders than with the complex nature of queenship. Stubbs's index refers to her as 'Eleanor, wife of Henry II', confirming her eclipse by a more constitutionally significant husband.[91] No mention is made of her role in the revolt of Henry the Young King, an event that is stigmatized as 'a Norman rebellion on English soil', a reaction of French feudalism against Henry II's development of English law and administration.[92] Stubbs was not unsympathetic to Eleanor, of whom he wrote that '[f]ew women have had less justice done to them in history',[93] but at the same time (as described in the previous chapter) condemned her 'undisguised flirtations' during the Second Crusade. J. E. A. Joliffe's mid-twentieth-century work on Angevin kingship had even less to say about Eleanor, who is mentioned only once.[94]

Eleanor as an alien, French queen could never be central to the narrative of the evolution of the British nation and constitution; she was a force for divisiveness and rebellion. Conversely, twentieth-century historians who are sympathetic to her have presented England (a land in which she spent twenty-six years and over which she was several times the *de facto* ruler) as a cold land of exile and imprisonment.[95] However, historians (predominantly) from the English-speaking world were to create a more positive image of Eleanor in the second half of the twentieth century as the feminist heroine.

The twentieth century: A feminist Eleanor?

If the nineteenth century had failed to free Eleanor from the Black Legend, the twentieth century reassessed her in a new, more positive incarnation: the Golden Myth. Two works that have arguably done most to form and popularize the image of Eleanor to the twentieth-century Anglophone reader were both by women writers: Amy Kelly and Marion Meade. Kelly's and Meade's biographies have never gone out of print, and are available in paperback to a mass readership. More recent popular biographies by the likes of Alison Weir and Douglas Boyd largely retread the ground covered by Kelly and Meade.[96] Both Kelly and Meade were influenced by the Second-Wave Feminist movement, Kelly writing during its pre-history at mid-century and Meade at its height in the 1970s.

Kelly's *Eleanor of Aquitaine and the Four Kings*, written in 1950, is still perhaps the most influential biography of Eleanor in the English language. Kelly had spent a lifetime in female education when she wrote this work, having been the head of Bryn Mawr School (a girls' school in Maryland, not to be confused with the women's liberal arts college of that name in Pennsylvania) and Professor of English at Wellesley College. She authored a report on liberal arts education for women in 1927, and this gives us some insight into her philosophy. For her, history was seen in materialist terms, as 'but the record of what men, with their pressing biological needs, have done to get on as practically as possible in an environment that limits them ...'[97] She believed that a history and social science curriculum 'should give intelligent students a very shrewd understanding of the causes of wars, the debasement of politics and statesmanship and the reasons for many social maladjustments, and should make them curious, critical and tolerant with respect to current social movements'.[98] Yet against this radical analysis, Kelly also advocated an education for women that reconciled their aspirations with the reality of their social condition 'so that conflicts do not arise to impair the quality of women's work or disturb social order'.[99] Kelly's materialist view of history is at odds with her desire, as cited in the introduction, to approach Eleanor's life 'as a study of individuals'. However, Eleanor does seem an ideal subject of study for a type of limited feminism that wishes to promote women without disturbing the social order. As a strong female figure, she offered a role model for women in a history dominated by men. Yet as a member of the ruling elite, she was still a figure from the Great Men (and, very occasionally, Great Women) school of history.

Kelly's biography was well received in academic circles on its publication. More recently, however, her work has been criticized as being overly imaginative – 'a biographer with a colourful imagination' in the words of Ralph Turner, who also argues that Kelly's background as a literature scholar led her to give too much credence to the courtly love literature as a source for Eleanor's Courts of Love.[100] Although more sober and scholarly than the Stricklands, and free of their judgemental tone, Kelly nevertheless repeats some of their errors. For example, the claim that Eleanor and her ladies dressed as Amazons on the Second Crusade reappears several times in the course of her book.[101] Some of her assumptions seem to have become the model for later, uncritical biographers. For example, she cites a diatribe of Bernard of Clairvaux against the attire of ladies, adding 'to whom if not the queen and her suite does the abbé allude?'[102] This attribution is taken as fact, without qualification, by the subsequent biographers Meade and Weir.[103] Meade presents Bernard's comments in his letter to the virgin Sophia as 'the only physical portrait of Eleanor'.[104]

But perhaps Kelly's greatest contribution to framing the image of Eleanor is her promotion of the idea of the queen as the leading patron of the troubadours and the Courts of Love alongside her daughter Marie, countess of Champagne. Kelly was a literary scholar by background, and seems to have been drawn to Eleanor via her interest in the literature of the twelfth century.[105] The question of the Courts of Love will be discussed in the next chapter; for now, it is sufficient to mention that their existence has been repeatedly challenged by historians and literary scholars, most recently by Jean Flori.[106]

Kelly's promotion of Eleanor as a hostess of the Courts of Love begins not in her 1950 biography, but in an article that appeared in *Speculum* in 1937.[107] This article displays much of the romanticization that would characterize Kelly's later Eleanor biography, and those of her successors. For example, describing Eleanor's return to Paris after the Second Crusade, Kelly asks,

> Was it not intolerable that the foremost queen in Christendom ... should lodge in the indifferent quarters of the king's routiers, while the empress of Byzantium dwelt apart from all vulgar contacts in purple pavilions, in harems rich with tapestries and silken hangings, among tiled fountains and chirruping golden birds ...?[108]

There is little critical analysis of courtly love in Kelly's *Speculum* article, which consists largely of a potted biography of Eleanor and an imaginative reconstruction of the process of one of the Courts of Love.[109] The author's reasoning that Eleanor and Marie de Champagne presided together at such courts in Poitiers is based on assumptions, not evidence. She begins by arguing that '[p]resumably, although Andreas does not so state, the place of assembly is Poitiers', and that Marie *could* have been present at Eleanor's court while the latter was governing Aquitaine between 1170 and 1174: 'Nothing we know of Marie's life precludes the assumption that she was in Poitiers in the period in question'.[110] By the middle of the article, Marie's supposed presence has become a fact, '*when* [my emphasis] she journeyed down from Paris or Troyes to assume her place at the court of Poitiers…'.[111]

It must be concluded that Amy Kelly is largely responsible for the longevity of the myth of the Courts of Love, which had been challenged as early as 1842.[112] It is possible that the myth would have died by the middle of the next century, had not Kelly given it new life. In the words of John C. Moore, reviewing a collection of papers on Eleanor's patronage published in 1976, '[t]he refulgent light that seems in these papers to be shining from Eleanor's court comes rather from the splendid prose of Amy Kelly…'.[113] June Hall McCash writes that 'Marie's function at the court of Poitiers was in large measure a product of the fertile imagination of Amy Kelly'.[114]

American author Marion Meade's biography of Eleanor was published in 1977. Meade seems to have been drawn to Eleanor on a feminist basis, viewing the twelfth century as a period that saw 'the burgeoning of a feminist movement'.[115] The choice of subjects of Meade's other works certainly reflect a feminist interest. They include *Stealing Heaven*, a novel about Héloïse and Abelard (the subtitle, significantly, gives their names in that order) that sympathizes predominantly with the former; a novel about a female troubadour at the time of the Albigensian Crusades; a biography of Dorothy Parker; and *Bitching*, a collection of interviews with women described by its current publisher as '[o]ne of the classic books from the Second Wave of Feminism'.[116] Her biography of Eleanor, however, reads, in places, more like romantic fiction than feminist history, reflecting perhaps Meade's background in journalism, rather than academia. In addition, her claim to bring a new female perspective to the subject ignored the fact that two women – Elizabeth Stickland and Kelly – had already written biographies of Eleanor.[117]

Her prose style makes Meade's one of the more readable Eleanor biographies, and she plays less fast and loose with history than some popular biographers.

For example, Eleanor's Amazonian exploits do not make it into her account. Despite her claim that 'I did not find it necessary to fictionalise Eleanor's life. Her history, what little is known of it, is novel enough',[118] Meade does, however, frequently flesh out details further than the evidence allows. For example, we are told that Eleanor, 'a highly literate woman, left no intimate record of herself, no letters, diaries, or poetry ...', leaving us to speculate as to how we know that she is highly literate.[119] After vividly describing Eleanor's early childhood, Meade tells us that '[h]er name first appeared in the records in 1129 ...' when she would have been, by Meade's account, at least seven years old.[120]

Meade admits in a note that her description of Eleanor's education is 'entirely inferential', and later informs us that Eleanor was 'exceptionally beautiful' before admitting that 'there is not a single word about what she looked like'.[121] Meade's feminism, set out in the introduction to the book, does not appear to inform the text itself beyond a restatement that Eleanor was a remarkable woman, 'one of the most politically astute women of the medieval era',[122] a contestable verdict given that Eleanor's misjudgement in supporting her sons' rebellion in 1173 led to a decade and a half of imprisonment and powerlessness. For a feminist author, she is remarkably quick to fall back upon clichéd ideas about gender roles, as seen in her treatment of Louis, whom she stereotypes as unmanly.[123] Her picture of Eleanor can occasionally be patronizing, as in her claim that she went on crusade out of boredom and a desire for adventure.[124] We see asserted again the Stricklands' image of the young Eleanor as a silly, flighty girl: 'her natural exuberance had reasserted itself, and she was ... enjoying herself to the utmost' and 'she planned to enjoy herself once she reached the pleasure palaces of Constantinople'.[125] Too often Meade, like many other popular biographers, falls back on references to Eleanor's character and personality to back her judgements, even though we can only make inferences about these traits. For example, we are offered this character sketch of the fifteen-year-old Eleanor, who at that age had barely appeared in the written record: 'Her restless temperament, her vanities and self-centeredness, her bold flirtatious manner, [were] combined with a certain tomboyishness ...' Later we are told that she 'had matured into a saucy, hot-blooded damsel ...'[126]

In the French-speaking world, Régine Pernoud was also developing the Golden Myth of Eleanor that had begun to appear in the pages of Amy Kelly's biography. In her *Aliénor d'Aquitaine*, published in 1965, Pernoud's Eleanor emerges as a cultured figure from the south who introduced the troubadour civilization of the Midi to a dour, barbarous north.[127] Pernoud's long career frequently revealed an interest in medieval women such as Joan of Arc and

Christine de Pisan, and in works such as *La Femme au temps des cathédrales*.[128] Her image of Eleanor was strongly influenced by Kelly's work, which she praised as 'quite outstanding in its soundness...'[129]

Her earlier work did not suggest Pernoud as an advocate of Eleanor. In the last years of World War II, she authored a brief history of France for the *Que sais-je?* series titled *L'Unité française*, later reissued in 1966 with the slightly less tendentious title *La Formation de la France*.[130] In this earlier work she had accepted the Black Legend, blaming Eleanor for the failure of Louis VII's crusade, and added some Orientalism into the mix.[131] Pernoud was perhaps referring to *L'Unité française* when she admitted in her biography of Eleanor that she had previously accepted the 'sorry reputation' of the queen 'without demur in one of my previous books',[132] a view that had been corrected based on a study of the original sources. Her *Eleanor of Aquitaine* was therefore presented as a work of scholarship in which 'the conversations and utterances reported in the text do not contain one word of invention'.[133] She criticizes other historians for having relied too heavily upon 'literary sources', and has been praised for 'her serious works of scholarship... [and for] writing for a popular and a scholarly audience'.[134] Yet many of these claims are contradicted by Pernoud's own approach. She clearly did invent many 'conversations and utterances' and other details that are not supported by primary source material. She describes Eleanor and Louis's wedding, about which we know virtually nothing, in enormous detail, down to the colour of Eleanor's robe and the expression on Louis's face.[135] Her detailed account of the siege of Vitry goes into similar, literally incredible, detail as she describes how 'Louis's companions grew alarmed at his stillness and silence. When they went up to him, they saw that his face was white and haggard and his teeth were chattering.'[136] Jacques Le Goff is particularly scathing about her scholarship, complaining that it was made 'without any serious documentation' (*sans une documentation sérieuse...*).[137] Pernoud makes it hard for the reader to check her sources, as she chose not to 'weigh the story down with notes and references...'[138]

Her portrait of Eleanor combines some elements of the old Black Legend while developing the new Golden Myth. So, on the one hand, we have the idea of Eleanor as a young, frivolous girl who was a bad influence on Louis VII. Far from being feminist, this interpretation borders on the sexist:

> Lurking behind every one of the decisions that had led to this imbroglio of private rifts and public outrages, of family squabbles and feudal wars, was the figure of Eleanor. In her pretty hands lay both ends of the skein which seemed to have been wantonly tangled for her own girlish amusement...[139]

When Louis comes into conflict with the count of Champagne over her sister Petronilla's marriage to Raoul de Vermandois, it is 'all because of a feminine whim'.[140] Elements of the Black Legend such as Eleanor's destructive role on the Second Crusade find their way into the work of Pernoud, albeit not in their crudest form. There are no Amazons, but 'Eleanor and the other women taking part in the expedition ... all doubtless led astray by her example – had insisted on bringing their chambermaids and were determined not to forgo a moderate degree of comfort during its long and arduous journey. Hence the daunting line of wagons ...'[141] Serious political decisions such as Eleanor's marriage to Henry are explained in terms that would be more suited to a romance novel.

> She was in love with him – so many different details prove that she was, and her love is attested to an even greater degree by the general tenor of her life ... As for Henry, he may have been swayed by the magnificence of her dowry ... but it would obviously be quite wrong to see his decision as the calculated act of an ambitious man. A passionate nature such as his was bound to respond to the beauty of this queen whose eventful history seemed to invest her with a special aura ....[142]

On the other hand, Pernoud views Eleanor as a 'woman beyond compare, towering over the age in which she lived'.[143] In this respect, Pernoud reflects not only the mildly feminist influence of Kelly, but the rise of an Occitan identity (to be discussed in the next chapter). Eleanor is identified as uniquely responsible for bringing the more advanced culture of the Midi north to the Île-de-France and England. The south is romanticized as a land of a relaxed troubadour culture: '[a]ll the gaiety of the south was given free rein before the young duchess of Aquitaine ...'[144] Pernoud claims that the troubadour Marcabru was brought to Louis's court by Eleanor, but was dismissed by the king out of jealousy (reflecting perhaps the legend of the troubadour Bernart de Ventadorn's love for Eleanor).[145] Louis's jealousy of Raymond of Antioch was rooted, according to Pernoud, in a culture clash, with Louis feeling alien at Raymond's Occitan-speaking court. 'It displeased [Louis] that anyone engaged on a mission of faith should even think of listening to troubadours ... [he] had felt left out during their conversations in *langue d'oc*, a language of which he had no command.'[146] Pernoud's Eleanor brings troubadours north to England: 'What did she make of England? How did her southern temperament respond to this kingdom, acquired after such a strenuous battle against wind and rain? Did her mind turn sadly to the smiling landscapes beside the Garonne or even along the Seine?'[147] Among the troubadours are Bernart de Ventadorn: 'Hereafter ... Bernard [*sic*] addressed all his verses to the woman who was indeed establishing herself as the most illustrious Lady of the West ... [in reality, he mentioned Eleanor in a single

verse] Was it really she whose praises he sang when he wrote of "*Mos Aziman –
my Magnet?*" ... Eleanor was certainly magnetic enough."[148]

These biographies reveal their limitations as 'feminist' interpretations of
Eleanor. Their authors are drawn to Eleanor as a powerful figure of female
authority, but struggle to free her (and themselves) from older interpretations
that focused on her emotions and personality, rather than on her as a serious
political actor, and which therefore tended to trivialize her motives and portray
her in gendered terms that are seldom applied to kings. Despite the influence
of feminism on authors such as Kelly, Pernoud and Meade, the nineteenth-
century portrayal of medieval queens as 'sentimental [and] passionate ... doing
unexpected things' identified by Theresa Earenfight still resonates in late
twentieth-century biographies of Eleanor.[149]

An interesting side-growth of the 'feminist' Eleanor of the late twentieth
century is the New Age or neo-Pagan Eleanor of the French Celticist Jean
Markale. I discuss Markale's work alongside feminist interpretations of Eleanor
because of the female-centredness of neo-Paganism which rejects the traditional
patriarchal structures of the Abrahamic faiths. Furthermore, Amy Kelly and
Régine Pernoud were also both major influences on Markale's work.

Markale was prone to mythologizing his own life, and he mythologizes
Eleanor's too. He was born in 1928, named plain Jean Bertrand, apparently
in Paris, although he later claimed to have grown up, or even been born in
the 'Forest of Brocéliande', and died in 2008 in the Morbihan department of
Brittany. He presented himself as a Breton, and more generally as a Celt; the
name 'Markale' came from King Mark of the Tristan and Iseult legend. While
predominantly a Celticist, Markale wrote on aspects of medieval history, often
including esoterica, as can be seen in the titles of works such as *L'Énigme du
Saint Graal: De Rennes-le-Château à Marie Madeleine*.[150] Among his medieval
output is a work from 1979 on Eleanor of Aquitaine.[151] While the French
original was published by the scholarly publisher Payot (which also published
the biography of Eleanor by Jean Flori),[152] the interest in Markale's work from
outside scholarly circles can be seen in the fact that the English translation of his
work (subtitled *Queen of the Troubadours*) was published in the United States by
Inner Traditions, a publisher of New Age and esoteric works.[153]

Markale was controversial, even within his own field of Celtic studies. The
Breton Celticist Christian-Joseph Guyonvarc'h is dismissive of Markale's
scholarship:

M. Jean Bertrand, called Jean Markale, sometimes passes himself off as a
professor of classical letters. He does not say where he studied ... he does not

know how to accentuate Greek, and is totally ignorant of Latin...he does not know how many cases there are in Irish (sometimes two, sometimes three)... All this is, at best, a joke.[154]

Many of Markale's claims are unsupported by references to primary sources, yet he is still on occasion cited by academic historians. For example, James Brundage cites Markale as a source for claims that allegations of adultery were raised against Eleanor during the proceedings to annul her marriage to Louis VII. However, Brundage in a footnote admits that 'I have been unable to verify Markale's source for this report.'[155] His arguments are often based on assertion and supposition, as when he states that '[t]here is a strong temptation to see in courtly love theories a survival, or rather a renaissance, of a Celtic mind-set that is more favorable to the female condition.'[156]

Markale's Eleanor is presented simultaneously as a Jungian archetype and a Hegelian figure of the spirit of the age. For Markale, she is literally a heroine, an individual who embodies an image 'compatible with that seen by the collective unconscious.'[157] Markale blurs the lines between history and myth – 'the hero...belongs to myth' – which a cynic might claim gives him license to indulge in unsupported speculations.[158] He not only compares her to the romance figures of Iseult and Guinevere, and to their Celtic archetypes, but also argues that Eleanor in turn inspired the representation of queens in twelfth-century literature. This position is not in itself unreasonable, and similar arguments have been made by literary scholars such as Margaret Pappano,[159] and by Jean Flori, who advises us not to dismiss too lightly the legendary or literary accounts of Eleanor's life.[160] However, Markale advances his argument much further to the 'fantastically developed'[161] idea that Eleanor also represented Pagan archetypes of the solar goddess, 'an ever-radiant Eleanor, a solar symbol inherited from the dawn of time, center of the world and keeper of powers that formerly devolved to the god-king...,'[162] the 'sacred prostitutes' of ancient Babylon, and the putative Pagan Great Goddess.[163]

The appeal of many of these elements to a New Age and feminist audience is obvious – the idea of Eleanor as an emanation of the Great Goddess, and as a proto-feminist heroine, for example. The English translation of Markale's *Aliénor* was well received in the US neo-Pagan media; Smokey Trudeau, reviewing the book in an issue of *Sage Woman* devoted to the figure of 'the Queen', wrote that 'for women who have sought a true queen who puts our childhood Disney princesses to shame, Eleanor is that queen'.[164]

Does the problem of the representation of Eleanor in popular histories (such as those of Markale, Pernoud and Meade) or in outdated scholarly works (such as that of Kelly) matter to the academic historian? Scholars have gone a long way in the last half century towards creating what one has called 'a realistic image' of Eleanor, as will be outlined in the final chapter.[165] Nevertheless, scholars are themselves not immune to the appeal of the Eleanor myth. Georges Duby writes of her legend that 'there are even serious historians whose imagination it continues to inflame and lead astray'.[166]

Martin Aurell has criticized the 'psychological approach' so often taken to the study of Eleanor,[167] and psychology can easily shade into misogyny, or at least into patronizing descriptions of Eleanor as an impressionable girl motivated by emotion rather than political calculation. In his recent book on the Angevin Empire, Aurell also cites similar recent examples by professional historians. David Crouch, referring to the young William Marshal, claims that 'Queen Eleanor of England was rather taken by his youthful charm.'[168] Jacques Le Goff, in an interview given to *L'Express* magazine about courtly love in 2002, went so far as to call Eleanor 'a real slut, motivated only by power and sex' (*une vraie garce, uniquement préocupée par le pouvoir et le sexe*).[169]

To conclude, historians of Eleanor have created an image of her, and of medieval women as a whole, that is misleading. The misogynist medieval and early-modern legends of Eleanor found their way into the Stricklands' disapproving Victorian accounts of the foolish and rebellious young Eleanor, and Michelet's attacks on the vindictive, Mélusine-like southern queen. Eleanor's reputation in the nineteenth century suffered from a combination of the low esteem in which women's history was held in the professionalizing academy, and the difficulty of presenting her as a heroine for either British or French nationalist history. Twentieth-century historians promoted a more feminist view of Eleanor, stressing her strengths and her power. But these accounts have themselves built on earlier legends, and too often rely on speculation and inference, and are frequently written in a tone that stresses the emotional and psychological traits of Eleanor in a manner that continues the nineteenth-century tendency to relegate women's history to the trivial and personal. The state of Eleanor scholarship in the twenty-first century, and the efforts of historians over the last sixty years or so to provide a corrective to both the Black Legend and the Golden Myth, will be discussed in the conclusion. But before returning to the search for a 'realistic image', we will trace the development of two meta-Eleanors – Eleanor the heroine of Occitan identity and Eleanor in the arts.

Eleanor of Aquitaine
(and Languedoc and Provence…):
The Southernness of Eleanor

Eleanor of Aquitaine is frequently claimed as a representative of southern culture. Her supposed connections with the more enlightened and cultured world of the lands of *oc* are frequently contrasted with the dour northern world of the *langue d'oïl*, represented by her husbands King Louis VII of France and Henry II, king of England, count of Anjou and duke of Normandy – all of them lands of the north. This image of a southern Eleanor incorporates many elements: Eleanor as patron of Occitan culture, specifically the poetry of the troubadours; Eleanor as ambassador of that culture in the less enlightened north; and Eleanor as defender of the south's independence against the centralizing ambitions of the Kingdom of France and the 'Angevin Empire'.

The idea of a southern Eleanor is perhaps best represented by popular historians, who find it hard to resist the romantic image of the troubadours, or of Eleanor as queen of the Courts of Love. Added to this is the romantic image of the south as a lost cause – an enlightened and cultured world destroyed by the Albigensian Crusades in the decades following Eleanor's death. To take but one example, Douglas Boyd in his recent biography of Eleanor takes the image of the 'April Queen' as the title of his book, as a symbol of Eleanor bringing the fresh and budding culture of the south to the dark, wintry north.[1] Boyd was clearly influenced by the romance of the Occitan culture: a former BBC producer, he retired to the south of France where, according to the publisher's blurb, 'he came across what remains of the ancient Occitan language, the language of Eleanor of Aquitaine'.

Eleanor's ambiguous cultural identity: Between *oc* and *oïl*

Yet Eleanor's identity was far from being an unambiguously southern one. She was probably born in the vicinity of Bordeaux, but even this is far from certain, and is based on later tradition. Other traditions identify her birthplace as being in the County of Poitou.[2] It was upon this county that the political agglomeration known as the Duchy of Aquitaine was founded; Eleanor's ancestors, the counts of Poitou, had expanded their power southwards. Poitou lies to the north of the modern linguistic border between the lands of *oc* and *oïl*, making Eleanor arguably a northern as much as a southern figure. In the brief period when Eleanor was effective ruler of her own lands, her court was based in or around Poitiers, the 'capital' of Poitou, and her son Richard was, before his accession to the kingdom of England, referred to as count of Poitiers and not as duke of Aquitaine. It was Poitou, not the south-west, that was the heartland of Eleanor's realm, and where the dukes of Aquitaine held the greatest concentration of demesne lands.[3] Her power as duchess of Aquitaine was essentially limited to 'a Poitou widened to the Aunis and the Saintonge ...'[4] In the words of Ralph Turner, 'Eleanor's premier identity was more Poitevin than Aquitanian.'[5]

The far south was at best peripheral to the duchy and at worst provided a challenge to the power of the Poitevins. Men of the far south did not feature prominently in Eleanor's entourage,[6] and the Occitan-speaking regions of the Limousin and the far south were often a source of rebellion which claimed the lives of two of Eleanor's sons – Henry the Young King (who died of a fever while leading a rebellion) and Richard I (who was killed while attempting to suppress one). It would be wrong, however, to exaggerate the rebelliousness of the Occitan south: John Gillingham has pointed out that the idea of a lawless Aquitaine is to a large extent a creation of northern chroniclers.[7] The Plantagenets encountered opposition within Poitou itself, as well as from the far south; indeed, Henry II faced a rebellion in Poitou on average every three and a half years.[8] Nevertheless, there was – as in all great lordships – a tension between the lord and his vassals, and this did on occasion take the form of an opposition between a Poitevin centre and an Occitan periphery. Medieval commentators sometimes conflated 'Poitou' and 'Aquitaine', but on other occasions distinguished Poitou from the far south-west. The twelfth-century *Pilgrim's Guide* to the road to Santiago de Compostela distinguished the 'warlike and generous' Poitevins from the 'frivolous ... garrulous, mocking, debauched' Gascons.[9]

Poitou was in many ways part of the northern French world, bordering on the important northern entities of Brittany, Anjou and Blois. Poitiers is closer to the Angevin centres of Angers, Saumur and Chinon than to Bordeaux, closer to the cathedral schools of Paris and Chartres than to the centres of the troubadour culture in the Languedoc. Duchesses of Aquitaine were associated with Eleanor's burial place, the Abbey of Fontevraud in Anjou, before Eleanor linked her dynasty to that of the Angevins, and that abbey came under the ecclesiastical authority of the bishops of Poitiers.[10] Eleanor's grandmother had retired there,[11] and Eleanor herself had made a grant to the house while still queen of France.[12] There were therefore strong familial, ecclesiastical and linguistic links between Poitou and the neighbouring *langue d'oïl*-speaking territories of northern France.

Eleanor has often been closely associated with the Occitan language, as seen in Boyd's book. Alison Weir goes even further, and asserts Eleanor's 'lack of interest in learning the *langue d'oïl*'.[13] Her grandfather William (Guilhelm) IX was a pioneer of Occitan song, and has been dubbed with good reason as the 'First Troubadour'. This has led to many historians assuming that Eleanor was brought up in an Occitan-speaking milieu, yet it is far from certain that Eleanor even spoke the southern language (although it would seem a reasonable assumption that she did). Flori believes that both Occitan and the *langue d'oïl* would have been spoken at the court of Poitiers.[14] However, the editors of a recent collection of essays about Aquitaine in Eleanor's age argue that 'despite the patronage of troubadours that even medieval writers fondly (and mistakenly) attributed to her, she probably did not speak Occitan'.[15] They go on to point out that the poems attributed to her son Richard I were written in Poitevin, not in the Occitan of the south. John of Salisbury commended the Poitevin dialect as a good language for frankness or even deceit. Addressing his own manuscript of *Policraticus*, John wrote 'Leave and, wherever you go, say that you were born in Poitou, for they have permission to speak a more frank language'.[16] The exact status of medieval Poitevin is ambiguous, but it appears to have represented a transitional dialect between Occitan and the northern *langue d'oïl*. In modern terms, Poitevin-Saintongeais is seen as a northern dialect, while the medieval dialect had more Occitan features but was part of a 'zone of transition' between the Loire and the Gironde (a region that closely corresponds to Eleanor's duchy, with the exception of the far south). Place name evidence suggests a medieval border between *oc* and *oïl* that ran right through Poitou.[17] Nicholas Vincent has found that Eleanor's clerks were from a mix of ethnic backgrounds – English, Norman, Poitevin and Angevin – suggesting that 'Eleanor's court was far from being a monoglot, occitans-speaking [sic] institution … the linguistic mixture of her household renders even more improbable that Eleanor can have lived up to her later, entirely insubstantial reputation as a troubadour queen'.[18]

Queen of the troubadours?

Central to the image of the 'troubadour queen' is the question of her artistic patronage. One of the most enduring received images of Eleanor of Aquitaine is that of the queen of the troubadours – a patron of courtly love, even as a presider over actual Courts of Love. We see it in the titles of works such as ffiona Swabey's *Eleanor of Aquitaine, Courtly Love, and the Troubadours*, or Jean Markale's *Eleanor of Aquitaine: Queen of the Troubadours*[19] and, while the idea has frequently been challenged by academic historians and literary scholars, it endures in popular culture.[20] Elizabeth A. R. Brown states simply that the existence of the courts 'has no basis in fact'.[21]

The concept of courtly love has itself been challenged by scholars. In his 1979 article tracing the development of the idea at that point, John C. Moore addressed the problem of definitions, seeing courtly love as one of those historical terms – like feudalism – which are invented after the fact, and are imprecise, but will not go away as they are commonly understood and seem to serve a useful purpose: '[they] can be used in educated circles with the confidence that they will be met all around with knowing nods. They provide a bond of learned camaraderie among professionals and amateurs alike, since they create the illusion of shared understanding'.[22] Attempts to define the 'rules' of courtly love leave so many exceptions to the rule as to be virtually meaningless,[23] yet the term has stuck. Amy Kelly's work was influential not only in creating our image of Eleanor, but in popularizing the idea of courtly love as an organized set of practices and even institutions.[24]

The work of Andreas Capellanus is the key plank of the idea of Eleanor as a patron of the Courts of Love. Andreas's work is as controversial as the concept of courtly love itself. Andreas described 'courts' of noble ladies, including Eleanor and her daughter Marie de Champagne, to whom lovers brought 'cases' for which they sought judgement from the court. There is no evidence firmly linking Andreas to Marie, still less to Eleanor,[25] and the historicity of these courts was doubted from as early as the mid-nineteenth century.[26]

Nonetheless, Andreas's work was frequently viewed as an account of actual courts handing down real verdicts, and it was a key source for Gaston Paris when he formulated the concept of *amour courtois* in the 1880s.[27] The role of Eleanor in these supposed courts attracted attention from historians who saw her as a key cultural influence in the 'twelfth-century renaissance', reaching its peak in the works of Amy Kelly discussed in Chapter 2. 'Amy Kelly's influential book on Eleanor of Aquitaine explained the way in which formal courts of love defined and propagated the rules of courtly love. Eleanor and her daughter Marie, Countess of Champagne, were presented there as the true creators and patrons of courtly love.'[28] In the latter half of the twentieth century, however, this literalist interpretation of Andreas was criticized, with his work being treated as a satire (perhaps, even, a clerical attack on the decadent, adulterous world of the court), and the Courts of Love as an invention of the author. Critics pointed to Andreas's use of Latin (a clerical, rather than a courtly language) and the lack of evidence for Eleanor, Marie and the other noble ladies having ever come together to form these courts.[29] John F. Benton wrote in 1961 that '[t]here is no evidence to show that Marie ever saw her mother or communicated with her after Eleanor left the court of France when Marie was seven …'[30] Despite this, the idea of Eleanor's association with the Courts of Love has proved tenacious. The legend continues to reassert itself, particularly in association with Eleanor, as if the combination of a romantic notion and a romantic queen is too much to resist. We see it in the titles of Markale's and Swabey's works, but it also persists in more scholarly circles. Moore, writing in 1979, expressed regret that '[a]t a 1973 symposium on Eleanor of Aquitaine, nearly all the papers hailed her as the patron of courtly literature and courtly love.'[31] Given the stubborn longevity of this myth, it is not surprising that we detect a somewhat frustrated tone in the works of scholars who have to repeatedly refute it, as seen in the somewhat tautological title of Benton's article 'The Evidence for Andreas Capellanus Re-Examined Again.'[32]

Eleanor as literary patron

The association of Eleanor with the Courts of Love holds less sway today, with even popular historians and novelists less inclined to believe it. However, the idea of Eleanor as a patron of the arts on an exceptional scale has enjoyed more longevity and respectability. Not only was Eleanor not alone as a woman patron of the arts, there is very little evidence to suggest she was exceptional in the extent of her patronage – possibly the opposite, as she can be linked firmly to only a handful of medieval texts.

So uncontested has been the idea of Eleanor as a patron that as recently as 2003, a literary scholar was able to commence a paper with the words 'Eleanor of Aquitaine has long been regarded as a great patron of the literary arts at the Angevin court.'[33] Rita Lejeune, the Belgian scholar of medieval French literature, made extensive claims for Eleanor's role as a patron.[34] She saw Eleanor as an importer of the more refined culture of the south to a less cultured north, an idea which became firmly implanted in many historians' views of the queen. Lejeune's opinion has been neatly summarized thus:

> After her marriage to Louis VII, she would have attempted to surround herself with people speaking her maternal language, the *langue d'oc*, and to try to recreate, in the drab Parisian court, something reminding her of the court of Aquitaine.[35]

This view, as we have seen, became 'mainstream' via the popular histories of Kelly and Pernoud. However, contrary to the stereotypes about Louis's dour court, Paris was already a cultural centre when Eleanor arrived there in 1137, as shown, for example, by the songs of Peter Abelard that were circulating widely at the time.[36]

At times, the Eleanor of literary scholarship falls victim to the Eleanor of myth. In the absence of firm evidence of Eleanor as a literary patron, we have come to read her influence or presence into many works of twelfth-century literature. This is not to say that Eleanor could not have been a patron or at least an influence over later twelfth-century writings in England and the Angevin lands in France, but we need to be perhaps a little more wary than some scholarship has allowed. For example, Margaret Pappano sees the figure of Eleanor in two of the *lais* of Marie de France, *Lanval* and *Chèvrefeuille*.[37] It is certainly possible to see Eleanor in the images of the queens Guinevere and Iseult, but Pappano's argument is undermined by her own acceptance of the idea of Eleanor as a warrior queen who dressed as an Amazon, an idea which we have seen to be a post-medieval myth.[38] It is true that there are interesting parallels between Eleanor, who was accused of adultery by clerical chroniclers, and the adulterous queens Guinevere and Iseult. However, given Eleanor's long and active career as queen of two realms, there is a danger of seeing her in *any* queen represented in Arthurian literature.[39]

So, was Eleanor a patron of literature at all? Layamon, in his Middle English *Brut*, stated that Wace's Norman-French *Roman de Brut* had been dedicated to Eleanor. There is, however, no independent confirmation of this from any of the manuscripts of Wace.[40] The *Roman de Rou* contains praise of Eleanor, but only in conjunction with Henry, suggesting that Eleanor's patronage of Wace was carried out jointly with her husband. The Nun of Barking's *Life of St Edmund* was dedicated to both Eleanor *and* Henry. Philip of Thaon's *Bestiary* was dedicated to Eleanor, but only in one of three manuscript versions; the work was originally dedicated to Adeliza of Louvain, the second queen of Henry I.[41]

Eleanor has often been discussed in relation to the *Roman de Troie* of Benoît de Sainte-Maure. The composition date of this Old French version of the Troy legend has been identified as c. 1165–70,[42] making the reference to 'a rich lady of a rich king' (*riche dame de riche rei*) likely to refer to Eleanor, although even this is uncertain, merely a reasonable assumption given that 'the term *riche rei* was associated with Henry II'.[43] This is not a conventional dedication, however; it is buried deep in the body of the text, following an 'anti-feminist diatribe' for which Benoît apologizes to his intended royal audience. It is as if Eleanor were a reader rather than a dedicatee of the work, with Benoît fishing for patronage.[44] As with the *lais*, Eleanor has been identified with the adulterous Queen Briseida of the *Roman de Troie*, on similar grounds as her identification with Guinevere or Iseult.[45] It is also tempting to link Eleanor to the Amazon Queen Penthesilea who appears in the *Roman*, but 'our caution in this instance cannot be too extreme', given that the idea of Eleanor as an Amazon is a post-medieval invention.[46] Benoît also wrote a vernacular verse translation of Robert de Torigny's *Gesta Normannorum Ducum*, which described Eleanor in unflattering terms for her role in the rebellion of the Young King.[47]

It is worth remembering that the presence of her name in a text only makes her a dedicatee of the work, not necessarily its patron. Writers might dedicate their work to a powerful figure in the hope of future patronage rather than in acknowledgement of patronage received. For example, the *lais* of Marie de France were dedicated to a '*noble roi*', usually identified as Henry II (or possibly his son Henry, the Young King). This does not, however, mean that Henry or Eleanor were active 'patrons' of Marie, and there is no evidence to believe that Eleanor commissioned the *lais* or many of the other works attributed to her patronage.[48]

There has in recent years been a shift towards viewing Henry's, or Henry and Eleanor's court jointly, as a source of cultural patronage, rather than Eleanor personally. The mid-twelfth century was an era in which a king was expected to be learned, not simply a war-leader. 'An illiterate king', wrote Peter of Blois, 'is a ship without oars or a bird without feathers'.[49] Bénédicte Milland-Bove argues that comital courts such as that of Marie de Champagne, rather than the royal courts of England and France, were the centres of literature in the *langue d'oïl*. Milland-Bove sees the spread of this culture to the court of Henry and Eleanor as being a result of cultural diffusion rather than the personal intervention of Eleanor.[50]

These examples relate to the literature of (northern) French, including its Anglo-Norman dialect. But what of Eleanor's role in the troubadour culture of the south? When it comes to the issue of her literary patronage of Occitan, the evidence is sparse. The 'only explicit and apparently secure reference to Eleanor in the troubadour lyric corpus' is the dedication of a song by Bernart de Ventadorn (or Bernard de Ventadour, as he is known in northern French) 'to the queen of the Normans'.[51] Other than that – despite the claims made for her as 'queen of the troubadours' – there is little to no evidence firmly linking her to the Occitan lyric culture: 'Nothing in the works of Marcoat, Alegret, Peire de Valeria, Peire Rogier or Bernart Marti indicates any kind of association with Eleanor.'[52] Connections between Eleanor and other troubadours are circumstantial or nonexistent, and there is no evidence that she brought troubadours from the south to Louis VII's court upon her first marriage: 'If Eleanor was accompanied by troubadours when she went to Paris, we cannot trace them.'[53] If anything, Eleanor's marriage to Louis led to a break between the Poitevin court and the troubadours, who looked to patronage from the lords of the far south, including rulers of Narbonne, Toulouse and Barcelona who were not vassals of the dukes of Aquitaine.[54]

Even more problematically for the image of Eleanor as a patron of Occitan literature and song, there is little evidence that her court was a centre of the troubadour culture during her residence at Poitiers in 1168–73. '[W]here is the evidence?' asks Ruth Harvey. Only one troubadour can be linked by documentary evidence to Eleanor at that time.[55] There are references in troubadour lyrics to other female patrons, but none to Eleanor. 'The basis for Eleanor's modern reputation … evaporates the harder one looks.'[56] Alfred Jeanroy's studies show that only 180 out of 2,023 Occitan poems could be identified as composed in Poitou, and only eleven out of 156 from the period 1140–80.[57] Ironically, there is firmer evidence linking Bernart de Ventadorn to the Anglo-Norman world than to Eleanor's Aquitaine. The dedication of Bernart's poem to the queen of the Normans is telling; Bernart was operating in the world of Henry II's literate court which he seems to have accompanied on its many travels.[58] We know that Poitou *was* a cultural centre, but for Latin ecclesiastical learning: 'By the eleventh century the most important cultural centre south of the Loire was the school of Saint-Hilaire in Poitiers …'[59]

Even more extensive claims have been made for Eleanor's literary influence beyond Occitania, France or the Anglo-Norman world. Peter Volk has argued that she introduced the courtly love lyric into Germany following her presence there en route to the Second Crusade.[60] Volk links Eleanor to the early German poet der von Kürenberg, who is illustrated appearing alongside a queen in the *Codex Manesse*, a later (c. 1300) collection of Middle High German poetry.[61]

There is, however, no compelling evidence to link Eleanor with von Kürenberg, to identity her as the queen in the *Codex Manesse* or to suggest – as Volk does – that they met.[62] The dating of von Kürenberg's work to c. 1160 makes it tempting to suggest that it was inspired by Eleanor's passage through Germany in 1148, but stylistically there is little sign of French or Occitan influence.[63]

Likewise, another German lyric, from the *Carmina Burana*, has been linked to Eleanor:

Were the world all mine
From the sea up to the Rhine
I'd give it all
If so be the Queen of England
Lay in my arms.[64]

Given Eleanor's fame, and the probable late-twelfth-century composition of the poem, it is not unreasonable to assume that Eleanor is the subject of this 'naïve' (in Waddell's words) lyric. However, it is 'about' Eleanor in only the most generic sense, and is certainly no indicator of her literary influence. Moreover, the original lyric may have referred to the *King* of England before being altered by the anonymous monk who recorded it in the *Carmina Burana* manuscript.[65]

A southern Eleanor?

Despite the attempts of modern biographers to turn her into a carrier of southern culture into the north, contemporaries did not stress the 'southernness' of Eleanor. In the words of John Carmi Parsons, 'explicit contemporary associations between Eleanor's behavior and her Occitan origins are lacking'.[66] As we have seen, Bernart de Ventadorn did not associate Eleanor with his Occitan homeland, but referred to her as the 'Queen of the Normans' (*reïna dels Normans*), while the *vida* of Bernart describes her as 'Duchess of Normandy'.[67] Richard le Poitevin, in a sympathetic account of Eleanor's later imprisonment by Henry, calls the latter 'King of the North'. Much is made of this reference by historians who wish to promote the idea of Eleanor as a romantic southern queen. His lament may even be the original source of the idea of Eleanor's glittering troubadour-laden court of Poitiers, where, according to Richard, 'young girls surrounded you playing the tambourine and the harp, singing pleasant songs'.[68] However, Richard seems to see Henry as a 'northerner' in relation to Poitou, rather than to the Occitan south, and was sympathetic to the Capetian Louis VII, so this can hardly be seen as an expression of Occitan nationalism against the northern French.[69]

If the literature of the troubadours does not point to a 'southern' Eleanor, then neither does the evidence of her charters. Vincent argues for an Eleanor who, as queen, took a great interest in her northern realm, and for whom captivity in Salisbury was not necessarily a cruel exile in a foreign land.[70] Her ecclesiastical patronage showed strong favour for Fontevraud, a house closely associated with the Angevins, while nearly half of her secular charters were for English beneficiaries. '[E]ven before 1174, and certainly after 1189, the majority of Eleanor's disposable resources lay in England or Normandy rather than south of the Loire.'[71]

Hivergneaux's work reveals Eleanor's concerns as being far more focused on Poitou than on Aquitaine as a whole. During a brief period of effective personal rule in Aquitaine between her divorce from Louis and the accession of Henry II to the English crown (1152–4), 'it would clearly appear that Eleanor's power rested on the same bases, *essentially Poitevin* [my emphasis], as that of her predecessors'.[72] Poitevin nobles and lesser lords were at the heart of her court in this period.[73] Her second period of effective rule in Aquitaine, from 1168 to 1173, follows a similar pattern. Her Poitevin uncle, Raoul de Faye, was seneschal in this period, and witnessed eight of the twelve charters that she issued at that time. Her entourage was drawn from the Poitevin nobility; no Gascons, and few Normans or Englishmen, appear in her charters from this time,[74] confirming the picture of Eleanor at the head of a court that was Poitevin rather than representative of Aquitaine as a whole or of the 'Angevin Empire'. Even if we extend her 'southernness' to an identification with Aquitaine as a whole (including Poitou), we still encounter problems; she seems not to have visited Aquitaine at all between 1160 and 1168.[75]

Eleanor made a rare visit to the south during a tour of her duchy in spring and summer of 1199, at a time when she was rallying Aquitaine to recognize her son, John, over the claims of Arthur of Brittany. She seems to have focused her efforts on the margins of the duchy – its southern and eastern lordships – rather than on Poitou. Ironically, as Nicholas Vincent points out, she was able to use the resources of her England to impose her authority on 'her' Aquitaine.[76] She met with Gascon and other south-western lords, but was less successful, however, in the other Occitan-speaking area of Aquitaine, the east, where the viscount of Limoges and the count of Angoulême appear not to have answered her call.[77] As Hivergneaux points out, the majority of her following continued to be drawn from Poitou and the neighbouring lordships of Saintonge and Aunis; 'the establishment of convincing ducal power remained limited to these regions'.[78] The members of her personal entourage were principally Poitevins.[79]

The northern bias of ducal power in Aquitaine is confirmed by the (few) charters concerning Aquitaine that were issued by Henry II, nineteen of which (out of twenty-six) concern Poitou.[80]

A new factor on the political scene enabled Poitevin power to be both strengthened in its heartland and asserted in the far south, however – the rise of town communes. These new institutions might have represented a challenge to seigneurial authority, but they also provided an opportunity for kings or the higher nobility to restate their feudal rights. Even in the Poitevin heart of the duchy, Eleanor recognized the commune of Poitiers which had bloodily been suppressed by her first husband, Louis VII, shortly after their marriage.[81] The commune of La Rochelle was recognized in 1175, as a reward for its loyalty to Henry II in the revolt of 1173.[82] While acts such as this might be seen as undermining ducal authority, they created a direct link of loyalty between the urban merchant class and the crown. Eleanor, during her period of effective rule of Aquitaine in the 1190s, granted or confirmed charters to Poitiers, Oléron, Saintes and La Rochelle – all of them in Poitou or Saintonge. The last of these is interesting, given that it was a confirmation of the charter granted by Henry for the town's loyalty against Eleanor and her sons. It should be noted that these grants were not so much acts of royal or ducal generosity as admissions of the reality of communal power.[83] The policy also helped extend Poitevin authority into the far south. Cities such as Bordeaux and Bayonne became islands of royal-ducal authority in Gascony, foreshadowing the position in the thirteenth century where Gascony remained as the Plantagenets' sole continental possession long after Poitou had been lost to the Capetians.

If the charters explode the myth of a southern, Occitan Eleanor, they do however seem to confirm the idea of a divide between an Anglo-Norman-Angevin north and a Poitevin-Aquitanian south. This divide, however, does not reflect a division between the *langue d'oïl* and *langue d'oc*, nor any personal animosity between Henry and Eleanor. Rather, it reflects the institutional difference between the different parts of Henry II's 'empire'.

It has often been suggested that Henry II intended to rule the 'Plantagenet space' as a federation of distinct territories, rather than as a unified 'empire'. That conception does not always accurately describe Henry's policies, and there was also a tendency towards 'colonial' policies on Henry's part, with the appointment of Anglo-Normans or Angevins to positions in Poitou (seen, for example, in the appointment of the Englishman Jean Bellesmains to the episcopate of Poitiers).[84] But the 'federal' model goes some way towards explaining the government of the Angevin lands. In the words of John Gillingham, Henry did not treat his possessions as an empire so much as 'a partible family estate'.[85] This may explain the lack of an Anglo-Norman or Angevin presence among Eleanor's entourage.

Conversely, Nicholas Vincent has demonstrated the equivalent lack of a Poitevin presence at the court of Henry II.[86] Unlike in the reign of Eleanor's grandson, Henry III, when Poitevins were stereotyped as a horde of office-seekers descending on England, the men of Aquitaine barely figure in the presence of Henry II: 'There were no Poitevins at the court of King Henry II, or at the very least there was not one single Poitevin who deserves to be ranked amongst those courtiers who regularly witness the charters of the King'.[87] Furthermore, the charter evidence suggests indifference on the part of Henry not only to Poitevins, but to Poitou (and Aquitaine) itself; only twenty five of Henry's charters were issued in Aquitaine, and Poitevins or Aquitanians scarcely ever appeared as witnesses to Henry's charters outside Aquitaine.[88] When they did appear, it was as witnesses to charters concerning Poitou.[89]

The romantic myth of Eleanor's southernness is often accompanied by a desire to make her a feminist heroine, with the south portrayed as a region in which women enjoyed greater rights than in the north. For example, Marion Meade wrote that 'the position of women in Aquitaine was, everything considered, remarkably high. Perhaps because the power of the Church was relatively weak there, its customary Puritanism and fierce misogyny had less influence...'.[90] However, it is far from clear that there was a north-south divide in the rights of aristocratic women. When, in 1164, a vassal of Eleanor's southern contemporary Ermengarde of Narbonne appealed to Louis VII that he could not be legally subject to a woman, the French king ruled in favour of Ermengarde. In the words of Linda Paterson, 'although Ermengarde is often cited as an example of female authority in Occitania, Louis supports her in the name of the custom of the French kingdom as a whole, against a legal system [Roman law] that was gaining ground more strongly in the south than the north'.[91] For Eleanor's part, there were plenty of precedents for a powerful female queen of England from the northern world, as discussed in the introduction.

While the idea of an 'Occitan' Eleanor is hard to sustain, it would be wrong to dismiss the idea of a 'southern' Eleanor entirely. There was on occasion a tendency to conflate all 'southerners' in the mind of medieval northern French writers. Ralph Glaber, writing in the tenth century, engaged in an anti-southern invective, in the context of King Robert's marriage to Constance of Arles, of whom Ralph heartily disapproved. He complained of the hordes of southerners who came with Constance to the Capetian court – 'For her sake a great flood of strange men from Auvergne and Aquitaine began to flow into France and

Burgundy' – and of the strange and decadent customs they brought with them.[92] Aquitainians and Auvergnats have been conflated with a queen from the Arelate (the remnant of the Carolingian Kingdom of Burgundy, roughly equivalent to Provence) to form a single body of 'strange men'. It should be noted that Ralph does not refer to them specifically as southerners, although they are clearly seen as alien to 'France' (Francia, i.e. the Île-de-France).

Eleanor and Occitan regionalism

Wherein lies the allure of Eleanor as a 'southern' woman? Partly there is the inherent romance of the exotic foreigner, which has so often been a trope of western culture. As we have seen, for Michelet, Eleanor was a 'passionate and vindictive' southerner. Around the time that Michelet was promoting his nationalist view of French history, educators were promoting the use of Parisian French, and deprecating regional languages, including Occitan, as peasant *patois*. The nationalist view of French national unity lived on into the following century: P. Belperou, writing (perhaps significantly) at the time of the Vichy regime, felt able without irony to title a book *La croisade contre les Albigeois et l'union du Languedoc à la France*.

Bull and Léglu point out that the 'exotic' southern woman mirrors the Saracen princess of medieval romance. But there is also an attachment to the romantic ideal of the lost cause of the Occitan South, a world of

> relative openness to exchange with foreigners and those of other cultures and faiths ... a relative absence of personal subjection ... [where] women have some power and influence ... and social freedoms less accepted in other parts of Europe ... Occitania was no Utopia, nor was it free from Original Sin. But it was the first spectacular casualty of the 'formation of a persecuting society', the victim of a desire on the part of outsiders to dominate and control.[93]

This view, expressed by Linda Paterson, is not necessarily wrong, and the violence of the Albigensian Crusades would seem to lend support to the idea of a society brutally ruptured by a less tolerant invader. But it is easy to see how such a view can become sentimentalized or tied to a modern Occitan cultural nationalism. In this atmosphere Eleanor could, in the words of Georges Duby, become for many 'the first heroine of Occitan independence'.[94]

The concept of Occitania is, however, a modern invention. In the words of Robert Gildea discussing modern French regionalism, '[i]f the tragedy of Alsace was to be torn between two states, and the regret of Breton autonomists was to have lost their own state, then the problem of those living in the south of France was not to be able to look to the shadow of a former state at all'.[95] Even the Occitan nationalist Robert Lafont admitted that 'Occitanie never was a nation-state'.[96] At no time in history were the Occitan-speaking lands both united and independent, nor were they ever controlled by a single feudal entity in the High Middle Ages. In the twelfth century, the west of the region was nominally part of the Kingdom of France, and was in turn divided between the two principal powers of the Duchy of Aquitaine and the County of Toulouse, while the east (principally, Provence) was part of the notional Kingdom of Burgundy, under the even more tenuous authority of the Empire. Furthermore, powers from outside the region had an important impact: the Duchy of Aquitaine was arguably a northern entity, with its power-base in Poitou, while the kings of Aragon periodically controlled Provence and a number of territories on the northern side of the Pyrenees. To further complicate the political picture, several small counties in the far south-west were effectively independent entities, as were many of the cities of Languedoc. The one unifying factor of Occitania that its modern champions would locate in the medieval past was 'one of having been at the receiving end of the Albigensian Crusade in the thirteenth century', and even that only affected the County of Toulouse and its dependencies (in terms of the modern regions, most of Languedoc-Roussillon and parts of Midi-Pyrennées).[97]

So if there never was an Occitania, where does the concept come from? Dante was the first to draw attention to the difference between the 'lingua d'oco' of southern France, and the languages of 'oïl' in the north, and 'si' on his own side of the Alps. The term 'Occitan' first appeared in the fourteenth century.[98] So if the idea of Occitania is artificial, it is at least one with a long history. The Occitan language is itself an amalgam – to be precise, a *koine*, a common literary language based on vernacular dialects – but no more so than the 'national' language of French. But the modern concept of Occitan is, like many national identities, a creation of nineteenth-century cultural revivalists. The poet Frédéric Mistral was arguably the reinventor of Provençal in 1854 when he and his associates created a brotherhood known as the Félibrige, ten years after the completion of Michelet's pro-centralist *History of France*. Mistral 'was hostile to the Jacobinism, anticlericalism and urbanism of the Third Republic' but favoured federalism over separatism.[99] Mistral's ideas were influential in ultra-conservative circles: Charles Maurras, who went on to become leader of the far-right royalist Action Française, was a member of the Félibrige in his youth, while Marshal Pétain praised Mistral in 1940 as 'the sublime evocator of the new France that we found'.[100] Mistral compiled the first Provençal dictionary, creating a composite language based on the dialect of western Provence, but incorporating other Occitan dialects, and designed the orthography for it, which is known to this day as the Mistralian system.

Other Occitan revivalists rejected Mistral's catholic and conservative model. Louis-Xavier de Ricard, a veteran of the Paris Commune, argued that '[t]his bourgeois, royal, unitary France, as it was made, was made not by the Midi but actually against it... Unfortunately northern France crushed our hopes of political liberty as it crushed the religious liberty of the Albigensians and the Reformation'.[101] He identified with a broader Occitan world over Mistral's narrow Provençalism: 'To counterbalance the reactionary Félibrige which Provencalised [*sic*] and Papalised in Avignon ... we asserted ourselves, somewhat roughly, to be freethinkers, republicans and Languedocians'.[102]

The political divide within Occitan regionalism was reflected by the emergence of two rival linguistic strands: those who favoured Provençal as the designation for the language and those who favoured Occitan. Broadly, this reflected a political divide between conservative adherents of Provençal as a 'pure' form of the language and liberal supporters of the more inclusive Occitan. Canadian journalist Mark Abley encountered a teacher of Provençal who deplored the diluting cultural influence of North African immigrants, and who taught the language in a room decorated with a map of French Algeria. But he also met a 'left-leaning' Occitan activist,[103] who 'talk[ed] about François I and Eleanor of Aquitaine before jumping ahead eight centuries to the Institute of Occitan Studies'.[104]

If French nationalist historians portrayed the 'union' of southern France with the north as part of a good (and inevitable) process, a countervailing tendency has been to promote Eleanor as part of a romanticized southern culture. She represents a problematic figure for southern regionalism, not only for the reasons outlined earlier, but because she and her duchy were not part of the narrative of the Albigensian Crusades. Catharism did not take hold in Aquitaine, and the Plantagenets played no role on either side of the Albigensian Crusades. If anything, Eleanor was a hereditary enemy of the counts of Toulouse, and both her husbands attempted (unsuccessfully) to assert in arms Eleanor's inherited claim to the county.

Eleanor was not always used in the twentieth century as a symbol of Occitan nationalism, however. For Louis Aragon, writing under the Vichy regime and the German occupation during World War II, Eleanor represented French national identity. The poem 'Crusaders' celebrating Eleanor as 'queen of the Courts of Love' was part of the collection *Le Crève-Coeur* (published legally in 1941, but immediately suppressed by the authorities).[105] The Marxist Aragon makes reference to the Second Crusade as 'that pilgrimage insane' (l. 29), in which men pledged to fight for the Church and for their queen:

> But her adorers, barons, knights, for years
> Remembered following Peter the Hermit, lean
> Lost troubadours of an accursèd queen (ll. 9–11)

By the end of the poem however, Eleanor, banished from 'her France' (l. 34) is turned into a patriotic symbol as Aragon reflects on a 'heart too full of a new defeat' (l. 31):

> They only understood the syllable clear
> When dying in some Syria. Not before
> The end did they know that Eleanor
> Was your name, Liberty oh Liberty so dear (ll.41–5) ['Liberté, Liberté chérie' in
> the original French, a quotation from *La Marseillaise*]

Nevertheless, French and Anglophone historians alike have promoted Eleanor as symbol of Occitania. Régine Pernoud, who was born in the Nivernais but brought up in Provence, dedicated her 1965 work on Eleanor to a southern scholar '[To] André Chamson, who can still speak the language of Eleanor, [I dedicate] this evocation of the Queen of the Troubadours',[106] which neatly sums up the romanticized image of the Occitan Eleanor.

Pernoud emphasized the contrast between a bright south and dour north, a flavour of which can be seen in the following passage, in which she imagines the scene when Eleanor marries the young Louis VII:

> Louis, like the knights who surrounded him, felt a little disconcerted by the entourage; the exuberance of the crowd, bolder, more lightly-clad than the people of the Ile-de-France or of Champagne, the speech in the *langue d'oc* that he understood poorly, the louder manners, the more heated exclamations – all of this left them taken aback, and it was only slowly, over the course of the banquet, in an atmosphere of general joy, that the distance between the people of the North and the people of the Midi was bridged.[107]

Eleanor in contemporary Occitania

Eleanor's image continues to have a strong influence on the modern imagination of Occitania. One example of this can be seen in institutional names. I have been able to locate at least twelve institutions of education named after Eleanor. Their distribution illustrates how Eleanor has come to be viewed as a figure of regional pride not only in the lands over which she ruled, but across areas of the south that were never part of her duchy. Not surprisingly, most schools and colleges named after her are within the borders of her Duchy of Aquitaine: six in Bordeaux and the Gironde,[108] and one each in Poitiers,[109] the Dordogne (approximately medieval Périgord),[110] on the island of Oléron (Charente-Maritime, historically part of Saintonge)[111] and in Landes *département* in south-west Gascony.[112] However, the École Maternelle Aliénor d'Aquitaine in Montpellier lies outside historic Aquitaine in Languedoc, part of the medieval County of Toulouse that actively opposed the efforts of Henry II to incorporate the region into his wife's duchy. One school even lies in the north (but also within the 'Angevin Empire'): the École Maternelle Aliénor d'Aquitaine at Domfront near the Normandy-Maine border, and site of an important castle of the dukes of Normandy. Bordeaux also has a restaurant named in her honour, as well as an obstetrics unit at the university hospital – appropriate, given that she was the mother of ten children.

Non-governmental organizations have also named themselves after Eleanor. La Rochelle (Charente-Maritime) is home to a Free-Mason Lodge 'Aliénor d'Aquitaine'.[113] The lodge was named in her honour because she confirmed the charter of liberties granted to the city by her father, William X: 'Eleanor and her father made La Rochelle a *free* town for *free* Men. It is appropriate that the *free rochelaise* Lodge should take for its distinctive title the name of that Lady' [original emphasis]. As such, the masons make a claim of continuity with the bourgeois founders of the commune and with its ducal patrons. But in a blog entry by the lodge's Supreme Commander Jean-Claude Villant, 'Eques a Leopardo aureo' the organization also lays claim to a lineage linking the masons to the Templars. In March 2011, the lodge hosted a presentation on 'Les Templiers à la Rochelle' by a local historian. Eleanor and Louis VII issued a charter in favour of the Templar house of la Rochelle in 1139,[114] so through the lodge's adoption of Eleanor's name it lays claim to a link with La Rochelle's Templar heritage as well as its communal one.

A recent artistic representation of Eleanor as a figure of the South in general can be seen in the 2009 play *Aliénor d'Aquitaine, ou a l'entrada del tems clar* (the title is a reference to a thirteenth-century Occitan lyric). The play was created and performed by the group Compagnie Gargamela, based in St-Hippolyte-du-Fort (Gard) in eastern Languedoc. This location, and the performance of the play in Toulon in Provence, again demonstrates the interest in Eleanor as a symbol of southern identity outside her home territories. In the play's online description, the performers are described as 'troubadours', and Eleanor as

'Occitan, French, and English wife and queen' (*épouse et reine occitane, française, anglaise*), recognizing her role in national and international politics, but also asserting her Occitan identity.[115]

The borders of Eleanor's Aquitaine have become very flexible in the popular imagination, to embrace most of the western Midi. So, for example, a newspaper story about English immigration into the south-west, headlined 'les Anglais envahissent l'Aquitaine d'Aliénor', refers not only to the modern regions of Aquitaine and Poitou-Charentes, but to Midi-Pyrénées and Languedoc-Roussillon, which lie partly or wholly outside the medieval Duchy of Aquitaine: 'the British have not only established themselves in the little Aquitaine of today [i.e. the modern administrative region], but across the greater "Guienne" that they formerly occupied – the Aquitaine of Eleanor. There are 8000 in Poitou-Charentes, 6000 in Midi-Pyrénées and 4000 in Languedoc-Roussillon' (a region that was never ruled by Eleanor or the Plantagenet kings).[116] The author is a little ambivalent as to whether the English are invading or reoccupying Aquitaine, but it serves as a reminder that the region is associated in the popular imagination with an 'English' presence from its time as part of the Angevin Empire.

An unsettling example of the use of Eleanor to assert an Occitan identity is her embrace by far-right *identitaire* groups. These organizations identify themselves as Occitan but assert that identity in an anti-immigrant and anti-Muslim way, rather than in an anti-French or anti-Paris context. They represent a throwback to the conservative cultural Provençalism that pre-dated the leftist Occitan nationalism of the twentieth century. In March 2012, the far-right Ligue du Midi organized a conference in Toulouse on 'la culture occitane d'Aliénor d'Aquitaine au bûcher de Montséur, la résistance Occitane' (Occitan culture from Eleanor of Aquitaine to the massacre of Montségur, [and] Occitan resistance).[117] The theme linked two (unrelated) medieval touchstones of Occitanism: Eleanor and the Cathars. In the same month, the Ligue attended a march in Lyon, photos of which appeared on the organization's Facebook page captioned 'En souvenir d'Aliénor d'Aquitaine!'[118] The page does not make clear why such a march would be in her memory, although reported chants of 'Islam hors d'Europe' might suggest a link to her role as a crusader – an identification reinforced by another photograph of an *identitaire* placard beneath a street sign designating the 'Quai des Croisades' in Louis IX's crusading port city of Aigues-Mortes.[119] The Ligue's emblem depicts a mounted knight, underlining its medievalism. The championing of both the Cathars *and* the crusaders is, of course, highly ironic. Nor is there any link between Eleanor and Catharism; on the contrary, the dukes of Aquitaine seem to have opposed the rise of heresy in the south.[120]

Eleanor and diverse French regionalisms

The 800th anniversary of Eleanor's death in 2004 provided the opportunity for assessments of her life and patronage, and these included reflections on her role in French regional history. The French cultural journal *303* published a special issue to coincide with an exhibition at Fontevraud marking the anniversary. The journal is supported by the council of the Pays de la Loire, one of the 'new' French regions established in the 1960s and 1970s.[121] These regions are a mixture of new 'artificial' creations with no historical predecessors, regions based closely on pre-revolutionary entities, and those that have historical names but bear little resemblance to the regions whose names they bear. 'Aquitaine' is an example of the last category, consisting of only the south-westernmost *départements* of Eleanor's duchy. Pays de la Loire is an artificial creation, but this region includes many of the heartlands of the 'Angevin Empire' including Maine, Anjou and parts of Brittany and Poitou (although not Poitiers, which belongs to the Poitou-Charentes region). The *Eleanor of Aquitaine* volume therefore reflects an interest in her not just as part of English or French (or, for that matter, Occitan) national history, but as part of the regional histories of the western provinces of France. Significantly, another regional centre of the Angevin 'Empire', Poitiers, has become a focus for recent studies of Eleanor, including those of Martin Aurell and Jean Flori. Further back, Edmond-René Labande's *Pour une image véridique d'Aliénor d'Aquitaine*, which arguably pioneered a more sceptical approach to Eleanor studies, was first published in a regional history journal of the west.[122] These reminders of Eleanor's presence in the north-west of France challenge the perception of her as a primarily southern or Occitan figure.

We can see similar identifications with a 'western' Eleanor in the world of popular history. The Rennes-based newspaper with the appropriate name *Ouest-France* produced a tourist guide *Sur les pas de Aliénor d'Aquitaine* in 2005.[123] The publisher's blurb states that Eleanor 'was closely involved in the affairs of western France' (*a été mêlée de près aux affaires de la France de l'Ouest*), yet also describes her as a 'Princess of Occitania' (*princesse de pays d'oc*). The newspaper's catchment area covers much of the northern part of the former Angevin Empire – Brittany, Maine, Anjou and Lower Normandy – but none of Aquitaine except the Vendée. In a similar spirit of Eleanor tourism in north-west France, the American historical novelist Sharon Penman led an 'Eleanor of Aquitaine tour' to Paris, Normandy, Angers, Fontevraud and Poitiers in 2011.[124]

However, it is, unsurprisingly, in Aquitaine that Eleanor's name has the most resonance in the modern world. At an official level, the regional council of Aquitaine supports an Eleanor of Aquitaine website, which is maintained through the region's heritage department.[125] The modern region of 'Aquitaine' is a much-truncated version of Eleanor's duchy, excluding Poitou, the Limousin, Auvergne and eastern Gascony but including Béarn, which was not part of Eleanor's duchy. 'Aquitaine is not the only French region to be an administrative and planning construct, without any possible cultural justification .... *Eleanor, called "of Aquitaine", was more Poitevin than Bordelaise*... [my emphasis]'.[126] Claiming Eleanor (who was probably born in Bordeaux but spent most of her life outside the region) as one of its own is perhaps a way for the modern rump 'Aquitaine' to claim an historical affinity with its much larger medieval namesake.

Long before the establishment of the *régions* by the Mitterand government, the Gaullist politician Jacques Chaban-Delmas had carved out a fiefdom (the medieval term seems appropriate in this context) in Bordeaux, the probable city of Eleanor's birth. Nicknamed the 'duc d'Aquitaine', Chaban-Delmas was mayor of Bordeaux continuously from 1947 to 1995, and viewed Bordeaux as a cultural centre for the region.[127] He was also at various times a Resistance fighter, government minister, prime minister, president of the Assemblée nationale, Gaullist presidential candidate and – significantly – president of the *conseil régional* of Aquitaine. It is perhaps appropriate that the 'duc d'Aquitaine' should have written a biography of its most famous duchess in 1987 which, as we have seen, stressed her southern and Aquitanian identity. It was published by a southern (or to be precise, Monégasque) publisher as part of a series entitled 'Les grandes figures du Midi'.[128] *La Dame d'Aquitaine* is no great work of scholarship, and is heavily dependent on Pernoud, even to the extent of sharing some of the same language to describe the impact of Eleanor at her wedding to Louis VII.[129] He shared with Pernoud the idea of Eleanor as a bringer of an open and refined southern culture, including more revealing dresses (*les robes ... plus décolletées*) to the austere north.[130] Nevertheless, the former Resistance fighter Chaban also located Eleanor within a French nationalist context, as discussed in Chapter 2.

Eleanor's name lives on in a project that identifies her with the modern 'little' Aquitaine, and more specifically with the far south-west. Work began on a new toll road, Autoroute A 65, in 2008. Linking Langon (just south-east of Bordeaux) with Pau, the road – officially named the 'Autoroute de Gascogne' – is operated by a private company named Aliénor. Again, we see the use of Eleanor's name as a badge of south-western identity, albeit in a region only tangentially connected with her. The company's logo shows the road's route within the modern region of Aquitaine on a stylized map of France.[131]

Eleanor's name has also been applied to a tourist project that recalls the medieval heritage of Aquitaine. Castillon-la-Bataille in Gascony (in the modern *département* of Gironde) is the site of the decisive French victory that ended the Hundred Years' War in 1453. It is also the site of a medieval-themed tourist attraction based on the battle, which includes a 'medieval' village called 'Aliénor'. An animated presentation on the website informs the viewer that 'for three centuries Eleanor's Aquitaine belonged to the English crown'.[132] As with the story about English migration into the south-west, there is a sense that the 'English' are foreigners to *Eleanor's* Aquitaine. Eleanor is claimed for French, rather than simply Gascon, history, the implication being that the victory at Castillon represents a vindication of Eleanor, not the dispossession of her Plantagenet descendants.

In conclusion, Eleanor of Aquitaine can in no way be considered a southern figure in an alien and hostile northern world. Her native duchy straddled the divide between the north and the south, and its main power centres were closer to Paris than to the Mediterranean. Poitou had close connections with Anjou – its neighbour – even before Eleanor's marriage to Henry II. Eleanor cannot be convincingly represented as a patron of the troubadours, and her links to the Occitan troubadour culture were small. Her 'southernness' can scarcely be perceived in medieval accounts, and was more a product of nationalistic nineteenth-century French historians, who linked her to the 'loss' of Aquitaine to the Plantagenets, and of a distaste for regional particularism. In more recent times, a reaction set in, which linked the romanticized view of Eleanor to an equally romanticized image of a prelapsarian Midi that was tolerant, cultured and progressive. Both images are equally false. However, Eleanor's name has lived on into the modern era as a symbol not only of Occitan identity but also of different regional identities within south-western and western France. In a France which is rediscovering regionalism but whose official *régions* are often artificial modern creations, an appeal to Eleanor can be useful in creating a regional identity grounded in a mythic past.

4

'A Canker'd Grandam':
Eleanor on the Stage before 1900

The Black Legend that had been developing in popular culture took centre stage – literally – in dramas and operas featuring Eleanor of Aquitaine from the sixteenth to the nineteenth centuries. Spanning Elizabethan to Victorian England, but also embracing Spain, France and Italy, these performances reflected the hardening of the Black Legend of Eleanor in early-modern, Enlightenment and nineteenth-century Europe, in particular the Fair Rosamond legend that would become the subject of several plays and operas in the eighteenth and nineteenth centuries.

The first appearance of Eleanor as a character in a stage drama occurred in 1591, with the publication of the anonymous *The Troublesome Reign of John, King of England*.[1] This was not the first stage treatment of that king's reign, however; John Bale's *Kyng John*, written in the late 1530s in the context of Henry VIII's reformation, had presented John as a proto-Protestant martyr, murdered by the clergy. Structured as a morality play, it contained characters representing qualities rather than historical figures: so Eleanor makes no appearance.[2] Both plays are remembered chiefly as precursors to Shakespeare's *King John*.

The Troublesome Reign of King John, rather than Bale's work, is probably the major source for Shakespeare's *Life and Death of King John*, along with Raphael Holinshed's *Chronicle*, Foxes' *Book of Martyrs* (which also portrayed John as a proto-Protestant martyr) and possibly Ralph Coggeshall's *Chronicle*.[3] While *The Troublesome Reign* shared Bale's patriotic and anti-Catholic sentiments, Shakespeare focused more on the politics of John's reign.[4] It has been argued that the question of succession that is at the centre of the drama reflects the anxieties in the 1590s over the succession to the childless Elizabeth I.[5] 'Shakespeare's play is…political. By representing the contentious, mystified passage of property, power and legitimacy from generation to generation, *King John* dramatizes – and thus both demystifies *and* makes unfamiliar – some of the most intensely serious cultural assumptions in late Tudor England.'[6]

As was common in his history plays, Shakespeare altered the timing and even the sequence of events to suit his dramatic purposes. For example, the deaths of Eleanor and of her daughter-in-law Constance, countess of Brittany, which occurred three years apart, are announced to John in the space of a few lines of a messenger's speech. This serves to dramatize the extent and speed with which John's fortunes collapse.[7] Events that covered the seventeen-year span of his reign are condensed into the action of a single play.

Eleanor in *King John* marks one side of an oppositional relationship between the mothers of two claimants to the throne. John's kingship is threatened by the claim of Arthur, count of Brittany (his nephew and Eleanor's grandson). Just as Eleanor champions John, so does Constance champion Arthur. A key element of the play is therefore the struggle between the two mothers. Indeed, the waters are muddied further by the presence of an illegitimate son of Richard I, the Bastard Faulconbridge. '[T]he presence of three mothers – Eleanor, Lady Faulconbridge, Constance – and a particularly freakish "son" – the Bastard – makes the play unique among the histories'.[8] Eleanor recognizes the Bastard as the son of King Richard and takes him under her wing, arguably allying herself with the cause of illegitimacy. She shows no such support for her true-born grandson, Arthur, and disputes his legitimacy. The play contains some memorable confrontations between Eleanor and Constance, which often focus on questions of motherhood, fertility and legitimacy. When Eleanor suggests that Arthur is illegitimate, Constance responds by both defending her honour and insinuating that it is Eleanor's that might be called into question:

> My bed was ever to thy son as true
> As thine was to thy husband; and this boy
> Liker in feature to his father Geoffrey
> Than thou and John in manners, being as like
> As rain to water, or devil to his dam.
> My boy a bastard! By my soul, I think
> His father never was so true begot:
> It cannot be, an if thou wert his mother.[9]

If Arthur is being punished for anybody's sins, it is those of his grandmother. When Eleanor says that he weeps because 'his mother shames him so', Constance replies:

> His grandam's wrongs, and not his mother's shames,
> Draws these heaven-moving pearls from his poor eyes,

Which heaven shall take in nature of a fee.[10]

…

Thy sins are visited on this poor child
The canon of the law is laid on him,
Being but the second generation
Removed from thy sin-conceiving womb.[11]

The countess further taunts the queen about her age and infertility, calling her 'a canker'd grandam'.[12] In contrast, Constance sees in Arthur's fair form proof of his legitimate royal lineage. If he were

grim,
Ugly and sland'rous to thy mother's womb,

…

I would not care; I then would be content,
For then I should not love thee. No, nor thou
Become thy great birth, nor deserve a crown.
But thou art fair, and at thy birth, dear boy,
Nature and Fortune joined to make thee great.[13]

As well as being the mother of one of the antagonists in a dynastic conflict, Eleanor is portrayed more broadly as a promoter of discord, and is compared by the French ambassador Chatillon to the Greek goddess of strife: 'An Ate, stirring him [John] to blood and strife'.[14] She is also a warrior-woman – 'I am a soldier now, and bound for France'[15] – which, given her baleful role in the action of the play, would seem to be marking her as an unnatural, unwomanly figure, rather than a thirteenth-century analogue of England's Virgin Queen. Despite the strength of their feelings and the seriousness of the issue at stake, the exchange between Eleanor and Constance in Act II, Scene 1, has been viewed as a stereotypically female squabble, in which 'they exchange bawdy insult and misogynistically conceived shrewish rant'.[16] I would, however, dispute the extent to which this exchange is any more shrewish than any similar exchange between male characters. References to motherhood and barrenness gender the exchange as female, but, as I have argued, it is in the context of a domestic dispute where paternity (and maternity) and legitimacy are central to the political question of succession.

Although there are many close similarities, the earlier play *The Troublesome Reign* had presented Eleanor in a different light. She is the first character in the play to speak, when she pronounces to the barons of England that although Richard is dead, 'yet give me leave to joy, – and joy you all!/That from this womb hath sprung a second hope [i.e. John]…'[17] Note that motherhood and succession are again central to Eleanor's role, but this time in a more positive sense; in place of the barrenness and infertility with which Constance confronts her in Shakespeare, the emphasis is on Eleanor's role as a mother of two legitimate kings. This contrasts with the opening speeches of Shakespeare's *King John* in which the king's 'borrowed majesty' is emphasized by the French ambassador Chatillon.[18]

The Troublesome Reign, like Shakespeare's play, sets up an opposition between Eleanor and Constance. The queen declares of Constance that

> Her pride we know, and know her for a dame
> That will not stick to bring him to his end,
> So she may bring herself to rule a realm.[19]

The exchange of insults between the two women is present in *The Troublesome Reign*, but with a different emphasis. The argument about whether Richard will leave the crown to John is there, as it is in Shakespeare; indeed the dialogue is very similar, with *The Troublesome Reign*'s 'A will indeed! A crabbed woman's will'[20] changed by Shakespeare to the more famous 'canker'd grandam's will'. Missing, however, are the references to illegitimacy, which seem to have been introduced by Shakespeare. The shift from a 'woman's will' to a 'grandam's will' emphasizes Eleanor's age and infertility further. Constance's accusations against Eleanor are more general, that she feigns love for a nephew whom she has betrayed. In a line that might allude to the Fair Rosamond legend, Constance declares, 'Sorrow betide such Grandames and such grief,/That minister a poison for pure love!'[21]

Eleanor plays a larger role in the scene where the Bastard of Faulconbridge is recognized as the son of King Richard. We are reminded, in a way that is not included in Shakespeare's dialogue, that Eleanor holds land, power and the potential for patronage in her own right: 'As long as Elinor hath foot of land;/ Henceforth thou shalt be taken for my son.'[22]

This change of thematic emphasis in Shakespeare away from John as a proto-Protestant hero may reflect the establishment in English culture of the 'Bad King John' image in Shakespeare's time. If the dating of Shakespeare's *King John* to the mid-1590s is correct, it appeared a little before Andrew Munday's plays *The Death of Robert, Earle of Huntington* and *The Downfall of Robert, Earle of Huntington* (1598). Munday's works created the idea of a noble Robin Hood fighting in the name of King Richard against the evil Prince John, which became more-or-less the 'standard' version of the legend until the late twentieth century.[23] They were part of the process by which Robin Hood and Maid Marian were becoming historicized, having previously been figures in popular ballads or the May Games.[24] Robin had been placed in his now-familiar setting of the reign of Richard I by the Scottish historian John Major in 1521.[25] Maid Marian was introduced into Robin Hood literature by Munday, who was influenced by Michael Drayton's poem *Matilda the Faire and Chaste Daughter of Lord R. Fitzwater*, 'a tragic story of a beautiful young woman pursued by the vile desires of King John, eventually to her death...'.[26] It would be wrong to see these works as a 'popular' tradition independent of Shakespeare, however; Stephen Knight describes much of Munday's work as a 'rehash of Shakespeare's *King John*' and points to the influence of chronicles such as Stowe's *Annales of England* on his work.[27] Taken together, however, we can see how an image of 'Bad King John' was being created in the 1590s and how Eleanor's reputation consequently suffered in connection to him.

Munday's play is of interest to us because it features Eleanor of Aquitaine, and in a slightly different form than Shakespeare's 'canker'd grandam'. 'Queen Eleanor ... is attracted to the Earl of Huntingdon and plans to disguise herself as Marian to elope with the hero'. This Eleanor is a sexual being; the line 'my roabe is loose, it shall soone be offe' is nominally about Eleanor preparing to swap clothes with Marian, but 'no doubt some vulgar stage business accompanied the line ...'.[28] But Eleanor is a figure of unjust authority, who threatens to accuse Robin of treason if he refuses her. When Robin sees Eleanor disguised as Marian, he condemns her as 'foule Marian, faire though thou be nam'd' and calls her a 'sorceresse' when he realizes her trickery. In Knight's words '[i]t is striking that as a noble, beautiful woman enters the outlaw tradition, the play realizes her opposite, a sexually aggressive, deceptive, dangerous harridan'.[29] Eleanor is sexualized, but in a manner that is repulsive, not erotic. The oversexed young queen of medieval clerical gossip has met the barren 'canker'd' old woman of Shakespeare to become an inappropriately sexual old woman.

It is unclear how influential *King John* was in shaping the image of Eleanor of Aquitaine. It seems likely that the play was performed in Shakespeare's own day and into the Restoration, and it 'survived in the post-Restoration theatre with only minor textual indignities'.[30] Excisions from the text in the eighteenth century acted if at all to downplay Eleanor's manipulative nature.[31] Elements that might have appeared pro-Catholic, pro-French or anti-English were downplayed, and an anti-Catholic reworking, *Papal Tyranny in the Reign of King John* was produced by Colley Cibber in 1737 against the background of the Jacobite threat. The play remained popular well into the nineteenth century, probably because of the potential for spectacle arising from its scenes of battle and siege.[32]

Holinshed's *Chronicle*, which was the major source of Shakespeare's history plays, and a probable source for *King John*, included the negative and misogynist view of the conflict between Eleanor and Constance that found its way into the *Troublesome Reign* and Shakespeare's *King John*:

> Surelie quéene Elianor the kings mother was sore against hir nephue Arthur, Quéene Elianors enuie against Arthur, rather mooued thereto by enuie conceiued against his mother, than vpon any iust occasion giuen in the behalfe of the child, for that she saw if he were king, how his mother Constance would looke to beare most rule within the realme of England, Constance dutchesse of Britaine till hir sonne should come to lawfull age, to gouerne of himselfe.
>
> *So hard it is to bring women to agree in one mind, their natures commonlie being so contrarie, their words so variable, and their déeds so vndiscréet* [my emphasis].[33]

The Elizabethan plays therefore portrayed Eleanor as a shrewd and ruthless old woman who was determined to secure her son's succession to the throne. It was, however, another aspect of Eleanor's reputation – one not mentioned in Shakespeare's *King John* – that would feature most prominently on the nineteenth-century stage: the legend of Fair Rosamond. Plays and operas either focused on Rosamond, or in which her story plays a key role, were common throughout the century, and not only (or even principally) in Britain. These representations of Eleanor as a jealous and murderous wife helped to reinforce the Black Legend and formed perhaps the most important image of Eleanor in the popular consciousness, before she was reconstructed in the following century as a proto-feminist heroine. Although Shakespeare did not make use of the Rosamond legend, it had made it into the print culture of his age through Holinshed,[34] Thomas Deloney's ballads 'The Faire Lady Rosamond' and 'The Imprisonment of Queen Eleanor', as well as possibly the popular ballad (collected by Child as no. 156) 'Queen Eleanor's Confession', depending upon its dating.[35]

A prologue of sorts to the nineteenth-century popularity of the Rosamond legend can be found in Thomas Addison's comic opera *Rosamond* of 1706, with music by Thomas Clayton. The tone of the libretto is light and pastoral, and as befits the genre, Addison altered the story to provide it with a happy ending: the poison that Eleanor administers to the heroine is only a sleeping potion, and Henry repents for of his adulterous ways and returns to Eleanor.[36] Addison introduced into the story an unnamed page who leads Eleanor to Rosamond's bower (the basis for the character of Arthur who would figure in later retellings of the legend), a knight named Sir Trusty, and his wife Grideline. The latter's jealousy over Sir Trusty's dalliances with women contrasts ironically with the more serious jealousy of 'Eleanora' towards Rosamond. The queen is jealous and vengeful ('My Breast with haunted vengeance burns') but this jealousy is tempered with sympathy, knowing that no woman could resist Henry ('One so great and so brave/All Hearts much enslave').[37] Nonetheless, she is intent upon revenge:

No, no, 'tis decreed
The traitress shall bleed;
No Fear shall alarm,
No pity disarm;
In my Rage shall be seen
The Revenge of a Queen.[38]

Unlike the later interpretations of the legend, where Rosamond is unaware that her lover 'Edgar' is the king in disguise, in Addison's libretto she knows his identity and pines for her 'absent Lord' and is also aware of the queen's jealousy.[39] Eleanor administers a sleeping draught to Rosamond, with the intention that her victim will wake up to find herself in a convent (an outcome closer to historical fact, even if it departs from the legend).[40] Henry and Eleanor reconcile, as do Sir Trusty and Grideline, following the example of their 'superiors'. Order – both marital and social – is confirmed, as Henry sings a song in praise of married love.[41]

Eleanor is described anachronistically as 'Britain's Queen' in the opera, which was published in 1707, the year of the Act of Union.[42] Addison was an English (later British) nationalist who disliked Italian opera, in part for its Catholicism.[43] A devoted Whig, he was part of a diplomatic mission to the court of the Elector of Hanover, Britain's future Protestant King George I.[44] He dedicated *Rosamond* to the duchess of Marlborough, resident of Blenheim Palace on the old royal manor of Woodstock, the supposed site of Rosamond's bower. It is possible that Addison was drawn to the subject of Henry II because he saw the king's military triumphs as analogous to the duke of Marlborough's victories over the French, for which Blenheim Palace and the Woodstock estate were gifts from the nation.[45] The ending of the opera openly refers to the building of Blenheim Palace on the ruins of Rosamond's bower.[46] Although the opera was not well received by the critics, '[a]s a theatrical occasion, the opening was a Whig triumph. William Walsh, one of the Whig oligarchy's most powerful cultural representatives, supplied a prologue, [f]iguring Marlborough as the God of War and comparing him to Henry II in amatory retirement with "*Rosamond* the Fair"'.[47] Brean Hammond argues that Henry and Eleanor's reconciliation is a direct appeal for support of the Act of Union, the English version of which

'received royal assent just two days after' the opera's first performance.[48] Who
or what does Eleanor herself represent? Hammond argues that she and Henry
represent the two realms, and Rosamund the opposition to the Act, which
Addison hopes will be set aside to allow the union to take place. I would suggest
an additional reading, however, in which Eleanor is Queen Anne, whose Tory
sympathies were a source of tension between her and her former friend the
duchess of Marlborough. If we follow Walsh's identification of Marlborough
and his wife with Henry and Rosamond in their 'bower' at Blenheim, then Anne
might be the jealous and vindictive Eleanor, with whom Henry wishes to be
reconciled.

Thomas Hull's play of 1773, *Henry II, or the Fall of Rosamond*[49] reinstated the
murderous nature of Eleanor's jealousy, and turned Henry's mistress back into
a tragic heroine, far from the 'rosa immunda' of Gerald of Wales; 'she is not the
wanton of legend, but an innocent girl who loves Henry for himself and not
because he is the King of England'.[50] Hull credits a play 'Mr. Hawkins's *Tragedy of
Henry and Rosamond*' which he had produced in 1761 as his source.[51] The play
was part of an eighteenth- and nineteenth-century trend of filling in the gaps
in the canon with plays modelled on (or even purporting to be) lost works of
Shakespeare. *Henry II* is written in iambic pentameters, and apes the bard to the
extent that 'had [Hull] not put his name to it, [it] might have been categorized as
a Shakespeare forgery'.[52] The play was also inspired by Henry Daniel's poem, *The
Complaint of Rosamond*.[53] Hull expands the *dramatis personae* in comparison to
Addison's opera, including the role of Clifford, Rosamond's father, who is angry
with the king for leading his daughter into sin.[54] He also historicizes the action,
placing it in the context of the coming rebellion by the Young King. The 'Prince
of Wales' [*sic*] complains of possessing only '[t]he empty Name and Title of a
King' and conspires with the Earl of Leicester, another historical figure who took
part in the rebellion of 1173–4.[55] His anger combines with that over his mother's
treatment:

> I have a double Cause to urge me on,
> A royal Mother's Wrongs join'd to my own.
> Do I not see her injur'd, scorn'd, abandon'd,
> For the loose Pleasures of a Wanton's Bed.[56]

Eleanor is motivated not just by her jealousy of Rosamond, but by maternal
anger when her son, the young Henry, is sent away to France by his father.
The Rosamond legend only takes centre stage later in the play, from Act III
onwards. Rosamond repents of her life of sin with Henry but dies of poison at

Eleanor's hands before the queen knows of this. Henry and Eleanor seem ready to reconcile; but Eleanor cannot bring herself to place '[t]he hand that's foul with murder' into that of her husband, and instead enters a nunnery to repent of her deeds.[57]

The tragedy of Fair Rosamond made its way into theatre and opera in continental Europe in the early-nineteenth century. A French verse-drama *Rosemonde* by Émile de Bonnechose opened in Paris in 1826.[58] Bonnechose came from a 'fervently royalist stock' who had been *émigrés* under the First Republic and First Empire, so it is understandable that history centred on the royal families of medieval Europe might appeal to his sympathies. However, Bonnechose avoided involvement in the 'outré political activities' of his ultra-royalist family and dedicated himself to a life of scholarship and letters.[59] Alexander Weatherson, in his study of the play and its influence on Italian opera, argues that Eleanor was treated with hostility as the woman who had alienated French territory to England, and that 'every character in [the play] ... – except Rosamund – was viewed in a distinctly unflattering light'.[60] However, Eleanor is represented sympathetically at the beginning of the play, as a French stranger in a strange land – a 'foreigner, without support under the sky of the English' – and the drama opens with the queen and Henry's page Arthur (who is secretly in love with Rosamond) reminiscing about their homeland of France.[61] This reflects the anti-British sentiment of the time: 'Stories hostile to the victorious British were popular in the reign of Charles X'.[62] Some of the invective directed towards Henry by Clifford was, however, censored, as insults directed towards a king – even an English one – were a little too much for the *Restauration* stage.[63] Despite the initial establishment of Eleanor as a 'French' figure, she soon becomes the wicked queen of the Rosamond legend as she plays on Arthur's sympathy for her unhappiness in order to extract from him the secret of Rosamond's hiding place. The familiar tragedy then begins to unfurl itself with both Rosamond *and* her father being stabbed, by Eleanor and Henry respectively. The king and queen then 'join hands in a most mysterious flux of shared emotion'.[64]

Bonnechose's play may appear obscure, especially to Anglophone readers, but it was highly influential in sparking a short-lived boom of interest in the Rosamond legend on the stage in continental Europe. A Spanish rendering of the Rosamond legend appeared in the form of Antonio Gil y Zárate's *Rosmunda* in 1839, apparently taking Bonnechose as its source rather than the English ballads and plays.[65] The most high profile stage interpretation of the story, however, was Gaetano Donizetti's opera *Rosmonda d'Inghilterra* of 1834 with a libretto by Felice Romani.[66] A ballet *Rosamunda* had been performed at La Scala, Milan in 1828, and both the ballet and Donizetti's opera were based on 'a French intermediary [i.e. Bonnechose's play of 1826] that ultimately derived from Addison's 1707 opera-text on this subject'.[67] Romani had originally written the libretto for the opera *Rosmonda d'Inghilterra* by Carlo Coccia (1829), at a time when English themes were popular in Italian opera.[68] Indeed, English *medieval* themes were popular in the wake of the success of Scott's *Ivanhoe*, which was adapted into the opera *Ivanhoé* by Rossini and Émile Deschamps in 1826.[69] Donizetti and Romani may have also been influenced in choosing the Fair Rosamond legend as their subject matter by a previous collaboration, *Ugo, conte di Parigi* (1832), set in late-Carolingian times of Louis V, which was based on *Blanche d'Aquitaine*, a French play of 1827 by Hypolite Bis, which was also about a murderess-queen.[70]

Following the failure of Coccia's opera, Romani offered the libretto to Donizetti. The new version of the opera was first performed in February 1834 in Florence.[71] It was hardly a huge success and it was apparently only performed in full one more time in the nineteenth century, at Livorno in 1846, although extracts were performed in Milan in 1834, 1851 and 1852. The opera was also reissued in 1837 entitled, interestingly from the perspective of this book, *Eleonora di Gujenna*, and was apparently performed only once in 1839. The plot is based reasonably closely on that of Bonnechose's play, including the element of disguise whereby Enrico (Henry) woos Rosmonda under the pseudonym 'Edegardo' (Edgar). The jealous Eleanora slays Rosmonda using poison, before trying to pass the blame on to Enrico. In a tradition of Eleanor passionately facing up to a female rival that dates back to Shakespeare, '[t]here is an effective duet for Rosmonda and Eleanora, "Tu morrai, tu m'ha costretto", where the accents on the unstressed beats suggest the contortions of Eleanor's jealousy ...'.[72]

Although not one of Donizetti's better or more frequently performed operas, it had some modest influence in the middle of the century. Another opera also called *Rosmonda d'Inghilterra*, by Jules-Eugène-Abraham Alary (also known as Giulio Eugenio Abramo Alari) was performed at the Pergola, Florence in 1840 – the same house in which Donizetti's version had opened six years earlier.[73] Celestia Bloss's novel *Heroines of the Crusades* (1853), discussed in the Chapter 6, contains a Fair Rosamond episode that seems indebted to Donizetti, as it includes the king's use of a pseudonym to woo Rosamond.

Alfred, Lord Tennyson's *Becket* of 1884 presents Eleanor within the 'Fair Rosamond' legend. Although Rosamund does not die, ending her days instead in Godstow nunnery, the confrontation between her and the queen is included, with Eleanor threatening to stab her rival. Tennyson was drawn to medieval subjects, most famously the Arthurian cycle in his *Idylls of the King* but also in lesser known works including the plays *Harold* (1876) about the last Anglo-Saxon king, and the Robin Hood-themed *The Foresters* (1894). He was probably influenced in his portrayal of Eleanor by the Strickland sisters.[74] The play was not performed until 1893, and was not especially well-received by critics; the *New York Times* reviewer who attended the show's opening in London felt that the play's Shakespearian blank verse 'once or twice touches the point of sublimity, and more frequently just misses dramatic grandeur. In many places, however, the drama shows a threadlike weakness...'[75] A critic defending Tennyson's dramas in 1901 admitted that they 'may not be among his greatest works... Their limitations are many, it is true...'[76] 'Tennyson's genius was lyrical, not dramatic' wrote another Edwardian critic.[77] Others, writing privately, were less polite; Henry Irving, who starred in the London version of *Becket*, told a friend 'Tennyson is a great poet, but he cannot write plays; what a pity he tries, they are the greatest rubbish!'[78]

Tennyson handles the themes in *Becket* somewhat clumsily, leaving little to the imagination. The action opens with Henry and Becket playing chess, with rather obvious references made to the players moving the pieces of bishop and king across the board, as Henry talks about the need to appoint a new archbishop, and his anger that clerics are not subject to his law.[79] It is established early on that Henry fears that Eleanor is plotting to kill Rosamund: 'I fear the queen would have her life.'[80] Henry 'loves Rosamund, my true heart-wife/Not Eleanor...' He has built a bower to protect Rosamund and thereby save 'the soul of Eleanor from hell-fire.'[81] We first meet Eleanor as she sings a song that ominously foreshadows Rosamund's death; 'Over! The sweet summer closes/and the reign of the roses is done.'[82]

Tennyson's purpose in this medieval play was to show 'the awakening of the English people and clergy from the slumber into which they had for the most part fallen' after the Conquest. 'In "Becket" the struggle is between the Crown and the Church for predominance...'[83] Eleanor is presented as a southern figure, who complains that 'I would I were in Aquitaine again – your north chills me.'[84] In contrast to the romanticism of the southern queen that has been a product of the twentieth-century writing on Eleanor, for Tennyson this marks her as an alien figure. 'I am a troubadour you know...but my voice is harsh here, not in tune...'[85] In her confrontation with Rosamund in the bower, Eleanor's foreignness is further emphasized by her becoming orientalized; she taunts the younger woman by telling her that the king has many mistresses, 'as many as your true Mussulman...but so it chances, child,/That I am his main paramour, his sultana.'[86] She tries to kill Rosamund using a dagger that she acquired 'from an Arab soldan', possibly a reference to her legendary liaison with Saladin.[87] Rosamund, in contrast, represents Englishness. She welcomes the fact that simple wildflowers are in her bower: 'I brought them in from the wood, and set them here. I love them/More than the garden flowers, that seem at most/Sweet guests, or foreign cousins, not half-speaking/The language of the land.'[88]

The conflict between Eleanor and Rosamund is a subplot that parallels the main conflict between Henry and Becket, and the two overlap. Eleanor's desire to remove Rosamund is tied to the eventual murder of Becket; the queen fans the flames of Fitzurse's dislike of the 'plebeian' Becket, as well as urging him to '[f]ollow me this Rosamund day and night', and in doing so exploits Fitzurse's own former love for Rosamund and encourages his jealousy of the king.[89] Fitzurse is a horrible mutation of the figure of Arthur from Bonnechose. Whereas the latter is the unwitting cause of Rosamond's demise, Fitzurse is cynically and deliberately violent. The four murderers later declare 'Remember the Queen!'[90] Crucially, it is Eleanor, not Henry, who urges Fitzurse and his fellow knights to kill Becket; hearing Henry shout, Fitzurse asks the queen 'What made the king cry out so furiously?' to which she replies that the Henry is angry with Becket, and urges Fitzurse to 'Strike at once; the King will have him!'[91] Conversely, Rosamund is identified with Becket, and like the former chancellor, she is converted to the side of church after she becomes a nun. She visits Becket on the day of his martyrdom, and ends the play as a 'mater dolorosa, kneel[ing] by the martyr's body'.[92]

Eleanor's hatred of Rosamund is political, not personal; 'I would she were but his paramour, for men tire of their fancies; but I fear this one fancy hath taken root, and born blossom too, and she, whom the King loves indeed, is a power in the State'.[93] Becket, conversely, offers protection to Rosamund as she tries to escape Fitzurse, and later stays Eleanor's hand as she is about to stab Rosamund.[94] John of Salisbury is assigned the duty of escorting Rosamund to her bower, another parallel to Becket's later murder which John of Salisbury witnessed. It may also be significant that he is one of the sources for Eleanor's alleged adultery with Raymond of Antioch.[95] Eleanor's own adultery is hinted at when Becket replies to her statement that kings should be 'faithful to their marriage vow' with 'Ay, Madam, and queens also'.[96] All the accusations of adultery ever made against Eleanor are made explicit by Rosamund, who threatens the queen that if she is killed she will fly to heaven shrieking

'Eleanor of Aquitaine, Eleanor of England!
Murder'd by that adulteress Eleanor,
Whose doings are a horror to the east,

A hissing in the west!' Have we not heard
Raymond of Poitou, thine own uncle – nay,
Geoffrey Plantagenet, thine own husband's
father –
Nay, ev'n the accursed heathen Saladdeen. Strike![97]

Tennyson's Eleanor is heavily influenced by the idea of the courtly, literate Eleanor that had taken hold in the nineteenth century. Eleanor is a 'troubadour' who translates lyrics from the Provençal, and she refers to her Courts of Love.[98] However, this is not presented in a wholly positive way: Rosamund complains to Eleanor that that she is 'a troubadour – you play with words'.[99] Her troubadour status is another way of marking the queen as alien and threatening.

The relationship between Henry and Becket is a close, homosocial one, which interferes with Henry's love for his women; Becket refers to himself as a 'statesman who loves his king, and whom the king/Loves not as statesman but true lover and friend'.[100] Both Henry's wife and mistress are threatened by the men's closeness, and later, by their enmity; 'Always Becket/He always comes between us!' complains Rosamund when Henry mentions his conflict with the archbishop.

Rosamund stands in contrast to the old queen – '[o]ur waning Eleanor' – in that she has a young child, Geoffrey, who is introduced at the start of Act III.[101] There is perhaps a slight echo of the confrontation between Eleanor and Constance in Shakespeare, where the younger woman taunts the older 'grandam'. When Eleanor tries to win young Geoffrey's trust by claiming to be a 'good fairy' come to visit his mother, the boy replies that 'you don't look like a good fairy. Mother does. You are not pretty, like mother'.[102] When threatened with poison by Eleanor, Rosamund appeals, unsuccessfully, to their common motherhood of Henry's children.[103]

We therefore see in Tennyson's *Becket* many of the themes that helped shape a negative image of Eleanor in the nineteenth century: nationalism (as she is presented as a foreign queen), misogyny, Orientalism and the Black Legend. More sympathetic portrayals of Eleanor, such as that of Addison, had been offered, but over the centuries her image as the wicked old queen had set in stone, to the extent that the murderous Eleanor of the Fair Rosamond legend was perhaps the defining image of her by the late nineteenth century. By this time, academic history had reinforced this image, and Michelet's reference to Eleanor as 'passionate and vindictive' could serve as a description of the Eleanor of nineteenth-century drama and opera. However, Tennyson did at least give her a major part in the action, the only time that she would play such a significant role in a drama about Becket. Despite the similarities between *Becket* and Eliot's *Murder in the Cathedral* (1935),[104] she does not appear in the latter play. She would feature only marginally in Anouilh's *Becket* (1959) and its film adaptation, which are discussed in the next chapter. However, the twentieth century would introduce new portrayals and interpretations of Eleanor on the stage but also through the new media of film and television, including perhaps the most memorable dramatic portrayal of a medieval queen ever captured on celluloid.

A Lioness in Winter: Eleanor on Stage and Screen in the Twentieth Century

By the beginning of the twentieth century, Eleanor's popular image had already been shaped by the historical fiction and popular history of the nineteenth. The new century brought with it a new medium through which that image could be further shaped – film and, later, television. If, by 1900, Eleanor's image on the stage had been shaped by the Black Legend, stage and screen portrayals in the twentieth century reflected the reassessment of Eleanor as a strong female – even feminist – role-model. The visual image of Eleanor on the screen has arguably been as influential, if not more so, than that of the printed page. 'Thanks to the indelible image of Eleanor that Katharine Hepburn created in the film version of *The Lion in Winter* (1968), this queen was often among those singled out by the first generation of feminist historians.'[1]

Eleanor was, however, relatively late in making a significant appearance on either the silver or the small screen. The character of 'Eleanor of Aquitaine' appeared only once on film or television before World War II, in the 1923 film *Becket*, a silent picture based on the Tennyson play.[2] As we shall see, adapted stage plays including Shakespeare's *King John*, James Goldman's *The Lion in Winter* and Anouilh's *Becket* were a frequent source for Eleanor's appearances in TV or film.[3] From the 1950s onwards, however, we see a growing interest in Eleanor on the screen, as either an incidental (but usually memorable) character in films and series set in the Plantagenet era – and especially in Robin Hood stories – or at the centre of the action in two adaptations of *The Lion in Winter* and the BBC drama series *The Devil's Crown* (1978).[4]

Eleanor and Robin Hood

Eleanor appeared in two episodes of the television series *The Adventures of Robin Hood*, which ran on Britain's ITV network (and CBS in the United States) from 1955 to 1959. This was the first time Eleanor featured within the Robin Hood canon on the screen: she had not appeared in Douglas Fairbanks' *Robin Hood* (1922) or *The Adventures of Robin Hood* (1938) which memorably starred Errol Flynn. Subsequently, however, Eleanor has become almost an obligatory character – albeit one who usually plays a cameo role – in nearly all Robin Hood television series and some films. In part this could simply be down to the televisual medium: the longer running time of a TV series compared to a film allows for – and indeed, requires – more storylines and more characters. However, the specific circumstances that surround the creation of *The Adventures of Robin Hood* suggest that there may be more to it than this alone.

The placing of the Robin Hood legend in the context of Richard I's crusade is a product of Walter Scott's *Ivanhoe*. The potential for Eleanor to appear in the Robin Hood legend was, however, not exploited for some time. She did not appear in *Ivanhoe* or in early screen portrayals of Robin Hood. The introduction of Eleanor onto the screen in the 1950s may reflect a changing attitude towards the role of powerful women. According to Lorraine K. Stock, the 1952 film *The Story of Robin Hood and his Merrie Men* and television's *The Adventures of Robin Hood* 'mark the first cinematic appearance of Eleanor of Aquitaine … The Queen Mother's prominence in both vehicles surely reflects the iconic role of Eleanor Roosevelt in America during World War II'.[5] A specific link to Eleanor Roosevelt is hard to prove or disprove; even if her name did not directly inspire a renewed interest in Eleanor of Aquitaine, the model of a powerful and influential woman may have helped to do so. Although she had not been First Lady since FDR's death in 1945, Roosevelt was involved in the formation of the United Nations, and was politically active through the 1950s. More generally the 1950s, despite their reputation as an era of conservatism and the reimposition of traditional gender roles, was an era when opportunities were opening up for women: for example, the proportion of American women doing paid work outside the home by the end of the decade was double that of 1940.[6]

If popular culture was ready for a strong female character, the specific context for the creation of *The Adventures of Robin Hood* favoured a progressive and democratic retelling of the legend, which may account for the introduction of Eleanor as an independent-minded woman. Coming in the context of Britain's broadly social-democratic post-war consensus, ' "Adventures of Robin Hood" … came at a time and place where the restrained radicalism that had pervaded the myth from time to time was widely acceptable'.[7] The series was produced by Sapphire Films, established by American exile Hannah Weinstein who had left the United States to escape the McCarthyite witch-hunts.[8] The lead writer for the series was blacklisted Hollywood screenwriter Ring Lardner Jr., working in exile in the United Kingdom. 'Ring Lardner Jr. is on record as having written, with Ian McClellan Hunter, about twenty of the first year's scripts, using a number of pseudonyms. Many of the first episodes were by an otherwise unknown "Eric Heath"...'[9] 'Heath' wrote the teleplay for 'Queen Eleanor', the ninth episode of season one (originally broadcast in the United Kingdom on 14 November 1955; in the United States, the writing credit was given to 'Lawrence McClellan'). This is the first of two episodes in which Eleanor makes an appearance.[10]

The Adventures of Robin Hood created a template for the portrayal of Eleanor that would be repeated in subsequent television versions of the Robin Hood legend. As portrayed by Jill Esmond, she is strong, feisty, even a little flirtatious. Lardner's attempts to ground the show in a realistic historical setting led him to historicize some elements of the storyline and Eleanor's character, albeit sometimes reflecting received history rather than the medieval sources.

The setting for the story is based on one of Eleanor's activities that is reliably attested to in the historical record – her involvement in raising money for Richard's ransom. Lardner thereby introduces a context for Eleanor's involvement in the Robin Hood story that would be repeated in subsequent renditions of the legend. The treacherous sheriff attempts to seize the ransom for himself, but the outlaws help Eleanor to cross Sherwood safely, avoiding the sheriff's ambush. The sheriff learns of Robin's plan, but is double-crossed by the Queen, who is not part of Robin's party, but instead has formed a second group escorted by Marian.

The teleplay establishes several qualities of Eleanor that are common to her received image in the twentieth century. She is a formidable adversary: 'I don't relish a brush with Eleanor of Aquitaine' says the sheriff. She is intelligent; learning of her ruse to safely cross Sherwood, the sheriff remarks that '[t]his plan is worthy of her shrewdness'. She is sexual and flirtatious: 'If I were a few years younger', she says of Robin, 'I think he would interest me romantically. [But] I think I've met enough adventurous characters for one life'. She has a sardonic sense of humour; referring to John, she says 'when you've had nine children, stop. The tenth can be a terrible mistake'. Overall, she is someone who has to use a mixture of strength, intelligence and feminine charm to survive in the turbulent politics of the Angevin world; 'Sometimes I have had to make use of force, sometimes my sex, and sometimes what craft I have in this old head of mine'.

As well as placing the story in the historical context of raising Richard's ransom, the dialogue also invokes specific incidents in Eleanor's life. Her participation in the Second Crusade is alluded to several times, albeit incorporating the myth of her leading her 'Amazons'. Complaining of the costs of Richard's crusade, she recalls her own crusading exploits. 'You led a brigade of women soldiers', Marian reminds her. Eleanor responds that, unfortunately, the women's brigade was 'a disaster'. However, Lardner turns the misogynist myth of Eleanor's ladies' disruptive impact on its head; 'The women were fine', Eleanor explains, 'but the men weren't ready for the idea'. Her using Marian as an escort also recalls her 'Amazons', as well as establishing that Marian is herself a strong female character who is capable of courage and initiative. Lardner's Marian contrasts with that of Michael Curtiz's 1938 *Adventures of Robin Hood*.[11] Played by Olivia de Havilland, Marian displayed plenty of spirit, but was 'beautiful if immobile', wrapped in constricting clothing that would prevent her taking part in a sword fight even if she wished to do so.[12] The idea of an older Eleanor who is sexual yet remains a positive character is apparently a new element of her image. The lecherous old queen of Munday's sixteenth-century play *The Death of Robert Earle of Huntington* had been a threatening and tyrannical figure, inimical to Robin and Marian. In Lardner's version Eleanor is Marian's foil, not her rival.

Esmond reprised her role as Eleanor in the episode 'The Deserted Castle' (episode 15 of series one, first broadcast on 12 March 1956, also written by 'Eric Heath'). The Queen plays a lesser role in this storyline, but again shows her independence of spirit and her resourcefulness. After Robin's attempt to sabotage a treaty between John and Philip of France fails, Eleanor declares to Marian, 'I think this is the point for we women to take charge'. Eleanor exerts her queenly authority to take charge of the sheriff and his men, and some of her authority rubs off on Marian. After being advised by Eleanor to be wary of a 'handsome scoundrel' (i.e. Robin), she commands Robin to kneel so that she may mount her horse. However, Marian and Eleanor, although authoritative women within the storyline, are also in some ways peripheral to it – literally so in a scene where they secretly listen to the proceedings among the men from the sidelines.

Esmond had previously appeared in the 1946 film *The Bandit of Sherwood Forest* as 'The Queen Mother'.[13] The film features 'Robert of Nottingham', the son of Robin Hood, going to the aid of the Queen Mother and a 'Lady Catherine' who are being held captive by the 'regent' William of Pembroke. It is unclear whether the 'Queen Mother' is Eleanor: the appearance of Robin's son would seem to locate the film a generation after the reign of Richard, and 'William of Pembroke' may be a reference to William Marshal, earl of Pembroke, who was regent on behalf of John's son Henry III, which would make the 'Queen Mother' Isabella of Angoulême rather than Eleanor.

Eleanor makes a remarkable appearance in a 1997 episode of the American TV series *The New Adventures of Robin Hood*, which ran from 1997 to 1999.[14]

This series stood in the same tradition as the contemporary *Xena: Warrior Princess* and *Hercules: the Legendary Journeys* – shows based extremely loosely on Classical mythology that paid very little attention to historicity. *The New Adventures* had a medieval setting but borrowed widely from eras and cultures outside twelfth-century England: gunpowder, Mongols, magic, Merlin and King Arthur and Lady Godiva all made an appearance. In *The Legend of the Amazons*, the warrior women of classical mythology visit Sherwood, led by Eleanor. Curiously for a series that happily disregarded 'historical accuracy', this episode makes a clear reference to history – or at least to an incident from Eleanor's life that has become widely accepted as such. The 'cheaply and often clumsily-made series'[15] was widely criticized, but in presenting an Amazonian Eleanor it was arguably no more inaccurate than *The Lion in Winter*.

Eleanor of Aquitaine also appears in the BBC's *Robin Hood* series that ran from 2006 to 2009,[16] and her portrayal shows remarkable similarities to that of the *Adventures* in the 1950s. This may be deliberate; the writers of the twenty-first century series pay homage to Lardner in the title of an episode in series two, 'Lardner's Ring'. In 'Treasure of the Nation' (series two, episode 11, written by Simon J. Ashford, originally broadcast on 15 December 2007), Eleanor is played by Lynda Bellingham. As in the 1950s series, Eleanor's involvement with the outlaws occurs in the context of the collection of Richard's ransom, and the sheriff and John's plans to seize it. In this instance, however, the 'treasure' alluded to in the episode's title is Eleanor herself. Legrand, a member of King Richard's guard, is sent secretly to Robin to deliver a coded message that leads them and the outlaws to the *Thesaurus patriae* – Queen Eleanor, who has escaped captivity at the hands of John. The storyline is broadly similar to that of 1955's 'Queen Eleanor', with the outlaws attempting to prevent Eleanor's recapture by the sheriff. Many of the aspects of the Queen's personality are the same too: she is flirtatious, but this time with Little John, rather than Robin. When introduced to him, Eleanor remarks that 'I can't believe there's a part of you that's little' and she takes to calling him 'big bear', much to John's embarrassment. She is not keen to be reminded of her age; when Legrand remarks, in horror at the idea that John would imprison her, '[b]ut you're the Queen Mother!' she replies, 'less of the mother, thank you'. She is intelligent – 'provision has been made for all eventualities' she declares, before revealing a secret trap door that leads out of the church in which the outlaws are hiding – and intellectually curious, especially about other cultures – 'I should like to know you better' she tells Djaq, the Saracen woman among Robin's band. Bellingham's Eleanor shares her 1950s counterpart's low opinion of her son John; 'Alas, one can choose one's friends but not one's family.'

Although there are no references to her Amazonian exploits on crusade, she is presented almost as a masculine warrior figure. When the dying Legrand hears Little John remark admiringly 'a stronger man I never knew', he thinks at first that the outlaw must mean 'the queen', before Eleanor corrects him. As well as being a proto-feminist, Eleanor also seems to be a proto-socialist who approves of Robin's wealth-redistribution; handing him a purse of coins, she says '[t]he rich are rich. The poor are poor. Isn't that where you come in?' Eleanor again shares the story with a strong independent Maid Marian (Lucy Griffith). A storyline established in season one, in which Marian has a masked alter ego known as the Nightwatchman, reaches a critical point in a parallel plot within 'Treasure of the Nation' in which Gisborne learns the Nightwatchman's true identity. Lucy Griffith's character can be compared to the tougher Marians of the 1990s films *Robin Hood* (1991) (described as 'kick-butt' in the summary on Netflix.com) and *Robin Hood: Prince of Thieves* (1991) (where she fights in armour and 'make[s] a good job of it'),[17] but she has deeper roots in Lardner's 1950s series.

Ultimately, however, Eleanor is a peripheral figure who is limited to cameo roles in Robin Hood films and television dramas. She is entirely absent not only from the pre-war films mentioned above, but from the Robin Hood movies of the 1990s. Even *Robin and Marian* (1976), the screenplay for which was written by the same James Goldman who gave Eleanor her most memorable screen portrayal in *The Lion in Winter* in 1968,[18] has no place for the Queen. She features in only a minor role (played by Eileen Atkins) in the 2010 film *Robin Hood* which attempts rather awkwardly to give Robin (played by Russell Crowe) an origin story in historical events that seem to allude to Magna Carta and the French invasion under the future Louis VIII in 1216 (anachronistically placed early in John's reign). In Disney's animated *Robin Hood* (1973) she is alluded to by John (depicted as a lion but without a mane, in contrast to his hirsute brother Richard) being reduced to a state of thumb-sucking infantilism at the mention of 'mother'.[19]

Becket

Eleanor likewise plays a peripheral role in the major film of the early 1960s that centred on the life of Henry II; *Becket* (1964), directed by Peter Glenville, and based on Jean Anouilh's play of 1959. Eleanor (played by Pamela Brown), and her mother-in-law the Empress Matilda, are presented as shrewish older women working on embroidery. The dialogue between her and Henry (played by Peter O'Toole, who would portray the king again in *The Lion in Winter*) focuses on Eleanor feeling that the king has neglected her for Becket; he has been 'lured away from the duties that you owe me'. Henry views Eleanor as asexual, her role limited to that of producing heirs: 'I didn't need anyone to lure me away from the duties I owe to you. I made you four children very conscientiously. Thank the Lord, my duty is done!' When Eleanor defends herself, it is by reminding Henry that 'I ... gave you your children', to which he replies 'I don't like my children!'

The central relationship of the film is between two men, Henry and Becket; it is, in Anouilh's own words, a 'drama of friendship between two men, between the king and his friend, his companion in pleasure and in work'.[20] As Finke and Shichtman have pointed out, this relationship is profoundly homosocial, 'border[ing] on the homoerotic. Henry is never shown in bed with a woman without Becket present...During the French campaign, Becket and the king talk politics together in bed with a French whore...between them, the prostitute providing a heterosexual "cover" for the erotic charge between the two men'.[21] The main female agent in the film is not Eleanor, but Henry's Welsh mistress Gwendolen played by Siân Phillips (who, over thirty years later, would play Eleanor in the BBC adaptation of *Ivanhoe*). 'Henry jeers at their [Eleanor and Matilda's] "carping mediocrity", and, whereas Sian Phillips's Gwendolen is a heroically tragic figure, Eleanor and Matilda are represented as ineffectual shrews'.[22] They are presented as passive and domesticated and 'are swathed – literally hemmed in – by elaborate gowns and wimples...'[23] Kevin Harty complains that the film is 'excellent ... in every way, except for its reduction of Eleanor of Aquitaine to a simpering fool'. The marginalization of Eleanor is not a product of the film, however; it is there in Anouilh's original text. With the exception of one or two extra (and fairly inconsequential) lines, Eleanor's role is no larger in the stage play.[24]

The Lion in Winter

In contrast, Eleanor appears centre-stage in James Goldman's *The Lion in Winter*. This has been perhaps the most influential dramatic representation of Eleanor, and helped to shape perceptions of her over a quarter of a century. It is not much of an exaggeration to say, as Ralph Turner does, that '[s]he entered popular culture when she appeared on the screen, played by Katharine Hepburn, in the film *A* [sic] *Lion in Winter*. The 1968 film, however inaccurate and anachronistic in many aspects, vividly showed audiences that Eleanor and Henry II's marriage was not a happy one'.[25] *Lion* originated in 1964 as an unpublished play, *A Day in the Life of Henry the Second*, before appearing in its final form in 1966.[26] However, the 1968 film version of *The Lion in Winter* (directed by Anthony Harvey) has proven more famous and influential than the stage play. Goldman himself admits that the film was more successful than the play, which

> opened on March 3, 1966 to highly contradictory notices, including a thunderous dismissal by the New York *Times*. Eighty-three performances later, it closed and sank from sight ... Then came the film ... *Lion*, as a stage piece was more than reprieved by the movie. It was transformed into a theater work that has been performed all over the world.[27]

Without this success, Goldman doubted that he would have returned to the theme of the Plantagenets in his screenplay for *Robin and Marian* (1976) or his novel about King John, *Myself as Witness* (1979). The film version made Katharine Hepburn perhaps the definitive screen Eleanor of Aquitaine. In the words of Finke and Shichtman, '[i]n 1968 *The Lion in Winter*, based on James Goldman's 1966 Tony Award-winning play, restored to the figure of Eleanor of Aquitaine her historical grandeur by embodying her in the magisterial figure of Katharine Hepburn'.[28]

Goldman was clearly impressed by Eleanor; the notes in his stage play that describe Eleanor upon her entry are not so much stage-directions as a paean:

> She is a handsome woman of great temperament, authority, and presence. She has been a queen of international importance for forty-six years and you know it. Finally, she is that most unusual thing: a genuinely feminine woman thoroughly capable of holding her own in a man's world.[29]

Goldman's words are revealing: he shares the received idea of Eleanor's exceptionalism as a strong woman 'in a man's world', as well as expressing surprise – (it is 'unusual') that a powerful woman is able to remain feminine.

For many viewers, Hepburn *is* Eleanor. In an otherwise unfavourable review in *The New Yorker*, Pauline Kael commented that 'her accent is so peculiarly hers that we just accept it as the way she talks. And it seems proper for a queen to sound like Hepburn'.[30] Hepburn's biographer, quoting the glowing description of Eleanor from Goldman's stage notes, concludes that this 'was, of course, a description of Kate herself'.[31] Hepburn often attracted queenly descriptions: according to a 1930s magazine writer, the young Hepburn had been the 'uncrowned Queen of Filmdom'.[32] Hepburn researched her role as Eleanor extensively, reading 'every available book on Eleanor of Aquitaine' and visiting the tombs of Eleanor and Henry at Fontevraud.[33]

In his introduction to the published play, Goldman explained that he intended it to be historical, while also taking some artistic license with the history:

> This play – while simplifying the political maneuvering ... is accurately based on the available data ... The people in this play, their character and passions, while consistent with the facts we have, are fictitious ... Those [anachronisms] the author is aware of – the way, for instance, Christmas is celebrated – are deliberate and not intended to outrage the historical aspects of the script.[34]

Goldman's meeting of the family at Chinon for Christmas 1183 is fictitious; Eleanor was in England – on a slightly longer leash than usual during her captivity – in 1183.[35] Taken more broadly, however, Goldman does capture the real political manoeuvres as Henry sought to reshuffle the cards of his sons' inheritance following the death of the Young King in the summer of 1183, with Richard and Eleanor clashing with Henry over his desire to reallocate Aquitaine to John.

The deliberate anachronisms are designed to remind the audience of the distance between themselves and the medieval past. This distancing is highlighted most forcefully when Eleanor, in response to John's outrage that 'he [Richard]'s got a knife!' says, '[o]f course he has a knife. He always has a knife. We all have knives. It's 1183 and we're barbarians'. The audience is reminded of the (supposedly) violent and 'barbarous' Middle Ages; Goldman's twelfth century is not that of the twelfth-century renaissance.[36] As Kevin Harty has observed, medievalist film is often characterized by '[t]he use of the Middle Ages as a means to enter a barbaric world ...'[37]

Stripped of its medievalism, *The Lion in Winter* is essentially a family drama. Finke and Shichtman describe it as 'a dynastic struggle over an empire that stretched from Italy to England [that] is reduced to a medieval *Who's Afraid of Virginia Woolf?*' The play blurs the personal and political, reducing motivations of characters to 'a pop psychology reading of family dynamics, of familial "dysfunction".'[38] The apparent universality of family dynamics (and dysfunction), allied to the play's self-conscious use of anachronisms such as the giving of Christmas gifts beneath a tree, gives the drama its apparent timelessness. '"What was fascinating about the play", Hepburn told her friend A. Scott Berg many years later, "was its modernness. This wasn't about pomp and circumstance but about a family, a wife trying to protect her dignity and a mother protecting her children" '.[39] Yet when opened up on the big screen, the film is at pains to look and feel medieval, or at least what a twentieth-century cinema audience perceives to be medieval. Castle interiors are bare and grey, animal and peasant life clutters Chinon's bailey, and the characters' clothes are often in drab shades. This matches one of the signs of the medieval identified by Finke and Shichtman: '[w]e would correlate the amount of filth present in a medieval film with the film's view of the Middle Ages ... The insistence on the filthiness of the Middle Ages seems to stem from a need to counter the romanticized, nostalgic view of the period, to proclaim its barbarity as a "dark age" '.[40] The squalor projected in director Anthony Harvey's twelfth century matches Goldman's view of it as an age in which 'we are barbarians', and the actors wore their costumes prior to filming in 'so that they looked rubbed and frayed'.[41] Vivian Sobchak argues, however, that the audience of 'historical' films is well aware that what it is seeing on screen is not necessarily the 'real' history; 'filmgoers know that histories are rhetorically constructed narratives, that "events" and "facts" are open to various uses and multiple interpretations'.[42] Conversely, some historians have taken the 'filthy' Middle Ages of the film as an indicator of its historical veracity. One (unnamed) H-Net user cited by Sobchack suggested *The Lion in Winter* as an example of a film that depicted the Middle Ages 'realistically': 'There seems to be enough muck and dirt and rushes on the floors to suggest something of the twelfth century'.[43] Roger Ebert also perceived the dirt and clutter depicted in the movie as a token of its realism:

> Henry II rules a world in which kings still kicked aside chickens on their way through the courtyard, and he wears a costume that looks designed to be put on in November and shed layer by layer during April. In this England ... [sic; the film is set in Anjou], there are dogs and dirt floors, rough furskins and pots of stew, pigs, mud, dungeons – and human beings. We believe in the complicated intrigue these people get themselves into because we believe in them. They look real, and inhabit a world that looks lived in.[44]

The link between the individual and history, and between familial and political dynamics, is made clear at several points in the play and film. Eleanor explains to her sons that, '[i]f I had managed sons for him [Louis VII] instead of all those little girls [sic; Eleanor bore only two daughters with Louis], I'd still be stuck with being queen of France, and we should not have known each other. Such, my angels, is the role of sex in history'. Later, she remarks that '[w]e are the world in small. A nation is a human thing. It does what we do, for our reasons'. Following her declaration that 'we are barbarians', Eleanor explains that conflicts arise not from impersonal historical forces, but from squabbles among rulers:

> We are the origins of war. Not history's forces, nor the times, nor justice, nor the lack of it, nor causes, nor religions, nor ideas, nor kinds of government, nor any other thing. We are the killers. We breed wars. We carry it, like syphilis, inside. Dead bodies rot in field and stream because the living ones are rotten. For the love of God, can't we love one another just a little? That's how peace begins.

For Goldman's Eleanor, war originates not just in the ruling elite but in its families. Royal marriages 'breed war', just as they breed sons or the 'little girls' who were the cause of her divorce from Louis. War, 'like syphilis', is a disease that is spread through intercourse or heredity. (The reference to syphilis, incidentally, is another anachronism.)

Eleanor is memorable for Hepburn's spirited and witty portrayal of the Queen, which is drawn in part from Goldman's dialogue, and in part from qualities Hepburn brings to the performance that cannot be captured on paper, for which she won the 1969 Academy Award for best actress. Released during the rise of Second-Wave Feminism, in the revolutionary year of 1968, Harvey's *The Lion in Winter* presents perhaps the archetypal 'feminist' Eleanor. The Queen is proud and defiant, boasting of how 'I even made poor Louis take me on Crusade. How's that for blasphemy. I dressed my maids as Amazons and rode bare-breasted halfway to Damascus. Louis had a seizure and I damn near died of windburn...but the troops were dazzled'. This line of course makes reference to the 'fantastic story' that Eleanor dressed as an Amazon during the Second Crusade,[45] but it also establishes her as a strong and independent woman. Hepburn was an appropriate vehicle for such an interpretation, as she came from a social-activist family (her mother Katharine Houghton was a birth-control advocate).[46] In the 1930s and 1940s, Hepburn was regarded as a symbol of the independent new woman and often appeared on screen and in real life wearing trousers, a form of cross-dressing that seems appropriate to the Amazonian Eleanor alluded to in *Lion*. Contemporary media often referred to her as a tomboy.[47] She challenged the quasi-feudal studio system just as (in Amy Kelly's version, at least) Eleanor challenged a patriarchal feudal order. Hepburn's public persona as someone with 'a long-standing reputation for independence, assertiveness even' was somewhat at odds with that expected of a Hollywood 'star';[48] like Eleanor in the monastic chronicles of the twelfth century, she was perceived as a disturbing presence who challenged received ideas of appropriate female behaviour. Like the Eleanor of the Strickland sisters, she was seen to have progressed from a troublesome youth to an august maturity (Hepburn was sixty years old when *Lion* was shot in 1967–8; Eleanor would have been at least fifty-nine in Christmas 1183). Discussing media framing of Hepburn's persona in the 1940s and 1950s, Janet Thumim writes that '[b]y 1959 the "disturbing personality" of 1945 had become "America's great lady of the screen": this fifteen-year period, significantly, covers Hepburn's passage from the sexually active generation to the generation where, however spuriously, the conventional stereotyping has women safely desexed'. In the late 1950s and 1960s, Hepburn often starred in films that Thumim dubs her 'spinster cycle'.[49] Andrew Britten, in a feminist reading of Hepburn's work, argues that in some of these later films she came close to the stereotype of the 'demented, castrating mother', pointing to parallels between her role in *Suddenly Last Summer* where her character's 'emasculating properties manifest themselves in the homosexuality of their son' and her role in *Lion*, where her son Richard is represented as gay.[50]

Eleanor is not, however, utterly desexed in *Lion*: we are reminded of her sexuality when she recalls 'riding bare-breasted', when she taunts Henry by suggesting that she slept with his father (a reference to accusations made by Gerald of Wales) or when she recalls her first meeting with Henry, when they 'shattered the Commandments on the spot'. But these are recollections from her past[51]; she is no longer Henry's bed-mate or a potential mother. When Henry toys with the idea of disinheriting all his children and breeding a new heir, it can only be with his mistress, the much younger Alais of France, whom he plans to marry after divorcing Eleanor. If Eleanor is a 'feminist' figure in *Lion*, she still represents a woman whose independence is limited by biology and male power. The examples that illustrate her sexuality – her alleged affairs and her riding bare-breasted – are both drawn from the misogynist Black Legend. The sexlessness and infertility of the older Eleanor is a common theme in stage and screen portrayals, dating back to Shakespeare's 'canker'd grandam'. In Anouilh's *Becket*, when she defends herself against Henry by reminding him that she bore his children, Henry's rejoinder is that 'Your body is an empty desert, madam!'[52]

The Lion in Winter reappeared on the screen in 2003, in a television movie directed by Andrey Konchalovskiy, starring Glenn Close as Eleanor and Patrick Stewart as Henry II, and with a teleplay adapted by Goldman from his original play.[53] The 2003 version is opened up for the screen even further than the 1968 film, with added medievalist colour, such as jugglers and fire-eaters in the courtyard of Chinon castle. The interiors are more elaborate than in the 1968 film, but still spartan.

Both films added scenes before the first lines of the stage play, including Eleanor's entry on a barge, but whereas the opening scene of the 1968 film introduces the sons (who are summoned to the court by William Marshal), the added first scene of Konchalovskiy's film is centred on Eleanor. We see her during the revolt that led to her imprisonment a decade before the events of the play. Eleanor is fighting in male, Saracenic-looking, armour, before being captured and taken to 'Salisbury, England', where we see the beginning of her imprisonment. Her wearing armour alludes to the claim that she dressed as an Amazon on crusade (mentioned later in her line about 'riding bare-breasted half-way to Damascus'), but it also suggests that somebody involved in the film's production was familiar with Gervase of Canterbury's story of Eleanor being disguised as a man when she was captured. In reality, of course, she was captured attempting to flee to the French court, not in the thick of battle. Konchalovskiy simultaneously refers to an Eleanor myth (her being an Amazon), and to an historical reference (her capture while wearing men's clothes) and creates a new myth (a warrior Eleanor fighting Henry's forces in armour).

In its theatrical form, *Lion* still enjoys popularity and frequent revivals.[54] However, some critics regard the play, whose dialogue seemed daringly irreverent in the 1960s, as rather dated. A *Variety* review of 2011's West End revival (directed by Trevor Nunn) described the play as an 'old chestnut', and wondered whether the decision to revive it was made 'tongue in cheek'. The reviewer echoes Finke and Shichtman's description of the 1968 film as 'a medieval *Who's Afraid of Virginia Woolf?*': 'The daft conceit of James Goldman's play can be summed up as "At Home with the Plantagenets", or perhaps "Who's Afraid of Virginia Woolf?" with jousting poles'.[55]

The family-soap-opera nature of *Lion* was already being satirized in the 1984 comedy *The Zany Adventures of Robin Hood*, where Eleanor is played by Janet Suzman 'with controlled ironic comedy'.[56] Although obviously a parody of Robin Hood movies, the comic allusions to Plantagenet family dynamics are surely inspired by *The Lion in Winter*. The film opens with John, who in the opening credits has been described as 'neurotic', reclining on a couch telling his troubles to a bearded companion. The scene's humour comes from the comic anachronism of a twelfth-century prince in that most twentieth-century of settings, the psychiatrist's couch. John has issues with his parents: 'No wonder I'm crazy. You'd be a fruitcake too if you had someone like King Henry for a father or Queen Eleanor for a mother ... Is it any wonder I do such cruel things to people?' To paraphrase Sondheim, 'Bad King John' is only depraved because he is deprived – of parental affection.

The Devil's Crown

Given the drama and familial conflict surrounding Henry II, Eleanor and their sons, it is surprising that they have not featured more prominently in television drama. The exception is the 1978 BBC TV drama series *The Devil's Crown*. Running to thirteen episodes of a little under an hour each, the series starred Brian Cox as Henry and Jane Lapotaire as Aliénor [*sic*]. It is a British drama in the tradition of *I Claudius*, a low budget, studio-filmed historical drama characterized by a dry, cynical sense of humour, which ran on the BBC in 1976 to great critical acclaim. The setting is highly stylized; medieval manuscript illuminations of buildings or landscapes provide the backdrops to the studio sets, with little attempt at naturalism. Characters 'see' events happening in other places, such as when Henry (in Anjou) observes Louis VII's marriage (in Paris) to Constance of Castile. Expensive set pieces such as battles are avoided for budgetary reasons.

> On account of the vast geographical scope of The Devil's Crown, the series makers decided against location filming, in favour of a more innovative approach. As the *Radio Times* explained when the series was originally broadcast, medieval imagery inspired 'stylised backgrounds to the real drama taking place in the foreground'.
>
> The backgrounds represented many different locations, and were complemented by 'multi purpose units – turrets, battlements, arches – which could be moved about and fitted together in various combinations', depending on the demands of each particular scene.
>
> Together, the backgrounds and units emulate what appears to modern eyes as the strange perspective seen in medieval artworks: 'the scenery has a slightly out-of-proportion, two-dimensional look [...] to achieve that curiously distorted effect that you find in contemporary illustrations', the *Radio Times* explained.[57]

An example of this technique is the war between Henry and Louis, following the former's marriage to Aliénor that occurs in episode 1. The conflict is represented symbolically by Henry's brother Geoffrey striding across the set from a conversation with Louis (in the Royal Domain) to join in an attack on Henry and Aliénor's tent (in Anjou) with his sword, before being wrestled to the ground by Henry. Time and geography are collapsed, in keeping with the 'two-dimensional...curiously distorted' set. Even if the set design may have had its origins in the practical challenges of staging a drama spanning France, England and the Holy Land on a studio set, it is evident that the producers brought their own concepts of medievalism to the design. Manuscript illumination is one of the 'marks of the medieval' identified by Finke and Shichtman in their study of medievalism in film, one of the means by which the viewer 'knows' that the drama is located in the Middle Ages.[58] 'Few media seem further removed in time and form from film than manuscript illumination … The medieval illuminated manuscript both anticipates and provides inspiration for cinematic fantasy; the technology of film supplements the illuminated manuscript with sound and movement, all while enhancing the size and scope of display.'[59]

The drama of the earlier episodes is in a sense seen through Henry's perspective; each episode begins with voice-overs of remembered conversations from his life, while the camera focuses on his effigy. The first episode is, however, arguably all about Eleanor; it is titled 'If All the World Were Mine', a reference to a lyric from the *Carmina Burana* that is often identified as a reference to Eleanor (see Chapter 3). However, it is essentially about Henry's pursuit of Eleanor: she never appears in a scene in which Henry is not also present. The *Carmina Burana* lyric is about Henry's possession of her, and we are reminded throughout the episode that he is driven by the pursuit of earthly power. When he cites the lyric at the end of the episode, his brother and rival Geoffrey expresses scepticism as to whether Henry really would exchange the world for his queen: 'If she believes that, she'll believe anything!' Eleanor fears that Henry will neglect 'my glorious Aquitaine' in favour of his own ambitions: 'It isn't Aquitaine you see at all. Your thoughts are all of England.'

The show paid great attention to historicity. It was accompanied by a non-fiction book also titled *The Devil's Crown* by academic historian Richard Barber which set out the historical context.[60] Ironically, even though the book's cover image shows Jane Lapotaire as Aliéner alongside Brian Cox's Henry, she is absent from the subtitle *A History of Henry II and his Sons*. Events may be stylized or simplified, but the plotlines largely adhere to history. In episode one, the back-story to the events is introduced through the characters' dialogue, and the viewer is informed of such events or concepts as Eleanor's involvement in the Second Crusade, the fragmented nature of the French polity, Henry's claim to England and so on. Such familiar concepts (at least to readers of popular history of Eleanor) as her alleged adultery with Raymond of Antioch, Louis's wish that he 'had been a monk', and Eleanor's patronage of troubadours are all covered.

In its presentation of Eleanor, the series treads carefully between on the one hand using the accusations against her to add colour and on the other maintaining a scepticism about their veracity. In 'If All the World Were Mine', her Amazonian role on the Second Crusade, her alleged adultery with Raymond of Antioch and her intimacy with the troubadour Bernart de Ventadorn are all alluded to without being confirmed or explicitly denied. In perhaps the most stereotypically Eleanorian line of the series, Eleanor cries '[w]here's my troubadour? Bernard is his name. Bernard de Ventadour'. She discovers that Henry has sent him away to England; 'I don't like him hanging around you. I know about him.' This exchange illustrates the show's occasionally clumsy use of dialogue as historical exposition, as it introduces the idea of Eleanor's love of troubadour poetry and her alleged love affair with Bernard. Eleanor is identified as Amy Kelly's Queen of Courtly Love; for example, she and Henry swear oaths to the 'God of Love' in which they promise to be true to one another.

Eleanor would make a short but memorable appearance nearly twenty years later in the BBC mini-series *Ivanhoe* which ran in January and February of 1997.[61] While Eleanor does not appear in Walter Scott's novel, she makes a cameo appearance in the television series, played by Siân Phillips, who had appeared in *Becket* in 1964.[62] Phillips had also played the murderous empress Livia in *I, Claudius* (1976), and any viewers familiar with her role in that classic BBC historical drama would surely have had the image of Phillips as that strong, indeed ruthless, matriarch firmly in their minds. Her Eleanor is a tough, no-nonsense mother who is determined to knock some sense into her quarrelsome offspring Richard and John. She summons the two together in an attempt to make peace, and she is firmly in control of the proceedings throughout.[63] When Richard greets her with 'I trust I find your grace in good health' she replies that '[y]ou find your grace in a state of fury that would shake the foundations of hell and send the devil himself running for shelter!' She directs some put-downs towards the two that are worthy of James Goldman's Eleanor from *The Lion in Winter*:

> It matters not to me at all if all the nations of Christendom know that Queen Eleanor's sons are curdle-brained ninnies, so incapable of settling their differences that they have to send for their mother to do it for them … I am not your father. I have no patience with weak, vainglorious, self-indulgent men, however much they clothe themselves in boyish charm … You are two sides of the same, flawed, coin: weak, stupid and selfish. But I forgive you. For you both sprang from my womb and I must in part bear the responsibility. Embrace, and forgive each other. NOW! Or by the fires of hell I'll see the pair of you beneath the ground and put the king of Egypt in Westminster!

Eleanor's condemnation of Richard and John as two sides of the same coin reflects a revisionism that seeks to overturn the stereotypical Good King Richard/Bad King John dichotomy that the audience would know from Robin Hood films and television dramas, which in turn are derived from Scott's *Ivanhoe*.

Eleanor has also been the subject of works on the French stage. As noted in Chapter 3, she was recently the subject of a play locating her as an Occitan heroine. However, she has also been a subject of drama from a more broadly French perspective. The French interest in Eleanor and the Angevins can be seen in the fact that *The Devil's Crown* was also broadcast on French television by the TF1 network. French television audiences of the 1970s would have been familiar with medieval dynastic drama from the successful adaptation of Maurice Druon's *Les Rois maudits* that ran in 1972–3 on ORTF. Like *The Devil's Crown*, *Les Rois maudits* was shot using minimalist studio sets.

Eleanor on the modern (and post-modern) French stage

Eleanor has, however, been featured more on the stage than on screen in contemporary French culture. Zoé Oldenbourg's play *Aliénor* (1992)[64] is notable in that its author has also written historical fiction and non-fiction on medieval subjects, including the crusades and the Cathars.[65] As such, her view of the Middle Ages has proven to be highly influential in French popular culture. The title of her book on the Cathars' last stand – *Le Bûcher de Montségur* – has become almost the defining term to invoke that tragedy. The Google French corpus reveals the rapid rise in the use of the term after the publication of Oldenbourg's book.[66] Oldenbourg's first book, the novel *Argile et Cendres*, is set in France in the late twelfth century, and Eleanor is mentioned in it tangentially.[67]

The introductory scene of *Aliénor* features a debate between two *récitants* over the sins and qualities of Eleanor. Both pray for her soul, but the first is more judgemental about her sins than the second. For the first, Eleanor is guilty of sin: 'The sin of pride. The sin of luxury. The sin of insubordination' (*Péché d'orgueil. Péché de luxure. Péché d'insoumission*). His counterpart is more sympathetic, arguing that such sins are an occupational hazard of ruling – 'her faults were those of her calling' (*ses fautes étaient celles de son métier*) – and that 'she knew how to act, and reign, and love' (*elle sut agir, et régner et aimer*).[68] It is clear on which side of the argument the author's sympathies lie. She had a low opinion of aspects of medieval Catholicism, and her *Bûcher de Montségur* was sympathetic towards the Cathars to the extent that one reviewer accused her of 'a regrettable anti-Catholic bias' (*un parti-pris anti-catholique regrettable*).[69]

The play is set in Fontevraud towards the end of Eleanor's life, as she regretfully considers having to leave her sanctuary in the abbey in order to fight for John against Arthur of Brittany. She is visited by the shades of key male figures from her life; her grandfather William IX, Louis VII, Henry II and Bernart de Ventadorn. Oldenbourg's presentation of the characters is very conventional: William IX is the troubadour duke, who brings life and gaiety to the scenes (he is presented as always laughing); Louis is torn between his childlike love for Eleanor and his love of the church; Bernart is presented as her lover, following medieval legend. Her relationship with her two royal sons also matches the conventional image of Richard as her favourite and John as a runt for whom she fights begrudgingly. Richard is Eleanor's 'beloved' (*bien-aimé*) and we see her arranging for her tomb to be placed alongside his, not that of Henry.[70] Raymond, granted a vision of Richard's death from his place in Purgatory, compares Eleanor to a '*mater dolorosa*'.[71] John, however, is a king and son for whom Eleanor will fight only for lack of other options: '*faute de grives on mange des merles*'[72] (in the absence of thrushes one eats blackbirds: a French proverb meaning one must make the best of what is available). Oldenbourg interprets familiar controversies in much the same way as Kelly or Pernoud; for example, Eleanor explains that her familiarity with Raymond of Antioch on crusade arose from her joy at being reunited with her uncle and hearing 'our sweet *langue d'oc*' (*notre douce langue d'oc*) spoken once more.[73]

Despite her passive *mater dolorosa* role, Oldenbourg's Eleanor emerges overall as a strong (overpowerful in her enemies' eyes) woman, essentially the 'feminist' Eleanor of late twentieth-century popular history, the Eleanor of Pernoud or Meade. (Oldenbourg cites Pernoud as a source for her work on the Crusades).[74] For the second *récitant* (who favours Eleanor), 'she was as wise as any woman, and wiser than many men' (*Elle fut sage autant que femme peut l'être, et plus sage que beaucoup d'hommes*).[75] For the first, less sympathetic *récitant*, responding to his counterpart's praise of Eleanor because 'she knew how to love', retorts that 'her love was pride and a desire to dominate' (*Son amour fut orgueil et soif de domination*).[76] Strong woman, lover, mother … Oldenbourg's interpretation of Eleanor does not provide any advances or new dramatic insights compared to the popular view of her constructed by Kelly and Pernoud. Indeed, Oldenbourg even breathes life into old myths: while Eleanor denies any inappropriate behaviour with her uncle, she is credited with being the lover of Bernart de Ventadorn.

A recent French play takes up the debate format over the life of Eleanor used by Oldenbourg, but casts it in a modern setting, that of the academic colloquium. Laurent Rogero's *Aliénor exagère!* performed by the Anamorphose theatre company and directed by the author, is described as a 'conference-spectacle performed by three historians-comedians and a moderator, on the theme of the real personality of Eleanor of Aquitaine.'[77] The performance is a comic parody of an academic conference: the players wear serious business suits and sit along a table covered with a white tablecloth and bottles of mineral water, but act in unscholarly and indeed childish ways; for example, the 'academics' reenact events from the Young King's rebellion using plastic toy soldiers and a cardboard model castle.[78] They also break into a dance, accompanied by medieval music,[79] while a discussion of the meaning of the fresco of Ste-Radegonde in Chinon sees the historians present ludicrous interpretations; Hadrien Rouchard, purporting to be a medieval historian at the University of Bordeaux III, argues that Henry is running away, while his fellow scholar from the Catholic University of Louvain (played by Limengo Benano-Melly) argues that it depicts players in a game of polo.[80] The actors debate the accusations made against Eleanor and use contemporary parallels: Rouchard argues that Eleanor was unfaithful to Louis, and will not accept the absence of irrefutable evidence of Eleanor's infidelity as proof of her innocence; he compares her to 'Lady Di', saying 'nobody has ever given us proof that she cheated on Prince Charles!' (*personne ne nous a donné preuve qu'elle a trompé Prince Charles!*) but we all know she did. Rouchard's academic is pompous and defensive; he responds to the dissenting opinions of the audience by asserting in an outraged tone that 'I am an historian' (*je suis historien!*).[81]

Rogero's approach to Eleanor is far more fresh and refreshing than that of Oldenbourg. This is not another biographical overview, it is an attempt to dramatize the historical debate around her, and to do so with a humour that verges on the Pythonesque, satirizing the self-importance of academic historians. It belongs to a tradition of French comical medievalism, such as the film *Les Visiteurs* (1993), in which a knight and his squire are transported to the late twentieth century, or the TV series *Kaamelott* (2004–9), which employs anachronism, topical humour and modern demotic French dialogue for humorous effect.

In contrast to historical fiction, which I will argue can become too obsessed with remaining true to an 'historical accuracy' that is probably unobtainable, the Groupe Anamorphose acknowledges the debatable and contingent nature of historical knowledge and addresses that uncertainty head-on, making drama and comedy of it. The group's website explains that:

> In order to create this performance, we began by making use of the dramatic movement which is the driving force in the books historians themselves write: most claim objectivity while accusing their colleagues of being carried away by their sentiments. This plurality among historical analyses has led to the current controversies regarding the 'real' Eleanor. Among these are: did or did not Eleanor take lovers? Did Eleanor exercise power in her own name over these kingdoms?

Did Eleanor divide or unite her family? Leaving the historical facts, we proceed toward their uncertain interpretation, and emerge into collective dispute.

Yet in some ways the group seems to have missed the current state of Eleanor historiography, falling back upon ideas of Eleanor's exceptionalism and ahistoricism, 'a woman for all seasons' ('*une femme de tous les temps*'):

> What fascinates us about her is her singular position as a wife, as a mother, as a powerful woman. On closer inspection, we find that what is extraordinary is not the actions of Eleanor in themselves, but the actions of Eleanor in the specific context of that medieval society ruled by men, where women were expected only to play a secondary role.[82]

Film and drama in the twentieth and twenty-first centuries have portrayed Eleanor at both the centre and the periphery of the action. In the Robin Hood cycle, her role has been a cameo or a walk-on one; she is there to introduce a strong female character into the male-centred world of the outlaws. As such, she is part of a trend that runs alongside that of presenting a 'kick-butt' Marian, or of introducing female outlaws such as Djaq in the BBC's *Robin Hood* of the 2000s. She is also peripheral to the action in *Becket*, but the 'ineffectual shrew' is a minor character in a narrative that centres on the relationship between two men. These Eleanor cameos also help to historicize the action; by introducing Eleanor into the Robin Hood cycle or into *Ivanhoe* the writers help ground the drama in a specific historical context which is recognizable to those viewers who know that Eleanor was the mother of Richard and John.[83] In dramas such as *The Lion in Winter*, *The Devil's Crown* and Oldenbourg's *Aliénor* she is at the centre of the action, as part of the family dynamics of the Plantagenets. These portrayals present Eleanor as a powerful female figure, yet one whose power is still delineated by the familial role, and the relationship to her husband and male offspring. They aim at historical accuracy (*The Devil's Crown* and *Aliénor* more so than *The Lion in Winter*, with its deliberate anachronisms and self-consciously modern feel), and draw on incidents from the chroniclers to establish Eleanor's character. Yet although informed by the 'feminist' Eleanor of popular history, they reinforce the Black Legend with reference to allegations about her adultery or her behaviour on crusade. As such, they reflect the ambiguities of the late twentieth-century Golden Myth of Eleanor which presented her as a powerful woman while remaining grounded in the romanticized portrayals of the Black Legend. Maybe Eleanor, whose image has been shaped for so long by myth and conjecture, is best served by *Aliénor Exagère*, which foregrounds the problems of ever knowing the 'historical' Eleanor and lampoons those of us who try to do so.

Eleanor in Fiction

It is fitting that a figure so mythologized as Eleanor should be such a frequent subject of historical fiction. Just as more conventionally historical studies of Eleanor have reflected changing attitudes towards women, power and the medieval past, so has historical fiction, with treatments ranging from the historical to the fantastic, the romantic and even the erotic. Fictional representations of Eleanor also reflect, albeit imperfectly, 'historical' works, especially popular history and (less commonly) academic history. They illustrate, maybe better than academic history, the popular understanding of Eleanor, and how that understanding is framed and expressed. Historical fiction may be viewed as pure entertainment, but has often consciously articulated the author's didactic purposes, and unconsciously reflected post-medieval attitudes towards the medieval past.

Eleanor in eighteenth-century *romans*

As we have seen, Eleanor's life was, in a sense, fictionalized from an early period, with the creation of a mythologized Eleanor in medieval romance and early-modern folklore. Eleanor-based 'historical fiction', however, could be said to emerge with the appearance of the novel as a literary genre in the eighteenth century. Marxist critic George Lukács argued that it is only in the age of Romanticism and with the work of Walter Scott that true 'historical fiction' appears. The Enlightenment and the French Revolution created a sense of national identity and an awareness of history as a process, and it is only in this period that self-consciously 'historical' fiction replaces works in which the past is simply a colourful backdrop:

> The so-called historical novels of the seventeenth century (Scudéry, Calpranéde, etc.) are historical only as regards their purely external choice of theme and costume. Not only the psychology of the characters, but the manners depicted are entirely those of the writer's own day. And in the most famous 'historical novel' of the eighteenth century, Walpole's *Castle of Otranto*, history is likewise

treated as mere costumery: it is only the curiosities and oddities of the milieu that matter, not an artistically faithful image of a concrete historical epoch.[1]

However, more recent reassessments see the historical novel emerging in the eighteenth century, and dispute Lukács's judgement of the fiction of that century. In the words of Kate Mitchell and Nicola Parsons,

> [i]n recent decades, critics have challenged this focus on Scott as the progenitor of the historical novel, and the corresponding claim that a supplementary relationship to history is paradigmatic of the genre. Eighteenth-century novels that were once read as *historicized* fiction …. are now being read in new ways that suggest eighteenth-century readers and authors had a more nuanced understanding of fiction's relationship to history.[2]

The shift from 'costume dramas' to 'factual fiction' is located in the eighteenth century by Anne H. Stevens. Reviews of eighteenth-century novels, and the paratext of historical notes that frequently accompanied them, 'articulated a shared concern that readers might glean inaccurate information from novels and be unable to distinguish between historical fact and historical fiction', a concern that the authors addressed 'through the use of footnotes and other paratextual devices'[3] that foreshadowed modern historical fiction authors' 'historical notes' and their audience's interest in 'historical accuracy'. Medieval themes were popular in eighteenth-century British historical fiction, including that of Eleanor's crusading son in James White's *The Adventures of King Richard Coeur-de-Lion* (1791), 'a comic and picaresque novel depicting Richard's adventures across Europe while returning from the crusades'.[4]

We see a mixture of the Black Legend with a more historicist and educative intention in the first novel about Eleanor of Aquitaine that we know of. The anonymous 'Amours d'Éléonore d'Aquitaine, reine de la France, et ensuite d'Angleterre, et de Guillaume, comte de Ponthieu, et de Henri, duc de Normandie, manuscript' appeared in the *Bibliothèque universelle des romans* in July 1779, in the section categorized as 'Romans historiques'.[5] As the title implies, it was a romanticized version of Eleanor's life, with a focus on intrigues and love affairs. At the story's centre is a fictional set of romantic complications involving Eleanor, Henry II, Guillaume, comte de Ponthieu[6] and Amélie de Vermandois. Yet it was accompanied by some 'Observations et notes historiques sur la règne de Louis VII' by 'M. Mayer' (Charles-Joseph de Mayer, one of the most prolific contributors to the *Bibliothèque*),[7] that sought to 'correct' the historical errors of the accompanying *roman*.

Although the *roman* is full of inaccuracies and invented romantic episodes, it appeared in a work that reflected the Enlightenment approach to historical fiction of the late eighteenth century. The *Bibliothèque universelle des romans* was a major enterprise that published 926 *romans* in 112 volumes between 1775 and 1789.[8] Until 1778 it was edited by Antoine-René, marquis de Paubry, who is best remembered for having assembled the collection that would become the Bibliothèque de l'Arsénal – an indication of his serious academic intent.[9] Despite the unscholarly nature and low literary merit of some of its contents, the *Bibliothèque* was 'conceived as an encyclopedic compendium of important world literature'.[10] It featured works from a variety of world literatures, including some set specifically in the past, carrying on occasions the sub-title *ouvrage périodique, dans lequel on donne l'analyse raisonnée des romans anciens et modernes*. There was often a tension between a desire to 'please the reader' and to instruct him or her in history.[11] There was a strong medieval element to the collection; two of the eight categories into which the editors grouped the *romans* related to the Middle Ages: *romans mediévales* and *romans de chevalerie*.[12] The medieval *romans* chosen were a promiscuous mixture of original medieval romances and tales and novels of the sixteenth and seventeenth centuries, and Véronique Sigu argues that the readership would not have drawn a sharp distinction between the medieval romances themselves and later works with medieval themes.[13] We see in the inclusion of accompanying historical notes the editors' concern that the readership view the *romans* as sources of education as well as entertainment, and that any inaccuracies presented in the *romans* be corrected by the editorial paratext.

The Eleanor *roman* mixed attempts at historical objectivity with an essentially fictional story of star-crossed love, with Eleanor cast as the villainess who comes between the two lovers. The author is sympathetic to Louis, despite the fact that his divorce from Eleanor exposed him to 'the censure of his century and of posterity' for the loss of Aquitaine. His actions are seen as those of 'an honest man' who married without love, for the interests of the state,[14] a view that corresponds to the editors' desire to focus in the *romans historiques* on political figures rather than on the 'marvellous'.[15] However, we also see fully formed many of the attributes of Eleanor that would persist in fiction and popular history for the next two centuries or more; the Courts of Love, Eleanor's extra-marital affairs and the unsuitable nature of her match to the dour, monkish king of France. Eleanor's court is a 'Temple de la Poésie', and she is a patron of the troubadours, including Bernart de Ventadorn. She is an unruly young pleasure-seeking wife; 'young, beautiful, and lively ... She had a decided penchant for pleasure ...'[16] She and her ladies decide to go on crusade to 'follow their lovers' (*suivre leurs Amans*), and while on crusade Eleanor behaved '*less like a queen than a prostitute*' [original emphasis], had an 'intrigue' with her uncle Raymond and 'received gifts from a young Turk, called Saladin'.[17] In contrast, Louis 'was gentle, but cold; was wise, but modest; too much an enemy of pleasure, seeking out monks too much ...'[18]

The accusations about Eleanor's behaviour on crusade are, however, confined to a footnote and attributed to an unnamed historian. The author chooses not to believe them and to assign to her 'only two' lovers, 'Henri, Duc de Normandie, & Guillaume, Comte de Ponthieu'.[19] The identity of the 'historian' is unclear, but these accusations reflect ideas that had become commonplace by the eighteenth century. As we have seen, the claims that she had an affair with her uncle in Antioch date back to Eleanor's own lifetime, and were later inflated to claims of a liaison with a very young Saladin.[20]

However, the relationship between Henry and Eleanor is not the centre of the story's plot. Rather, it is the story of Guillaume and Amélie, in which true love wins despite the efforts of Eleanor to place obstacles in the way of the lovers. At one point she imprisons and attempts to poison Guillaume,[21] an element that surely reflects the Fair Rosamond legend, which would have been well-known in France in the eighteenth century, as Isaac de Larrey refers to it in his *Histoire d'Eléonore de Guyenne* of 1691.[22] Eventually true love prevails, as Louis learns of Eleanor's attempt to murder Guillaume, has him released and initiates divorce proceedings against his wife.[23] Henry leads a rebellion of French lords which Louis successfully suppresses, and the divorce is finalized, ridding the king of 'a wicked wife'.[24]

The 'Amours d'Eléonore' was followed in the same issue of the *Bibliothèque* by some 'Observations et notes historiques sur la règne de Louis VII' by Charles-Joseph Mayer,[25] who sought to 'correct' the historical errors of the accompanying *roman*. He clarifies that Eleanor and William of Ponthieu were not lovers, but rather undermines his claims to historical authority by asserting that Eleanor was, in fact, the lover of Thibaud, count of Champagne![26] Mayer introduces the legend of Fair Rosamond, complete with the labyrinth and Eleanor's poisoning of the girl, in order to demonstrate that Eleanor had an 'atrocious and jealous character' (*caractère atroce & jaloux*).[27] He also gives credence to her affairs with Raymond of Antioch *and* Saladin, as well as all 'the poisonings of which she was guilty' (*les empoisonnemens dont elle s'est rendue coupable*), and concludes that it is understandable that her reputation led to some invention among *romanciers*.[28] Mayer's view of the twelfth century is framed by an Enlightenment perspective that is anti-clerical (monks had 'a singular dominance over public opinion' (*une prépondérance singulière sur l'opinion publique*)) and nationalist (Henry II's acquisition of Aquitaine foreshadows 'Azincourt et ... Maupertuis', the battles of Agincourt and Poitiers during the Hundred Years' War).[29] Mayer viewed Louis VII as a cultured man who was unfortunately limited by the age in which he lived, and in particular by the influence of the Church. 'The Curia of Rome exercised an astonishing supremacy over the Court of France ... blind devotion had made the Crusades fashionable ...'[30] He praised Suger but not St Bernard, suggesting that Mayer found clerics who worked for the good of France acceptable but not those who involved French rulers in ultramontane adventures such as the Second Crusade, which Mayer blamed on Bernard.[31] Interestingly, given Mayer's hostility towards Eleanor, he does not blame her for Louis's war with Champagne, which he instead attributes to the king's youth and inexperience.[32]

Eleanor in nineteenth-century historical novels

The nineteenth century saw the further development of historical fiction with an emphasis on what we might call 'historical accuracy'. Ranke's belief that all ages were to be considered on their own merits also made the study of the Middle Ages more respectable, removing some of the stigma of 'the Dark Ages' that had attached itself to the period during the Enlightenment. Scott's medieval novels *Ivanhoe* (1820), *The Betrothed* (1825) and *The Talisman* (1825), although (unlike the BBC adaptation of *Ivanhoe* in the 1990s) they did not feature Eleanor, were important in creating the nineteenth-century reader's view of the Angevin period. An example of Scott's impact in shaping the views of the medieval period can be seen in his character Robert of Locksley from *Ivanhoe*, in whom Scott invents the concept of Robin Hood as a partisan for the Anglo-Saxons against Norman oppression in the reign of Richard I.[33] In doing so, Scott (a Scotsman born during the first century of the new state of Great Britain) was creating a specifically *English* ancestral hero for a nineteenth-century audience:

> Scott said that the characters of his novel [*Ivanhoe*] had manners and sentiments common to most Englishmen because he had them occupy 'that extensive neutral ground, the large proportion, that is, of manners and sentiments which are common to us and our ancestors, having been handed down unaltered from them to us [...]' ... Scott ... means that his novel is an historical reconstruction of twelfth century England in the spiritual image of the nineteenth.

In this twelfth century setting, he reconstructed the traditional hero into the figure of the deliverer; he is an ancestral hero of superhuman power used to deliver the English people from the misrule of evil men.[34]

As we have seen in Chapter 2, the French Revolution saw Eleanor cast as a criminal queen in the image of Marie Antoinette.[35] In the Restoration era, however, she became once again the inspiration for historical fiction, at the very time that Scott was popularizing that genre. In 1823, the Comtesse Palamède de Macheco's novel *Éléonore d'Aquitaine* was published.[36] Described as a *roman historique*, this was truly an historical novel in the sense that the 'Amours d'Eléonore' with its wholly fictional characters and blatant anachronisms (such as the use of a pistol by a potential assassin) had not been. Born Amicie Claudine Antoinette de Bataille, a member of a French aristocratic family, the author was the wife of a fellow aristocrat, Claude Palamède Louis, comte de Macheco. The count was an émigré who fought with Condé against the French Revolution, returned to France under Napoleon, then became a Field Marshal and a royalist deputy in the Assemblée nationale after the Restoration, before returning to private life after the revolution of 1848.[37] In the historical notes to her novel, Macheco reveals her royalism when she refers to the death of *l'aimable infortuné duc d'Enghien* ('the noble and unfortunate Duc d'Enghien'), who was executed by Napoleon in 1804.[38]

The countess was clearly drawn to novels about French queens, as she was advertised on the title page of her Eleanor novel as '[au]teur de *Blanche de Castille*, etc.,'[39] and given her royalist background, and the vogue for histories of French queens described in Chapter 2, it is unsurprising that she presents France's royalty and aristocracy in a positive light. Louis VI is a 'brave, politic, prince, with profound views' (*prince brave, politique, ayant des vues profonde*). Louis VII is presented as handsome and loyal, and his mother Adelaide of Maurienne is 'beautiful and virtuous' (*belle et vertueuse*).[40] Even Louis VII's faults are presented as virtues – he was too kind-hearted, and unable to commit evil himself, he did not suspect it in others.[41] The crown of France is the 'foremost crown in the world' (*premier diadème du monde*) and Eleanor is expected to embody the responsibilities of queenship, as her seneschal reminds her: 'Called to the foremost throne in the world, be both sovereign and model to your people; become through your virtues the pride of France…'.[42] Like the French queens of the contemporary popular history described in Chapter 2, she must be the model of bourgeois respectability for her people. In contrast to the Enlightenment suspicion of the Catholic church expressed in the 'Amours d'Eléonore', Macheco writes at length and approvingly of Bernard of Clairvaux's preaching of the crusade, and the response that it engendered.[43]

In line with the growing concern for accuracy in 'historical' fiction, Macheco is aware that she may be reproached 'for having written a *roman*', stresses that she has studied historical sources and explains which characters are historical and which her inventions.[44] She expresses an admiration for Walter Scott, while modestly denying that her writing could be compared to his.[45] She also includes a concluding section of 'notes' in which she gives the historical background to the events of the novel and cites her sources.[46] Her novel even contains footnotes giving it the appearance of a work of scholarship. Yet Macheco presents Eleanor in the stereotypical way that would become familiar in nineteenth- and twentieth-century fiction, as a light-hearted and irresponsible woman – with an emphasis on *woman*. She displayed 'all the passions of which the spirit of a young woman is capable; love, coquettishness, capriciousness, jealousy, ambition'.[47] The young Eleanor combines 'a mixture of coquettishness and capriciousness with profound ideas; [an interest in] politics, with the most frivolous occupations...'.[48] Macheco has a moralistic agenda, in contrasting the young queen with the older, mature monarch: 'There is great morality in showing, after errors and crimes, misfortune and repentance...'[49] This foreshadows the Strickland sisters' later judgement that Eleanor was 'among the very few women who atoned for an ill-spent youth by a wise and benevolent old age'.[50] Eleanor's *légèreté* (thoughtlessness) is tied to another supposed aspect of her personality that would become standard part of the popular image of Eleanor – her artistic tastes and her patronage of the troubadours, specifically Bernart de Ventadorn,[51] and Macheco was clearly aware of the medieval tradition that the troubadour was a lover of Eleanor.[52] She incorporated legends about Eleanor into her novel; in her historical notes, despite expressing doubts about its veracity,[53] Macheco gives credence to the story that Eleanor had Rosamond de Clifford murdered, arguing that 'the character of the queen, jealous and haughty, makes this story plausible'.[54] Eleanor's rumoured misbehaviour on crusade is also included,[55] notably her and her ladies' dressing as Amazons, her 'violent passion' for Saladin as well as a claim that Raymond of Antioch planned to arrange a marriage between her and a prince of the Sultanate of Iconium. Both of these claims are made not only in the text of her novel but in the historical notes that follow it.[56] The idea of the planned marriage to a Saracen appears to be Macheco's invention, but may be based on a similar scheme mooted during the Third Crusade, whereby Richard I's sister was to marry the brother of Saladin.[57] In sum, we have the stereotypical (even misogynist) view of Eleanor as a wicked, adulterous woman, albeit 'supported' by the appearance of scholarship. Macheco's work was very much of its time; while it lacks historical accuracy, she at least attempted to locate it in the genre of historical fiction pioneered by Scott, although her nostalgia for a monarchist, Catholic France reflected the conservatism of the *Restauration* period, and her own background in a royalist *émigré* family. Her judgements about Eleanor's character also reflect her transgressions against the respectable *bourgeois* image of French queens in the works of contemporary popular history.

A generation later, we see a fictional rendering of Eleanor by an author with a very different background and agenda. Where the Comtesse de Macheco was French, royalist and Catholic, Celestia Bloss was American, radical, feminist and Protestant. Bloss's novelized history *Heroines of the Crusades* was published in 1853, with Eleanor featuring prominently as one of these heroines.[58] A schoolteacher in Brighton, New York, Bloss had family connections with the abolitionist and temperance movements that were animating American reformers in the 1850s. She founded the Clover Street Seminary, a school for girls, and it was to educate her young female scholars that she wrote about history. Her most celebrated work, *Bloss's Ancient History*, was intended as a text for her students, and was adopted by other schools. To make it more appealing for adoption, the author's gender was disguised behind the initials 'C. A. Bloss'.[59] *Heroines of the Crusades*, by contrast, was a fictionalized work, but was also intended for her pupils, to whom it was dedicated.

Bloss was part of the movement known retrospectively as First-Wave Feminism, and upstate New York was at the heart of that movement as well as that for the abolition of slavery. The Troy Female Seminary, 'the first recognized institution for the education of girls' was established near Albany in 1821;[60] the first convention for women's rights met at Seneca Falls in 1848, a New York town that was the home of Elizabeth Cady Stanton; the African-American abolitionist Sojourner Truth was from Albany; Susan B. Anthony and Frederick Douglass made Rochester a base for their agitation, and it was in this city, next door to Bloss's home town of Brighton, that Anthony was arrested for attempting to cast a ballot. It is possible that Bloss and Anthony met, or at least knew of one another, as her brother was acquainted with Frederick Douglass.[61]

Closer to home, other members of Bloss's family were reformers. Her brother William Clough Bloss, also a teacher, was an abolitionist, and published an anti-slavery paper *The Rights of Man*. He acquired a tavern in Brighton, but later joined the temperance movement and marked his conversion by emptying his beer barrels and whiskey bottles into the Erie Canal.[62] Her brother-in-law was also an abolition and temperance activist, and is believed to have used his house as part of the 'Underground Railroad'. As for Celestia Bloss herself, although she was not a public activist, she has been described as 'an ardent feminist' by reason of her commitment to women's education and her retention of her maiden name after marriage.[63]

What did Eleanor of Aquitaine mean to Celestia Bloss? The Brighton schoolmistress would probably have agreed with Macheco in using Eleanor to provide a moral example, but her work displays a far greater admiration for the power of women. She sought to portray 'the true philosophy of female heroism',[64] and she cited the opinion of Jules Michelet that 'this was emphatically the era of women, and that for some years a female [Mélisende, queen of Jerusalem from 1131 to 1153] exercised the sovereign power over the territories of Islamism'.[65]

On the subject of Eleanor of Aquitaine and the other crusading queens Berengaria of Navarre and Eleanor of Castile, Bloss was indebted to the Strickland sisters, whom she cites in her introduction and in many of her notes.[66] She clearly based parts of her Eleanor section on the work of Elizabeth Strickland, as when she describes the incident where Eleanor's ladies dress as Amazons. Bloss repeats Strickland's reference to the noblemen who had the good sense to remain at home, but adds an extra touch that might reflect her own views on warfare; '[they] had the good sense to suppose that Heaven would be better pleased with their remaining in peace at home, than by their going abroad to destroy their fellow-men'.[67] She would also have been influenced by the anti-clerical attitudes of Enlightenment authors such as Hume and Gibbon (both of whom Bloss cited in her notes). As we have seen, Hume expressed a dismissive and stereotypical attitude towards Eleanor, which would have conflicted with Bloss's feminism.

Despite her desire to provide her young readers with female heroines, Bloss's account of Eleanor is generally negative, but is mitigated by a more sympathetic interpretation of some famous myths about the queen. The legend that she had an affair with Saladin while on the crusade is interpreted in such a way as to make Eleanor the innocent victim of malicious gossip. Bloss has her seeking to make peace with Saladin and convert him to Christianity, hence her need to make surreptitious visits to the Muslim leader.[68] Eleanor is in love with Saladin, but never acts upon her desires.

The Fair Rosamond legend is also interpreted in a more positive light by Bloss. Rosamond is treated sympathetically, as an innocent who is fooled by

Henry, who does not reveal to her that he is the king. Eleanor, while far from being presented as the innocent party, is shown at least to repent of her threat to kill Rosamond, who instead lives out her days at the nunnery of Godstow.[69] The fact that both women are portrayed as victims of Henry's deceit may reflect Bloss's feminism. As with several episodes in her account of Eleanor's life, she derives details from Elizabeth Strickland, such as the fact that Rosamond is hidden by Henry in a labyrinth, and that she is discovered when Eleanor observes a golden thread attached to Henry's spur as he leaves the maze, allowing the queen to follow the thread to the centre.[70]

Given that Macheco and Bloss had very different political agendas, there were clearly broader reasons that motivated both liberal and conservative women authors to write historical novels. Fiction – and historical fiction in particular – was a field in which it was possible for educated women to operate. The academic discipline of history, which was being created at that very time, was, however, male-dominated. Female authors of fiction and non-fiction alike were excluded from universities and archives, and had to rely upon male patronage to gain access to their sources. In the introduction to her *Heroines of the Crusades* Bloss thanks 'the gentlemen of the Rochester University, through whose politeness I have been permitted to consult several works …'[71] The university would not admit women scholars until 1900.[72] Historical fiction could therefore fill a vacuum for female writers – and readers – who were excluded from male academia. As we have seen, writers such as Bloss and Macheco were keen to present their works as historical, with supporting notes. Nineteenth-century historical writers saw themselves as writing to inform and morally instruct as well as to entertain; '[i]n Victorian times readers justified their reading of historical novels because they were educational.'[73] For Bloss, a woman teacher in a girls' school, Eleanor and other heroines of the crusades served a didactic purpose in the most literal sense, educating her charges about strong medieval female role models.

So the historical novelist (especially the female one) was excluded from an increasingly professional and male caste of academic historians, but that exclusion could in some ways be liberating. 'History had become the exclusive domain of the professional historian, and writers of historical novels were relegated to amateur status. This in turn gave writers freedom to explore new approaches and to look at the margins of societies rather than the main events.'[74] Jane Austen memorably voiced her frustration with the dull, male-centred conventional histories of her day: 'Real, solemn history I cannot be interested in … The quarrels of popes and kings, with wars and pestilences in every page; the men all so good for nothing and hardly any woman at all.'[75]

Standing in for women's history?
Eleanor in twentieth-century fiction

One 'margin' that was largely unexplored by historians of the 'main events' was women's history. As discussed in Chapter 2, a growth of interest in Eleanor occurred in the mid-twentieth century, and continued apace with the rise of Second-Wave Feminism in the 1970s. The study of queens, however, falls somewhat awkwardly between old top-down views of history, and more radical historians' focus on the history of the marginalized. The serious academic study of 'queenship' as a role or office is a recent development, dating from the last decade of the twentieth century (as discussed in the introduction). An anecdote helps to illustrate the suspicion felt by some academic historians towards the study of queens; a friend of mine who in the early 1990s approached a (male) professor to ask him to supervise a dissertation on Isabella of France was told that he 'did not do boudoir history'. In the eyes of some critics, even today in a world where women's and gender studies are included in academia, historical fiction too often has to (in the words of Lois Leveen) 'stand in for feminist history', especially for the general reader. 'Historical novels about women's lives are ever popular – histories of women far less so'.[76] The reading of historical fiction is still strongest among women. A survey conducted by Mary Tod in April 2012 found that '15.6% of men almost never read historical fiction', against only 4.5 per cent of women.[77] 18.4 per cent of respondents read historical fiction '[t]o understand the experience of those marginalized by history', reinforcing Leveen's contention that historical fiction has to 'stand in for' the history of those groups such as women who are neglected by academic history. The educative role is more important for women than for men: women gave 'bringing the past to life' as their main reason for reading historical fiction (79.3 per cent selecting this response), whereas men did so 'because it's a great story' (65.5 per cent). A plurality of all respondents named stories with 'a strong female character' as their favourite type.[78] Among male readers, however, such stories failed to make the top three story-types. Likewise, the majority of historical fiction authors are women; approximately 68 per cent of the members listed on the website of the Historical Novel Society are female (or at least use female *noms de plume*).[79]

We might also add that, just as women's history is underrepresented, so has historical fiction not been treated seriously as a literary genre, adding to the marginalization of its women readers and authors. When Hilary Mantel's *Wolf Hall* won the Man-Booker Prize in 2009, the fact that a historical novel had won the award drew widespread comment. The *Times* of London described a shortlist that included *Wolf Hall* and other historical fiction as 'dominated by a form once taboo',[80] while Allan Massey expressed a hope that Mantel's second Booker prize in 2012 with *Bring Up the Bodies* might finally give historical fiction critical recognition: "The genre has been a poor relation for too long, regarded by many as a bastard child, neither one thing nor the other, neither good history nor good fiction. At best it has often been treated with a lofty condescension.'[81] Women writing about women in the historical fiction genre could therefore be viewed as doubly facing marginalization from the academic and literary establishments.

The gap left by the paucity of serious historical studies was therefore filled for the general reader by popular history (discussed in Chapter 2) and historical fiction. Not all of the novels written about Eleanor can be dismissed as 'boudoir history', but they do tend to focus on the colourful and the 'exceptional' in her story. They have also been remarkably broad-ranging in their treatment of Eleanor, from the conventional 'historically accurate' to the fantastical and erotic.

Eleanor has inspired many works of what we might term conventional historical literature (by which I mean narrative biographical novels that attempt to remain true to history). Two twentieth- and twenty-first-century authors of historical fiction will be used as examples: Jean Plaidy and Sharon Kay Penman. Both authors belong to the tradition of novelists who pay careful attention to sources and to the historiographical literature, accompanying their works with the type of historical paratext that we first encounter in eighteenth-century fiction.

Eleanor Hibbert, who as Jean Plaidy was the author of ninety works of historical fiction, including several set in Anglo-Norman England, devoted a novel to Eleanor (*The Courts of Love*, published in 1987)[82] as well as a series, *The Plantagenet Saga*, that included novels covering the life and times of Eleanor.[83] Plaidy was the product of a world before Second-Wave Feminism: she wrote that 'married life gave me the necessary freedom to follow an ambition which had been with me since childhood, and so I started to write in earnest', yet was attracted to writing about 'women of integrity and strong character' who were 'struggling for liberation, fighting for their own survival'.[84]

Plaidy's presentation of Eleanor adheres to the popular image of the Queen that had become established in the nineteenth century; romantic, cultured, adulterous, irresponsible in youth but becoming an elder stateswoman later in life. According to the publisher's introduction, 'Eleanor grows into a romantic and beautiful queen, but she has inherited the will of a king, and is determined to rule Aquitaine using her husband's power as King of France. Her resolve knows no limit and, in the years to follow she was to become one of history's most scandalous queens'.[85] Plaidy includes many of the incidents that formed the image of the frivolous young queen of France – the crusading escapades of Eleanor and her ladies, her affair with Raymond of Antioch and a subsequent affair with Geoffrey of Anjou. Rosamond's bower is included in the story, but not her murder at Eleanor's hands. Plaidy's later novel *The Courts of Love* features, as the title implies, one of the most enduring elements of the Eleanor myths, the claim that she held actual Courts of Love at Poitiers. Eleanor rides to the crusade at the head of her ladies (although in Plaidy's telling they do not dress up as Amazons).[86] Her love affair with Raymond of Antioch is included, as is an unconsummated love for her brother-in-law (Raoul de Vermandois).[87] Plaidy's portrayal of Eleanor's two husbands reflects the standard popular dichotomy between a weak, ineffectual Louis ('there was something rather timid about him')[88] and a tempestuous and philandering Henry.

A rather different view of Eleanor is presented in the works of Sharon Kay Penman. Penman has written (to date) four historical novels on the Angevins[89] and four works of historical detective fiction in which Eleanor is a core character.[90] Eleanor's character in Penman's novels is a development from the more romanticized Eleanor of previous representations. She is more of a cool-headed politician, reflecting perhaps Penman's greater attention to recent scholarly sources that were unavailable to Plaidy. There is no Rosamond's bower, and no extra-marital affairs on Eleanor's part. For example, her decision to rebel against Henry (recounted in *The Devil's Brood*) is determined by political factors (such as the fear of losing Aquitaine to Henry), not out of anger at Henry's affair with Rosamond Clifford: 'Eleanor's greatest grievance was not a simpering lass with flaxen hair and smooth skin. It was Aquitaine, always Aquitaine'.[91] In other ways, however, Penman sticks to the more traditional approach to Eleanor; her marriage to Henry is presented not as a property transaction, but as a passionate love affair and Eleanor is still uniquely jealous of Rosamond among the king's mistresses.[92] There is a even a brief nod in the direction of the Courts of Love, with Eleanor's court at Poitiers presented as a southern world of troubadours and relative female equality, to the shock of a visiting Anglo-Norman kinswoman: 'This was an alien world ... Eleanor's Aquitaine'.[93]

Both Plaidy and Penman include historical paratext to illustrate their historicist seriousness. 'Jean Plaidy's novels are typical [of 'educative' historical fiction] in being all prefaced by a decent list of sources ...'[94] Plaidy's bibliography for *Courts of Love* included scholarly works by Norgate and Warren among other, dated works of history such as the Stricklands', and biographies of Eleanor by Kelly, Meade, Pernoud, Rosenberg and Desmond Seward.[95] Her Eleanor is essentially that of the popular historians. By contrast, Sharon Penman's writing reflects the advances in Eleanor historiography since Plaidy's time, allowing the historical novelist to create a more nuanced view of the medieval queen. Sources for Penman's novels include recent scholarly works on Eleanor such as those of Flori, Turner and the volume *Eleanor of Aquitaine: Lord and Lady*.[96] Her notes accompanying *The Devil's Brood* address directly the difference between the popular perception of Eleanor and the historical record.

> First of all, I want to address the queries of fans of *The Lion in Winter* … As I was writing this novel, I could hear their puzzled voices echoing in my ears. *Then Henry did not take Alys as his concubine? And Richard was not gay? He did not have an affair with the French king?*
>
> I defer to none in my admiration for James Goldman; *The Lion in Winter* remains one of my favorite films. But it came out in 1969, and what was accepted as gospel forty years ago is not necessarily true today.[97]

Penman's note reminds us that history is not fixed, that one generation's historical interpretations will find their way into popular culture and influence the next despite the history of academia having moved on. Penman cites a series of sources, both medieval (such as Gerald of Wales and Roger of Howden) and modern (scholars such as W. L. Warren and Judith Everard).[98] But it is likely that James Goldman (or Katharine Hepburn), rather than Warren or Everard will continue to have the greater influence on popular perceptions of Eleanor. Furthermore, given that the history of 1969 and that of 2008 (when *Brood* was published) are dependent upon the same medieval sources, it is problematic for Penman to declare that what 'was gospel' in 1969 is no longer 'true'. Historical fiction's concern for 'historical accuracy' locates it in a positivist tradition that, ironically, is no longer so widely accepted in the academy.

In the 1990s and early twentieth century, different types of interaction have become possible between author and readership. The 'Author's Note' to *The Devil's Brood* by Penman has been reproduced online as a guide (with additional questions) for members of reading groups,[99] while the 2006 paperback edition of Jean Plaidy's *Courts of Love* also contains questions for discussion, aimed at book groups, including the following:

> Eleanor has been described throughout history as one of the world's greatest female rulers, revered for her superior intellect, extraordinary courage, and

fierce loyalty to her children and her land. Does Jean Plaidy's portrait of Eleanor mirror history's 'snapshot' of her?[100]

The anonymous editor does not consider the extent to which the 'snapshot' view of Eleanor has been formed (or at least reinforced) precisely *by* popular fiction. The social aspect of book groups and social media has turned reading into the social act it was before mass literacy and affordable books turned in into an increasingly private activity in the nineteenth and twentieth centuries. A reader can now discuss a novel and the history behind it with other readers and directly with the author. Penman, for example, has a website, a blog, and both personal and 'fan club' Facebook pages. These media, which academic historians are less likely to utilize (or at least, to do so while attracting a comparable following), increase the possibilities for the general reader to 'receive' history from fiction writers. This does not necessarily mean that the public receive 'bad' or 'wrong' history, however; discussions on Penman's Facebook page often address questions of historical accuracy, and the author's and readers' opinions on what 'really happened'.

Eleanor in young adult fiction

A notable sub-genre of Eleanor literature is juvenile or young adult fiction. It is easy to see the appeal of Eleanor as a subject; she was queen of France at a similar age to the target readership (13 or 15, depending on the date we accept for her birth), and as part of the late twentieth-century reframing of Eleanor in a positive light, she might be considered a role model of a strong, independent woman for young female readers. Historical novels in the twentieth century continued to play an educational role for younger (and adult) readers; '[s]ome, like Helen Waddell's *Peter Abelard* become historical works in their own right. Historical novels bring with them an air of learning which has more weight and cachet than mere romances: they are genuinely informative'.[101] Mary Tod's survey of readers found that 76.3 per cent read historical fiction '[t]o bring the past to life, appreciating how people lived and coped in very different times', while 51.8 per cent did so '[t]o understand and learn about historical periods without reading non-fiction'.[102] So two of the top three reasons given for reading historical fiction reflected its role as education rather than entertainment, with '[b]ecause it's a great story' only in second place. For the adolescent reader in particular, historical novels 'were perhaps the ideal diet for the [mid-twentieth-century British] grammar-school appetite. Very closely researched and full of carefully chosen detail ... [p]art of their appeal was perhaps autodidactic and educative'.[103] The possibility that younger readers will learn about Eleanor through fiction is increased by the paucity of Eleanor-themed non-fiction for that age group, an absence that Mary Ann Capiello, author of a forthcoming chapter book on Eleanor, attributes to a wariness about addressing the sexual themes surrounding her life.[104]

In describing her reasons for writing a novel about Eleanor, E. L. Konigsburg, author of *A Proud Taste for Scarlet and Miniver* (published in 1973), explained that she 'was a woman not only of her times but a woman for all time ... I believe that what [the characters in the novel] say about themselves and their Middle Ages is as true for us as it was for them, as true for their times as it is for ours'.[105] The view of Eleanor as an historically transcendent character is reinforced by the memorable framing device that Konigsburg employs. Eleanor is in heaven, waiting for Henry to emerge from Purgatory.[106] This process takes many centuries, given Henry's manifold sins, so she spends her time reminiscing about the events of her life with her companions, the Empress Matilda, Abbot Suger and William Marshal. Their heavenly conversation clearly takes place during the later twentieth century, as the narrators, gazing down on the earth, are able to keep in touch with earthly events through newsreels on giant, drive-in movie screens.[107] Yet, she historicizes Eleanor and the Middle Ages as markedly different from the world of her readers. She relates in an interview that she was drawn to write about Eleanor after learning from her readers that they 'liked books that take them to unusual places where they meet unusual people'.[108] Eleanor's world is very different from our own, where 'a rather plain housewife' sits on the throne of Great Britain.[109]

Although Konigsburg has not made any explicitly feminist claims for her novel, *Scarlet and Miniver* can be located broadly within the interpretation of Eleanor that coincided with the rise of the feminist movement in the 1960s and 1970s. It has, for example, been advocated as a work for presenting a non-sexist view of the Middle Ages.[110] Konigsburg was clearly drawn to Eleanor as a strong female character – 'What a woman!' she writes in the notes that accompany the novel.[111] It appeared too early to be influenced by Meade's 'feminist' interpretation of Eleanor in 1977, but is clearly moved by a similar spirit. Konigsburg alludes to research that she carried out for the novel,[112] and it seems reasonable to assume that Amy Kelly was a source, given Konigsburg's emphasis on Eleanor's role in the Courts of Love; the author presents fully fledged Courts of Love, with Eleanor and Marie de Champagne drawing up their rules of conduct. 'The

Courts of Love had laws: the male must be polite, he must regard his lady-love as someone above earthly temptation ...'[113]

Following Konigsburg's lead, other novels about Eleanor have appeared for younger readers. Kristiana Gregory's *Eleanor: Crown Jewel of Aquitaine* was published by Scholastic in 2002.[114] Part of the *Royal Diaries* series, the novel focuses on the young Eleanor at the time that she learns she must marry Louis, in keeping with the intended audience (described by the publisher as ten years old and upwards). *Crown Jewel of Aquitaine* – unsurprisingly for a novel produced by an educational publisher – is in the tradition of didactic historical fiction, and comes accompanied by an 'Historical Note', a genealogical table, notes on the historical persons featured in the novel, maps and illustrations.[115] Like Konigsburg, Gregory mixes a historicist setting in the medieval past with a concern for the relevance of Eleanor to modern, young readers: 'I'm convinced many of the concerns and interests kids have today are similar to those of eight centuries ago: friendship, paternal love, curiosity about their future, yearnings for adventure and, of course, cool clothes'.[116] The book includes conventional markers of the medieval for a modern audience, such as dirt, rain and 'graphic depictions of squalor', alongside knights in armour[117] and Gregory invokes both the dreary and romantic images of medievalism in her opening sentence: 'It rains again ... I can see father's knights pace along the battlements. Their helmets look shiny gray in the rain'.[118] She also gives the reader a fair amount of medieval squalor in the form of rats and worms.[119]

Eleanor has also been the subject of children's literature in French. Brigitte Coppin's *Aliénor d'Aquitaine, une reine à l'aventure* (1999) tells the story of Eleanor during her marriage to Louis VII, focusing on her experiences on crusade.[120] The novel emphasizes Eleanor's strength and independence, and the cover blurb quotes a line that reveals her attitude towards Louis as 'you have no rights over me' (*Tu n'as aucun droit sur moi!*).[121]

Unconventional Eleanors

There is also a world of Eleanor novels beyond conventional historical fiction. The Black Legend of Eleanor became the basis for a sub-genre of erotic fiction in the 1950s. Bernard de Gélannes's *La Vie Galante de ... Éléonore d'Aquitaine*, issued in 1955 by pulp-fiction publishers Editions de l'arabesque, was part of a series of *La Vie Galante* titles, erotic fiction featuring women from France's history, including Isabeau of Bavaria as a fellow medieval queen.[122] Likewise, a

98-page novel that appeared in 1957, *Aliénor d'Aquitaine et les cours d'amour: la vie amoureuse* by Émile Brux,[123] was also part of a series of erotic historical pulp fiction titles, *La vie amoureuse*.

The erotic interpretation of Eleanor's life has been taken up more recently in French fiction by Mireille Calmel.[124] Her three novels present Eleanor as bisexual, but they also represent a departure from the 'historical' tradition in that they introduce an element of fantasy. Her Eleanor owes more to the 'new age' queen of Jean Markale than to the pulp fiction of de Gélannes. Calmel's version of Eleanor has proved to be a bestseller; *Le Lit d'Alienor*, the first novel in her trilogy, has been published in a dozen European countries and sold over a million copies.[125] Events are related from the perspective of Eleanor's (fictional) female counsellor Loanna de Grimwald, a witch who is the descendent of Merlin and 'inheritor of druidic secrets' (*héritière des secrets druidiques*)[126] and 'last descendant of the great priestesses of Avalon' (*dernière descendante des grandes prêtresses d'Avalon*).[127] Loanna's mission is to form an alliance between Aquitaine and Anjou, with the intention of creating a great empire over which Henry is to be 'a king educated in druidic learning' (*Un roi formé aux enseignements druidiques…*).[128] Calmel thereby introduces female agency to the creation of the Angevin Empire, while the reference to 'priestesses of Avalon' recalls the feminist recasting of the Arthurian legend by Marion Zimmer Bradley.

The esoteric or New Age themes of Calmel have been taken up by other fiction authors. Robert Fripp, self-published Canadian author of the Eleanor-themed novel *Power of a Woman*[129] has also published a book *Spirit in Health* which 'explores traditional shamanism and pre-technological healing methods …'[130] Fripp sees courtly love as a 'new paganism', and has the church view Eleanor 'as the Arthurian character Morgana le Fey, the witch'. This echoes Jean Markale's evocation of 'the fairy Morgana, incarnation of the original mother goddess …'[131]

Another popular novel of Eleanor, the Texan Margaret Ball's *Duchess of Aquitaine*, has (in the words of one reviewer) 'a slight pagan slant to it, starting off with a description of a dance to bring on the spring equinox which makes a pretty clear statement about the divinity of women'.[132] Perhaps significantly, Ball is primarily a writer of fantasy novels, some of which she has co-authored with Anne McCaffrey.[133] *Duchess of Aquitaine*,[134] which covers Eleanor's time as queen of France, presents the young Eleanor living in a world where the Pagan and matriarchal past lives on through folk wisdom and folk medicine. For example, the peasants of the Bordelais – much to the archbishop of Bordeaux's displeasure – venerate the Lady of the Cart, who must be appeased so as not to bring the blight of ergot to their grain.[135]

Eleanor also appears in a very modern form of literature, the graphic novel. *Aliénor: La Légende noire* was published in April 2012.[136] I have used Martin Aurell's term Black Legend in this book to refer to the negative myths that grew up around Eleanor. The graphic novel, however, appears to be taking the *légende noire* (Black Legend) at face value and uses it to create a sensationalist view of Eleanor. The front cover illustration shows Eleanor standing proudly in front of a burning city, while the publisher's blurb promises a story of a 'political schemer and a woman both treacherous and sublime in matters of love' (*Femme politique, intrigante, amoureuse perfide ou sublime*) who 'will determine the course of history' (*décidera du cours de l'Histoire*).[137] The novel perpetuates the notion of Eleanor as an evil influence upon Louis; as Vitry burns, Suger informs Louis that 'tonight, your soul is lost ... and for what, young king? For whom? You know for whom, Louis of France! She has bewitched you!'.[138] If many Eleanor novels have located her in a broadly feminist context, *La Légende noire* is a throwback to the misogynist tradition denigrating troubling and rebellious queens, forming part of a series *Les Reines de sang*, of which the other title published to date focuses on another scandalous medieval queen: *Isabelle la Louve de France* (Isabella, 'She-Wolf of France', wife of Edward II of England).[139]

Historical fiction or fictionalized history?

Sales figures of books are one, albeit crude, means of gauging how a popular readership receives its understanding of Eleanor. A comparison of sales figures from Amazon gives us a sense of the relative impact of fictional, 'popular' historical and 'academic' treatments of Eleanor; on 26 December 2012, Amazon.fr ranked the paperback edition of Jean Flori's *La Reine insoumise* its 110,179th best-selling book. In contrast, the new paperback edition of Régine Pernoud's *Aliénor d'Aquitaine* ranked a much healthier 11,364th, and the first volume of Mireille Calmel's series of novels ranked the 2,860th bestseller. If these figures are representative, we can say that a Francophone reader is more likely to have his or her perception of Eleanor shaped by a popular novel than by non-fiction, and in turn more likely to have it shaped by a fifty-year-old work (Pernoud's) than a more scholarly work (Flori's) that was written in the last decade.[140] A similar pattern emerges for Anglophone Amazon users. The current paperback edition of Alison Weir's *Eleanor of Aquitaine* ranks number 21,770, Ralph Turner's more scholarly biography comes in at number 1,335,739 (despite being a paperback and reasonably priced at $25), while Weir's *Captive Queen: A Novel of Eleanor of*

Aquitaine was the 74,304th bestseller. American readers appear to be informed about Eleanor more by popular history than by fiction compared to Amazon.fr users, but the 'academic' study by Turner comes in below such relatively obscure fictional portrayals of Eleanor as Robert Fripp's *Power of a Woman*, ranked number 773,457, and published by small New Age publisher booklocker.com.[141] The ranks for the British amazon.co.uk are respectively 42,873 (Weir, *Eleanor of Aquitaine*), 19,552 (Weir, *Captive Queen*), 402,520 (Turner) and 424,429 (Fripp).[142] Popular history is itself a major market for publishers; in 2003, £32 million worth of history books were sold in the United Kingdom, representing a record 3 per cent of book sales.[143] Weir, according to her official website, is the fifth best-selling historian in the United Kingdom, and has sold over a million books in the UK and 1.3 million in the United States.[144] Yet popular history is in turn outsold by historical fiction, at least when it comes to Eleanor. There is also some erosion of the distinction between popular history and historical fiction, as shown by Weir's publication of a novel about Eleanor in the wake of her successful biography of the same subject. For some readers, historical fiction takes the place of history – Mary Tod found that more than half those surveyed read historical fiction with the specific purpose of *avoiding having to read history* books![145]

As we have seen, historical novelists in different genres have treated the life of Eleanor with various degrees of license or of adherence to 'historical accuracy'. Ultimately, however, does it matter whether historical fiction is 'historically accurate'? James Forrester in the *Guardian* argues that '[h]istorical accuracy is like quicksand. Stay too long in the same place and it will suck you down and there will be no movement, no dynamism to the story. Too much attention to factual detail is undoubtedly an impediment to literary art'.[146] Philippa Gregory, author of the *Cousins' War* novels that are set during the Wars of the Roses, addressed the issue of historical accuracy in her novels (and more specifically, the television adaptations based on them) by arguing that '[i]t's not a history documentary. It's entertainment'.[147] Emma Frost, writer for the television series *The White Queen* that was based on Gregory's novels, defends fictionalizing history in a more sophisticated way that reflects our post-modern uncertainty over whether the past can reliably be reconstructed through partial (in both senses of the word) sources:

> There is this obsession people have with historical accuracy, and I think what I would say to that is, first of all, the history that we have is not what happened, it's what got written down. And what got written down is largely about men's lives, and what got written down is filtered through the lens of the particular prejudices of the person who wrote it down … There is no such thing as historical

truth – every single version of history says more about the era that history book was written than it does about the history itself.[148]

Yet many authors of historical fiction, with their notes and citations, tend not to take a post-modern or relativist approach to their work. On the contrary, they often display a concern for accuracy and 'the truth', and express a Rankean historicist aim to have their characters reflect life as it really was in their chosen period setting. When asked whether she projected her 'own wishes for society' onto her portrayal of the twelfth century, Ellis Peters, author of the *Brother Cadfael* series, replied that, on the contrary, 'I think I'm deliberately trying to place myself into the minds of people of the twelfth and thirteenth centuries.'[149] Historical films, like historical fiction, have often claimed an educational purpose; when promoting *The Adventures of Robin Hood* (1938) Warner Brothers 'issued special packages to educators in order to assist them in using the film in classroom lectures on medieval feudalism.'[150]

One of the purposes of this book has been to argue that Eleanor's myth is reshaped in every century, if not every generation, reflecting contemporary concerns. If both 'professional' and 'popular' historians have created or perpetuated myths about Eleanor, writers of fiction can scarcely be held to a different standard. The creation of 'what we know' about Eleanor is a complex process in which historical fiction (alongside stage, screen, and visual arts depictions discussed in other chapters) has played arguably a greater role than the work of academics. In the words of Richard Slotkin, '[a]t the core of culture is a continuous dialogue between myth and history, "plain invention" and the "core of historical fact".'[151] If historical novels fall somewhere between those two poles, so have the works of historians, who have given us, among other images, that of Eleanor riding with her Amazons on crusade, which has found its way via both academic and popular history into works of fiction and drama, from Niketas Choniates to Katharine Hepburn. History is a process of selection – as E. H. Carr observed, not everything that happened in history is an 'historical fact', and 'facts' are chosen[152] because they are deemed to possess some historical significance by those who we imbue with authority as 'historians'. To quote Slotkin again,

all history writing requires a fictive or imaginary representation of the past. There is no reason why, in principle, a novel may not have a research basis as good or better than that of a scholarly history; and no reason why, in principle, a novelist's portrayal of a past may not be truer and more accurate than that produced by a scholarly historian.[153]

While academic historians rarely venture into fiction, Alison Weir has bridged the divide between popular history and historical fiction. Her 1999 biography *Eleanor of Aquitaine, by the Wrath of God, Queen of England* was followed in 2010 by an Eleanor novel, *Captive Queen*.[154] Weir's non-fiction work is far from perfect, but at least displays a healthy scepticism towards some of the myths that have surrounded Eleanor. In her novel *Captive Queen*, however, using a fiction writer's license, she presents as true all the accusations of adultery that were levelled against Eleanor by near-contemporary authors. In the opening paragraphs of the novel, we learn that Eleanor has experienced 'a few stolen moments... [with the troubadour] Marcabru; with Geoffrey [count of Anjou]; and later with Raymond [her uncle, the prince of Antioch]'. She recalls 'coupling gloriously between silken sheets' with Geoffrey of Anjou.[155] She also employs the familiar (and highly gendered) dichotomy between a weak Louis and a strong Henry: in her Eleanor biography, Louis is 'sexually withholding', while Henry II is 'aggressively virile'.[156] 'Louis's conjugal visits were not frequent enough to fulfil their purpose... It became apparent only much later how deeply this sexual neglect affected the more worldly and passionate Eleanor'.[157] Although Louis is blamed for Eleanor's childlessness, and the wider problems in their marriage, Eleanor is still trivialized as a woman whose actions are driven by her emotions and sexuality. The *Captive Queen* reinforces this judgement in more graphic language; Eleanor has been unable to excite Louis's 'suppressed and shrinking little member to action very often'; Henry, by contrast is 'magnificent, a young red-headed lion...'[158] As in her historical writing, Weir in her novel fails to free Eleanor (and her royal husbands) from the gender-stereotyping of past portrayals.

The French author Jocelyne Godard has also crossed between historical fiction and non-fiction. Her non-fiction *Les Amours d'Aliénor d'Aquitaine: Prendre coeur et prendre dame* (2002),[159] focuses, as the title implies, on Eleanor's love life, with Eleanor's political decisions influenced by her emotional ones – 'prendre coeur et prendre dame'. Not specifically or even primarily an author on medieval subjects, Godard appears to have been drawn to Eleanor as a strong female character. Her novels focus on women; *Dhuoda*, on a woman writer from the reign of Louis the Pious; the woman Pharaoh Hatshepsut in *Les Thébaines*; women in a sixteenth-century tapestry workshop in her series *Les Ateliers de Dame Alix*; and women in World War I in her *Guerre et femmes* series. *Les amours d'Aliénor d'Aquitaine* is part of a series about the love lives of notable women in French history, including Isabeau of Bavaria and Margaret of Valois (Dumas's *la reine Margot*), wife of France's Henry IV, alongside more modern figures such as George Sand and Sarah Bernhardt.[160] Asked in an interview why she was drawn to write about women, she responded:

> It is true that this is a path I have chosen since the first book that I wrote about Dhuoda, the first Carolingian woman writer, in the time of Charlemagne. Since writing this first book I resolved to get to know all women who had an interesting, remarkable and rich life but who have been overshadowed over the course of the years. I have chosen to recount the lives of women who left a mark on their age but who have tended to be forgotten today.[161]

Although a 'popular' author, Godard expresses a serious interest in medieval studies, for example attending a symposium on the medieval book.[162] Yet, as in Weir's case, Godard's desire to portray a strong woman, and her serious historical interest in her subject matter, does not prevent her from presenting Eleanor in romantic and emotional terms.

These examples show that even at the beginning of the twenty-first century the educational aspiration of the nineteenth-century historical novelist still lives on, as do nineteenth-century views of Eleanor as a creature driven by emotions that owe more to the Strickland sisters then to modern historiography. In the twentieth and twenty-first centuries, there has been a tension between the older Black Legend, which is colourful and dramatic, and the more recent scholarship. For the novelist, an Amazon queen is clearly more appealing (and sellable) an image than the queen as administrator or patron of monastic houses. There is also a tension in fiction, as in popular history, between the desire to present Eleanor as a positive female role-model, and the fascination with colourful – but misogynist – stories about her scandalous conduct, which serves to undermine the authors' intentions to write about a strong medieval woman. Divergent views of Eleanor have also emerged in fiction, whether reinventions of the old Black Legend or new visions of Eleanor as a New Age feminist role model.

Eleanor in the Visual Arts

Once, in the course of an adult education day school on medieval queens and queenship, I was stopped by a student who asked of Eleanor of Aquitaine, 'was she beautiful?' Historians have often felt free to discuss her appearance; she had 'long auburn locks' according to Alison Weir,[1] while (perhaps a little more realistically) Kate Norgate argued that she 'was young and beautiful; [but] her personal charms were more than equaled by those of her two great duchies of Aquitaine and Gascony'.[2] In the course of research for her trilogy of novels on Eleanor, Elizabeth Chadwick found the queen described in *non-fiction* works as 'a black-eyed beauty' (W. L. Warren), with 'a curvaceous figure that never ran to fat even in old age' (Frank McLynn and Desmond Seward), yellow hair and blue eyes (Desmond Seward), long auburn hair and green eyes (Douglas Boyd), or 'blond with grey or blue eyes set wide apart' (Marion Meade). These (mostly) male historians' 'droolings over the curvaceous figure' of Eleanor 'would appear to be some sort of modern male wish-fulfillment', in Chadwick's words, as they express a fascination with the body of the black-grey-blue-green-eyed blond-auburn-haired queen.[3] There are in fact no true contemporary portraits of Eleanor of Aquitaine and, as Marion Meade candidly remarks, 'there is not a single word about what she looked like' although this does not prevent her from remarking that Eleanor was 'exceptionally beautiful'.[4] Queens were routinely described as beautiful in chronicles: so we should not read too much into comments such as those of Richard of Devizes that Eleanor was 'beautiful and modest', especially given his implied criticism of her behaviour on the Second Crusade.[5] Marion Meade presents Bernard's comments in his letter to the virgin Sophia as 'the only physical portrait of Eleanor'.[6] Yet the letter nowhere refers to Eleanor, and the sole reference to a queen or queens is a general and rhetorical one: 'The ornaments of a queen have no beauty like the blushes of natural modesty which color the cheeks of a virgin'.[7] Bull and Léglu agree with Elizabeth Chadwick, calling popular historians' fascination with Eleanor's supposed beauty 'a feature of women's objectification'.[8] Descriptions of their appearance could be used to blame as much as to praise medieval queens; Rachel Gibbons writes that 'the most accessible weapons for an historian to use against a woman were criticism of her looks and her sexual conduct...'.[9] While Eleanor was never accused of being ugly, she was accused of adultery, and any discussion of her looks must be treated in this context of moralistic criticism.

Medieval images

Portraiture as such did not exist in the twelfth century; kings and queens were portrayed visually as types, not as individuals.[10] But even if we include all contemporary visual depictions of Eleanor, portrayals of her remain few and problematic. We have the following contemporary or near-contemporary visual sources for Eleanor: her seals; a fresco in the chapel of Sainte-Radegonde, Chinon, that has often been interpreted as a depiction of the family of Henry II; a stained glass window of her and Henry II in the cathedral of Poitiers; and her tomb effigy in the abbey church of Fontevraud.

Seals were not intended to portray the issuer of the document as an individual but to convey a sense of his or her authority. A king's seal would typically portray him enthroned on one side and on horseback with a drawn sword on the other, conveying two of his major roles – as war-leader and as provider of justice and civil authority. What messages are conveyed by Eleanor's seals? She issued seals both in her own capacity as duchess of Aquitaine, as queen of France and as queen of England. Kathleen Nolan, in a recent study of the iconography of French queens, discusses Eleanor's seals, their symbolism and their relationship to the practices of contemporaries.[11] The images on the seals are not, of course, portraits, but rather convey images of authority which provide an insight into Eleanor's evolving role.

No royal seal survives for Eleanor from her period as queen of France. However, seal impressions or antiquarians' sketches exist of her seals as duchess of Aquitaine and queen of England. From 1151 to 1154, between her divorce from Louis VII and her second husband Henry's accession to the English crown, Eleanor enjoyed a period of effective personal rule over Aquitaine. A drawing survives of her seal from this period attached to a document of 1152. It describes her as duchess of the Aquitainians, and possibly (there is a section of the legend missing) as countess of the Poitevins.[12] It depicts her uncrowned, holding a foliate object reminiscent of a fleur-de-lis in her right hand and a bird in her left. The fleur-de-lis does not necessarily symbolize Capetian France, as similar images appeared in English queens' seals, including Eleanor's.[13] The bird is a common symbol of royal authority, perhaps representing the dove of the holy spirit. It began to appear on imperial sceptres in the mid-eleventh century, and Edward the Confessor's seal showed him with a sceptre of this type.[14]

Elizabeth A. R. Brown argues that Eleanor used a second seal, attached to a charter of 1153, with slightly different imagery in this period, showing her with an open, empty left hand, lacking the fleur-de-lis, and wearing a veil or cape.[15] Nolan, however, believes these originate from the same seal, with the differences due to different interpretations of old, damaged seals by the antiquarians who sketched them.[16]

Images of Eleanor's seal as queen of England show similar iconography to that of 1152, but Eleanor now appears crowned, and the bird sits on a cross that tops an orb. The orb and cross was a symbol of temporal authority that was part of a king's regalia, suggesting a quasi-royal authority for Eleanor, as does her 'branchlike scepter topped with a fleur-de-lis more impressive than the single fleur-de-lis she (like the queens of France) held on her seal of 1152'.[17] This reinforces what we know of her active role in the government of England during the reign of her second husband and her sons. In Nolan's words, 'Eleanor is the first Anglo-Norman queen, as far as we can determine, to exhibit the full, highly charged formula of bird, cross, and orb, attached to male monarchs' seals'.[18] Furthermore, the seal was double-sided, reflecting the practice of kings, a practice apparently initiated by Eleanor's first husband, Louis VII, to reflect his dual authority as both king of France and duke of Aquitaine.[19] Eleanor's seal has an identical image on each side, but one describes her as queen of England and duchess of Normandy, the other as duchess of Aquitaine and countess of Anjou.[20] Nolan argues that Eleanor had only one seal as queen, which was created at the beginning of her reign, so this enhanced image of her authority was present from the outset of her time as Henry II's queen.[21]

The image most frequently used by those seeking a contemporary portrait of Eleanor is the fresco from the chapel of Sainte-Radegonde in Chinon. It is popular as a cover illustration for books about her, for example, Roy Owen's scholarly work of 1993, and Sharon Kay Penman's 2008 novel *The Devil's Brood*. However, various identifications have been offered for the figures in the fresco, with no unanimity over the identity, or even the gender, of the figure identified as Eleanor.

The scene depicts five riders. From left to right, there is a pair of riders wearing caps, one of whom holds a falcon; another pair of riders in the centre, one with a crown, and one with long, uncovered hair; and a fifth, lone rider on the right, also wearing a crown. The central, crowned figure turns back, hand extended to the figure with the falcon. His or her gesture has been variously viewed as one of departure, or of somebody handing over, or about to receive, the falcon. It is this crowned figure who has commonly been identified as Eleanor.

The first scholar to attempt an identification of the figures did not associate them with Eleanor or Henry II. Albert Héron, who discovered the scene in 1964, hypothesized that three of the figures are John, his wife Isabella of Angoulême, and her second husband, Hugh of Lusignan. The art historian Ursula Nielgen, however, dated the painting to the late twelfth century, beginning the tendency to see it as a depiction of the family of Henry II.[22] Nurith Kenaan-Kedar interprets the scene as Eleanor bidding farewell to her sons before being taken into captivity. The central, crowned figure, according to Kenaan-Kedar, is Eleanor, and she is handing the falcon over to Richard, the rider behind her, symbolizing the transfer of authority over Aquitaine to her son. The crowned figure leading the group is, of course, Henry; the other figures are the Young King (the second capped rider) and Joanna (the rider with the long hair). This interpretation is appropriate to a chapel dedicated to St Radegund, who was a patron saint of prisoners.[23] It begs the question, however, of whether Eleanor would have considered this episode worthy of celebration. Kenaan-Kadar's reasoning relies on a certain subjectivity and sentimentality; the central, crowned figure is identified as Eleanor because she appears old and 'sad'. She argues that the painting was commissioned by Eleanor after Henry's death (and thus the restoration of her freedom) when she was resident in Chinon in 1194, as a response to a painting of Henry's sons' rebellion which, according to Gerald of Wales, the king had made in Winchester.[24]

There is no particular reason to believe that the falcon in the painting represents Aquitaine, as there are no other examples of the falcon being used as a symbol of the duchy. A bird mounted on an orb does appear in some of Eleanor's seals, but this appears to be a symbol of temporal power, not a symbol of Aquitaine *per se*.[25] The presence of a blue-and-white diamond pattern on the inside of the crowned rider's cloak has also been used to make a link between the figures in the fresco and the Plantagenets. A similar design appears in the funeral plaque of Geoffrey of Anjou (Henry's father). Kenaan-Kedar points out the similarity, along with the resemblance of Geoffrey's comital cap to the headgear worn by two of the Chinon riders.[26]

However, other, radically divergent, interpretations have been suggested of the scene. Ursula Nielgen argued that all five of the figures are, in fact, male; there is nothing about the clothing or hairstyles of the two 'female' figures that differentiates them from the other three. She identifies the figures as Henry II and his four sons, and the second crowned figure as Henry, the Young King, not Eleanor.[27] The two riders wearing comital caps are Richard and Geoffrey (counts of Poitou and Brittany respectively), and the remaining rider is John. Nielgen tentatively suggests a date after the 1173–4 rebellion, when the family members were reconciled with the exception of Eleanor.[28]

One of the few contemporary depictions of Eleanor that has been securely identified as such is the representation of her and her family at the base of a window in Poitiers Cathedral. This is a small scene, taking up the central panel of the bottom register of a much larger depiction of the Crucifixion. Eleanor, Henry and four children appear in the area reserved for the patrons, with the king and queen holding an image that represents the window itself. This image is not, however, part of the original artwork; it is a result of nineteenth-century restoration by Adolphe Steinheil.[29] As with seal images and her tomb effigy, this cannot be taken as a realistic portrait of Eleanor. The scene of dynastic solidarity, with the four children representing Henry and Eleanor's then-surviving sons, Henry, Richard, Geoffrey and John, locates the commission sometime between the birth of John in 1166[30] and the revolt of Young Henry and Eleanor that began in 1173.[31]

The antiquarian Jean Bouchet, writing in 1525, identified Eleanor as responsible for the rebuilding of the choir of Poitiers Cathedral in 1162. The design of the window, with Eleanor on the right, the place usually reserved for the patron, suggests Eleanor's initiative in her capacity as duchess of Aquitaine and countess of Poitou.[32] However, there is no corroborating evidence from before 1525 for Bouchet's claim, and Eleanor was in England in 1162.[33] Claude Andrault-Schmitt argues against the whole concept of a programme of art associated with Eleanor and Henry in north-western France. While he accepts the identification of Eleanor as the patron of the window in Poitiers Cathedral, he points out that 'this type of commission is a limited operation, without any relationship to an architectural 'programme'', and the subject matter was probably determined by the bishop of Poitiers, Jean Bellesmains, not the royal couple.[34] The design of the window mirrors the contents of Bellesmains's letter *de officiae missae*.[35] It is interesting to note that the bishop was critical of Eleanor's rule in Poitou. In a letter to Thomas Becket, he complained of the influence of the queen's uncle, Raoul de Faye.[36] In a more general sense of course, Eleanor was a patron of the Church, as were all aristocrats, male or female. Her charters reveal extensive donations to religious houses, both in England and in France. But her patronage was 'neither especially generous nor especially extensive' given her vast income.[37] Eleanor has also been suggested as the person responsible for the ducal palace in Poitiers, but without conclusive evidence.[38]

As in discussions of Eleanor's literary patronage, some arguments made for her role as a patron of the visual arts appear to stretch the evidence to fit prior assumptions about her. For example, an article by Sara Lutan identifies aspects of the decoration of an Angevin Abbey with Eleanor and her family. She cites, among other evidence, a scene of a knight slaying a dragon, which she identifies with St George and, by extension, with King Richard I. In a scene of a harp player and a queen, the latter is identified as representing Eleanor.[39] While both of these identifications may be correct, they smack a little of the perceived image of those two figures – Richard the red-cross clad crusader king, and Eleanor the queen of the troubadours. The earliest reference to St George as a patron of England occurs in 1351, while, as I have argued above, the association of Eleanor with the troubadours is largely a modern construct.[40]

One image that, like her seal matrices, unambiguously represents Eleanor is her tomb effigy at Fontevraud. The modern-day arrangement of the effigies of Eleanor, Henry, Richard and Isabella of Angoulême does not represent the original placement of the tombs, which were disturbed during the revolution. Eleanor is shown holding a book. The original book was destroyed, and this is a restoration, but it probably faithfully represents what was originally there, as her hands are too far apart to have been depicted in prayer.[41] She does not wear any symbols of authority other than a crown, marking her as having less authority than the kings Henry and Richard, although, as Kathleen Nolan reminds us, the book that she holds marks her as possessing a different type of authority – religious or intellectual.[42]

This depiction is remarkable in several ways: it is the earliest funerary monument that we know of to depict a woman with a book, and apparently the only one to depict a man or woman in the act of reading.[43] Contrary to the popular image of Eleanor as predominantly a patron of secular literature, the book is probably (given its setting in an abbey of which Eleanor was a patron and, at the time of her death, a resident) a devotional work.[44] There are compelling reasons for believing that Eleanor was responsible for the commissioning of the effigies (except, obviously, that of Isabella of Angoulême, who died more than forty years after Eleanor). Stylistic similarities suggest that the effigies of Henry and Richard were commissioned at the same time (i.e. after Richard's death, when Eleanor played a key role in defending Anjou for John), and Eleanor's presence at Fontevraud in her last years places her in the right location at the right time. If so, this is one of the few instances when we can securely identify

Eleanor as an artistic patron.[45] They must have been created between the death of Richard in 1199 and the fall of Anjou to the Capetians in 1204 (also the year of Eleanor's death), reinforcing the belief that Eleanor may have been the person who commissioned them.[46]

Modern representations

Eleanor has frequently, if inconsistently, been portrayed in post-medieval visual art. The nineteenth century saw a huge revival of interest in the medieval past among the artists of Western Europe. The reasons for this were manifold, and cannot be discussed in any detail here, but they included a romantic rejection of industrial modernity and a desire of nation-states to trace themselves back to their supposed medieval origins. Britain, France (under the Restoration and the July monarchies) and (more indirectly) imperial Germany could all cite forebears in the monarchies of the high Middle Ages, but even newly 'invented' nations looked back to medieval examples to legitimize themselves; for example, in 1848 Belgium commissioned an equestrian statue of Godfrey of Bouillon, one of the leaders of the First Crusade and one of the 'Nine Worthies' of medieval tradition, to stand in the Place Royale in Brussels.[47]

The crusades were a popular source of inspiration for those artists who were commissioned to glorify the nineteenth-century nation state. As well as providing a suitably heroic backdrop for the deeds of medieval monarchs, they also provided a precedent for rising European colonialism. The British Houses of Parliament and the restored imperial palace at Goslar were both decorated with crusading scenes to cast reflected glory on Victorian Britain and the Wilhelmine Reich. This was especially true for France, which began to build an empire in the Arab and Muslim world with its invasion of Algeria in 1830, as well as intervening in Syria and Lebanon in 1839–40. In 1843, King Louis-Philippe opened the Salles des Croisades in the palace of Versailles, dedicated to 120 paintings on the theme of the crusade, and to the names of French crusaders (many of them based on the wholly fictitious Courtois charters). The Salle des Croisades paintings had 'a clear purpose, namely to emphasize the continuity of French history under Louis Philippe' who had come to power through the July Revolution, and whose claim to the throne was disputed by 'legitimist' royalists, 'and there is a clear coincidence in timing between a number of the crusade paintings and the king's renewal of Charles X's crusade in Algeria'.[48]

Two of these painting included Eleanor: Émile Signol's *St Bernard Preaching the Second Crusade in the Presence of King Louis VII, Queen Eleanor of Aquitaine and Abbot Suger at Vézelay, 31 March 1146*, and Jean-Baptiste Mauzaisse's painting with the equally long-winded title *King Louis VII takes the Oriflamme at St-Denis in the presence of Queen Eleanor of Aquitaine and receives the pilgrim's staff and scrip from the hands of Pope Eugenius III* (each was commissioned in 1838 and exhibited in 1839).[49] Understandably, these French artists wished to avoid the controversial aspects of Louis and Eleanor's crusade. Both surviving paintings portray Eleanor in an essentially passive role.[50] In the Signol painting, Bernard preaches to the crowd from the steps of a dais on which the royal couple are enthroned. Louis stands, gazing nobly into the distance while Eleanor sits to his left, hands clasped in prayer, with her eyes raised towards heaven. In Mauzaisse's picture, Eleanor once again is seen in an attitude of prayer, and to one side of the main actors in the scene. On the left of the painting, Louis kneels before the pope, receiving the latter's blessing, while holding a pilgrim's staff and scrip. Eleanor is on the opposite side, kneeling on a prie-dieu, again with hands in prayer and eyes cast down. In both images, she is presented as pious, passive, beautiful and essentially an accessory to the main events – very different to the scandalous figure presented by the chroniclers.

A third Eleanor painting from the Salles has disappeared. Franck (*recte* Franz) Winterhalter's *Éléonore de Guyenne prend la croix avec les dames de sa cour* (1839) is listed in a catalogue of 1842,[51] where it is listed as painting number fifty-six. It would appear from the 1842 listings to have been located between Signol's and Mauzaisse's paintings. A nineteenth-century tourist guide also describes the painting.[52] Another guide to the paintings, by Eudoxe Soulié, added disapproving remarks about Eleanor's supposed warrior exploits, which perfectly reflect her image in contemporary novels and history books:

> Eleanor of Guyenne, a bold and enterprising woman, wished to follow her husband, King Louis VII, perhaps not so much out of religious enthusiasm as to satisfy a taste for adventure. Her frivolous conduct during the expedition later led to an impolitic divorce that saw Guyenne pass to the house of Plantagenet. Recent excavations have uncovered breastplates from that period, the design of which suggests that they were worn by women. We must suppose that they belonged to the women warriors who accompanied Eleanor of Guyenne.[53]

Soulié writes in the tradition that disapproved of Eleanor from a patriotic French perspective for having alienated lands to the English crown though her 'impolitic divorce'. His is, to the best of my knowledge, the only source that claims archaeological proof for the existence of Eleanor's crusading Amazons. Given

Soulié's commentary on this lost third painting, it is possible that it was removed because it presented a more dangerous view of Eleanor as an embodiment of female authority and an insufficiently 'French' figure.

An interest in the crusades was equally evident in mid-nineteenth-century Britain. The Great Exhibition of 1851 may have celebrated the excitement of Victorian technology, but it also reflected the prevailing romantic medievalism of the era. Exhibits included Simonis's statue of Godfrey of Bouillon, Marochetti's statue of Richard the Lionheart that would later stand outside Parliament and 'a decorative panel of Queen Eleanor by W. F. d'almaine, imitating the style of Edward I' executed in a style that 'reflected a certain Pre-Raphaelite influence'.[54] Given the association with Edward I, this 'Queen Eleanor' may be Eleanor of Castile – the only queen of England other than Eleanor of Aquitaine to go on crusade – but it indicates the contemporary interest in medievalism and the crusades.

From the second half of the nineteenth century Eleanor became a popular subject for British Victorian and Edwardian artists, but they cast her in a very different role. Ten such paintings addressed the subject of the Fair Rosamond legend, and several of these paintings include Eleanor. One includes Eleanor alone, but the composition strongly alludes to the Rosamond legend. Curiously, these paintings come in two distinct time periods – five in the 1850s and early 1860s (the early decades of the movement), and four in the first two decades of the twentieth century.

The first period coincides with what has been called the heyday of history painting in Britain during the period 1840–70.[55] This was the age of Walter Scott's continuing popularity, and of the birth of the Pre-Raphaelite movement with its medievalist nostalgia. The Fair Rosamond story's appearance in early-modern ballads may also have inspired the Pre-Rapaelites, as D. G. Rossetti and Holman Hunt had listed the 'Early English Balladists' among their 'immortals' in 1848.[56] In 1854, Arthur Hughes's *Fair Rosamund* and William Bell Scott's *Fair Rosamund in her Bower* appeared. Scott was a friend of pre-Raphaelite Dante Gabriel Rossetti, and would work on other medieval themes including *Return from a Long Crusade* (1865).[57]

Frederick Sandys's *Queen Eleanor* of 1858, while presenting Eleanor as a young queen, alludes to the Rosamond story by showing her with a goblet in hand, presumably containing poison. Sandys was attracted to the subject of female enchantresses; other subjects of his painting included Cassandra, Vivien, Morgan le Fey and Medea, and he seems to be placing Eleanor in that company, given that legend had often identified her as a supernatural or even demonic figure.[58] Dante Gabriel Rossetti's 1861 painting *Fair Rosamund* does not include Eleanor, but Edward Burne-Jones portrayed the queen and Rosamond twice, in his *Fair Rosamund and Queen Eleanor* of 1861 and *Fair Rosamund* of 1862. Both these paintings represent the moment when Eleanor enters Rosamond's bower, having discovered her hiding place. An older, dark-haired Eleanor, holding the thread that has allowed her to uncover Rosamond's hiding place, bursts into the scene, head thrust forward. A blonde Rosamond cowers in the right of the painting. Eleanor appears as (literally) a dark invasive force, and the viewers' sympathies are drawn to the mistress, not the wife. In the 1862 painting, she is literally entrapped in the incriminating thread, which loops around her waist, and whereas in 1861 she is shown turned towards Eleanor; in the later painting her vulnerability is further emphasized by her turning away as if in an attempted flight from the queen.

The Eleanor–Rosamond story was popular in other cultural spheres, as we have seen in Chapter 5. Tennyson's *Becket* possibly accounts for the second wave of Rosamond-related paintings that began in 1905, with Herbert Sidney's *Fair Rosamund* and Evelyn de Morgan's *Queen Eleanor and Fair Rosamund.* John William Waterhouse's *Fair Rosamund* appeared in 1916, and Frank Cadogan Cowper's *Fair Rosamund and Eleanor* in 1920.

These paintings reflect the low esteem into which Eleanor had fallen in the late nineteenth and early twentieth centuries, thanks to the popularity of the Fair Rosamond legend. There are, however, occasional exceptions to this theme. A painting by Edmund Blair Leighton of Eleanor knighting a young Richard the Lionheart provides a rare Victorian example of the queen depicted as an authority figure, rather than the evil murderer of Rosamond or simpering consort of Louis VII. Perhaps because it better fits the modern view of Eleanor as a strong woman, this has been reproduced in contemporary culture, including as the cover image for Calmel's *Le Lit d'Alienor* and even as a resin statuette!

On the other side of the Channel, there are two interesting examples of Eleanor being celebrated in civic art. A window in the *mairie* of Poitiers, by the nineteenth-century French artist and restorer Adolphe Steinheil,[59] shows Eleanor confirming a charter of liberties to the city. A fresco depicting 'queen Eleanor granting a charter to the burghers of Niort' (*La reine Aliénor octroyant commune et franchise aux bourgeois de Niort*) by Charles Fouqueray was created in 1901 for the council chamber of the Hôtel de Ville in the Poitevin city of Niort.[60] These scenes illustrate another aspect of the modern memory of Eleanor, as a symbol of civic pride. As discussed previously, Eleanor has become a symbol of regional identity for the South and West, and here we see her as a symbol of local pride for the communes of Poitou to which she granted charters. However, it is arguable whether Eleanor is shown as a specifically Poitevin figure of regional pride, or as an authority figure legitimizing the freedom of the commune. As in the crusade paintings, she is of course presented in a positive light.

The Poitiers window, which features as the cover image of Ralph Turner's biography of Eleanor, depicts her standing, crowned, on a dais, with her right hand on a book, facing a group of citizens, one of whom holds the charter in his right hand. Steinheil was a noted restorer of medieval paintings and glass, who had worked on the cathedrals of Laon and Bayonne, although he is better remembered as one of the victims in a sensational murder.[61] Most significantly in this context, Steinheil restored the scene of Eleanor and Henry as patrons of the Crucifixion window in Poitiers Cathedral.[62] Although Steinheil could not be said to have captured a twelfth-century artistic style in his Hôtel de Ville window, the influence of the cathedral window is obvious. In both, Eleanor is depicted wearing a blue gown, white veil (or rather, a cloak in the cathedral window) and a gold crown. These colours may also have been inspired by those of Eleanor's tomb effigy at Fontevraud.

The Niort painting depicts a similar scene, with a rather stern-looking Eleanor handing the charter to a kneeling *bourgeois*. The scene is labelled with a scroll-like legend in pseudo-medieval Latin above the central group, which includes a bishop and other clerics. The composition of the scene is very similar to Steinheil's window at Poitiers, with Eleanor standing on a dais at centre-left, with the grateful bourgeois to the right and below her. It is curious to find such images of royalty and the clergy in the municipal art of secular Third Republic France. It is possible that this is simply a medievalist device to legitimize and celebrate the city's medieval origins, lacking in any conservative political overtones. Romantic Victorian-era medievalism was still in vogue in 1901. On the other hand, it may reflect a conservative royalism particular to the region, Niort being close to the conservative bastion of the Vendée.

Book illustrations and covers

Book covers and illustrations have been a major source of imagined portraits of Eleanor in the nineteenth and twentieth centuries. The nineteenth-century works of Elizabeth Strickland and Celestia Bloss (discussed in Chapters 1, 2 and 6) quite literally portray Eleanor in different ways through their engraved illustrations. The 1897 condensed edition of Strickland's work, by an unknown artist, shows Eleanor as coquettish, leaning forward (in a pose reminiscent of the female fashions of the 1890s and Edwardian era, with their bustles and corsets) and raising a finger and giving a sideways glance at the reader.[63] Bloss's book, illustrated by S. Wallin and J. C. Buttre, also shows Eleanor in a rather frivolous light, as leader of her 'Amazon' ladies on crusade, but this is at least a more assertive view of the queen, spear in hand at the head of a body of armed women – the type of 'fighting woman' of whom Elizabeth Strickland disapproved.[64] The image of a woman holding a lance also appears on the cover of Bloss's book. Mid- to late nineteenth-century illustrations of Eleanor were not, however, confined to works of fiction. In 1875, Joseph Michaud's *Histoire des Croisades* appeared in a new edition illustrated by the engravings of Gustave Doré, one of the great engravers of the age, famous in part for medieval themes such as his illustrations of Dante's *Divine Comedy*. However, Eleanor is absent from the scene depicting Louis taking the cross from Saint Bernard, perhaps reflecting the author's low opinion of the queen as outlined in Chapter 1.[65] John Ridpath's *Cyclopedia of Universal History*, on the other hand, included an image of 'Queen Eleanor and her Troubadours' by Doré, where the queen and her ladies are shown relaxing in a rustic glade listening to the music of three troubadours, reflecting the more romantic image of the queen, although it does accompany a passage relating Eleanor's behaving 'not after the manner of a queen' in Antioch.[66]

The twentieth-century view of Eleanor as an assertive woman has, as we have seen, created a veritable industry of Eleanor books and corresponding cover images. Non-fiction works about the medieval queen tend to advertise their claims to serious scholarship by choosing photographs of medieval images (possibly) of Eleanor, notably the Sainte-Radegonde, Chinon, fresco (used by Blackwell for Owen's work, Livres de Poche for Pernoud's biography and the History Press for Boyd's *April Queen*), the stained-glass window of Poitiers Cathedral (chosen by Jonathan Cape for the 1999 first edition of Weir's Eleanor biography), the image from the *Codex Manesse* (a richly decorated early fourteenth-century collection of High German poetry) of a medieval queen alongside the poet von Kürenberg, which has come to be identified with Eleanor (the US edition and UK paperback editions of Weir),[67] and a different *Codex Manesse* image of a young man and woman on horseback for both the original French edition and the English translation of Flori's *Aliénor d'Aquitaine: la reine insoumise*. These images are, presumably, employed to give a sense of authenticity and scholarship, in contrast to the more imaginative covers employed by publishers of Eleanor fiction. However, as we have seen, all these images are more or less problematic: the Chinon fresco may portray Eleanor's son, Henry the Young King; there is no reason to believe that either image from the *Codex Manesse* is Eleanor; even the Poitiers window, which is securely identifiable as a representation of Eleanor, was not intended as portraiture. It is perhaps surprising that Eleanor's tomb effigy at Fontevraud is underused as a book cover: maybe the passivity of the image fails to match the perception of her as an assertive woman?

Works of fiction are more likely to use modern images of Eleanor, such as Margaret Ball's *Duchess of Aquitaine*, which employs a dynamic painting of Eleanor by the Japanese-American artist Kinoko Craft. The queen appears on horseback, crowned, with a falcon on her left wrist and long red hair flowing behind her. This image matches the modern perception of Eleanor as an active, confident female authority figure. The falcon and the appearance of Eleanor on horseback both recall the Sainte-Radegonde fresco, although Craft states that she was not influenced by it.[68]

Kristiana Gregory's young adult novel of Eleanor employs a cover image representing a rosy-cheeked young princess looking, despite her twelfth-century clothes, rather like a modern American teenager, with a book clutched to her bosom but appearing before a backdrop of a castle and a knight, perhaps the two surest markers of medievalism for a modern audience. Brigitte Coppin's novel *Aliénor d'Aquitaine, une reine à l'aventure* (1999) is also aimed at a young readership. Flammarion's choice of cover illustration for the original edition reflects the modern image of Eleanor as a strong woman, showing her as a dynamic and warlike figure, seated on horseback with a determined expression on her face, with two armed, mounted men behind her, against a backdrop of a Middle Eastern city (identifiable as such by domes and minarets). The cover art for the 2011 edition, however, has softened the image of Eleanor. She now appears wearing a long dress, crown and wimple, standing alongside her horse. Possibly the change is to appeal to a female readership, replacing a warlike image of Eleanor with a more soft-focus one, or maybe it was intended to play down the anti-Muslim nature of crusading, following the Iraq war, and the 2005 riots in the *banlieues*.

The cover images of many works of historical fiction aimed at adults fetishize and objectify Eleanor's body. Few books about Eleanor express the frank sexuality of 1950s soft-porn titles such as *La vie galante de Eléonore de Guyenne*, or *La Vie amoureuse: Aliénor d'Aquitanie et les cours d'amour*, with their covers showing a scantily clad queen. The *La vie galante* series is remembered – insofar as it is remembered at all – more for the cover art by Jef de Wulf than the novels themselves.[69] De Wulf's covers are in a lurid 'pulp' style, emphasizing the subjects' *décolletages*. Eleanor herself is depicted not so much wearing as falling out of a corset, wearing a long, diaphanous skirt that covers only one of her legs, with a white surcoat bearing a red crusader cross (presumably worn by Eleanor herself, and later removed by her or a lover) in the background. The setting is clearly the Second Crusade, with Eleanor's alleged misdemeanours with Raymond of Antioch clearly alluded to. Likewise Émile Brux's 1957 novel, *Aliénor d'Aquitaine et les cours d'amour*, came adorned with a cover image of Eleanor in a tight-fitting, *décolletée* green dress.[70]

Covers of twenty-first-century novels about Eleanor may be less pornographic, but they are nonetheless problematic in their portrayal of women's bodies. In a common trend in contemporary historical fiction publishing, women are literally effaced and figuratively beheaded by images that focus on the heroine's body but leave out her face. The US edition of Weir's *Captive Queen*, the e-book *Gilded Cages: The Trials of Eleanor of Aquitaine* by Ellen Jones[71] and Christy English's novel *To Be Queen*[72] all have covers that show a woman in a period dress, with her face wholly or partly cut off at the top of the image. This trend has been remarked upon by many online commentators, with different explanations offered, including economic considerations (it is cheaper for the publisher not to have to pay the model for image rights) or psychological (the reader, presented with a literally faceless heroine, is free to place herself in the character's place). Another possibility is that the focusing of the image on the 'exotic' period dress is a signifier of the medieval period for the reader. It is hard, however – especially given the frequent focus on the heroine's *décolletage* – to deny the possibility that the central female character is being objectified. There appears to be no equivalent epidemic of faceless men, nor do explanations based on commercial image rights, or the desire to represent 'Everywoman', account for the cutting or disfigurement of older portraits of historical figures such as Catherine of Aragon.[73]

> The headless woman is a potentially inflammatory image, in part due to the history of crude jokes about the 'ideal' woman.
>
> 'I think it's worth saying that [the headless book cover] is not too far away from the well-known sexist image of the male fantasy of the woman who's totally available and can't talk back and doesn't think and doesn't judge,' says Deirdre English, director of the Felker Magazine Center at the University of California at Berkeley Graduate School of Journalism.[74]

The literal, visual image of Eleanor has evolved alongside her image in history and literature. The medieval Eleanor appears on occasion as a female authority figure, exemplified in her seals, while her tomb at Fonetevraud hints at a different form of authority, that of a dynast and patron. However, the contemporary visual evidence – like the written evidence – on close inspection proves to be more sparse and problematic than would appear from post-medieval authors' accounts. Just as many biographies of Eleanor have made tendentious claims about her nature or the events of her life, so do they often feature problematic images on their covers and misleading physical descriptions of her between the covers. The development of post-medieval depictions of Eleanor also reflects the evolution of her image in text – the pious crusader queen, the queen of the troubadours or the murderer of Rosamond in the nineteenth century giving way to more positive (or at least more diverse) images in the twentieth. However, just as the rise of the Golden Myth of Eleanor has not seen the end to a fascination with her sexuality in fiction, so does the cover art of modern Eleanor novels continue to suggest an objectification and marginalization of women.

Conclusion: Eleanor in the Twenty-First Century

In this work, I have attempted to trace the evolution of both the Eleanor of history (or at least, of historiography) and the Eleanor of fiction and the arts to the end of the twentieth century. As we have seen, some myths of Eleanor have stubbornly refused to die (such as the 'Amazon Queen' idea), while on the other hand her image has evolved in new and sometimes surprising directions (like the New Age heroine, inheritor of druidic knowledge). Where does the image of Eleanor stand in the early twenty-first century?

The origin of modern, sceptical approaches to Eleanor was marked by Edmond-René Labande's essay 'Pour un image véridique d'Aliénor d'Aquitaine' in 1951. Labande sought to challenge the old mythologies about Eleanor, and to turn back towards well-attested documentary sources to assess her life. Despite appearing in a somewhat obscure journal of French regional history, Labande's article has been highly influential on recent Eleanor scholarship, and was republished as a stand-alone volume in 2005.[1] However, even Labande emphasized the exceptionalism of Eleanor, and recapitulated elements of Eleanor's image that later scholars have treated more sceptically. He echoed Richard of Devizes in seeing Eleanor as 'an incomparable woman', and gave credence to the Courts of Love.[2]

In the half a century or so since the appearance of Labande's work, how successful have academic historians been in fulfilling his hope for a 'realistic image of Eleanor of Aquitaine'? Early signs of a critical reassessment were seen in a landmark essay of 1976 by Elizabeth Brown, in which she sought to contextualize and demythologize Eleanor.[3]

Serious Eleanor scholarship of the last decade has produced a number of book-length works. Two scholarly biographies of Eleanor have appeared, by Jean Flori[4] and Ralph Turner,[5] as well as two major collections of essays, one each in English and French.[6] This suggests a revival in scholarly interest in Eleanor on both sides of the English Channel, aided by the 800th anniversary of her death in 2004. *Eleanor of Aquitaine, Lord and Lady*, edited by Bonnie Wheeler and John Carmi Parsons, is a collection of essays addressing the full range of Eleanor's activities – political, dynastic, literary and artistic. The title suggests Eleanor's dual role, crossing (perhaps problematically?) the line between the 'male' world of power and the domestic female realm. In 2004, two years after the Wheeler and Parsons volume was published, the French cultural journal *303* published a special number to coincide with an exhibition at Fontevraud marking the 800th anniversary of Eleanor's death. This work reflects an interest in her not just as part of English or French (or, for that matter, Occitan) national history, but as part of the regional histories of the western provinces of France. While it may still be impossible to avoid the misleading popular biographies that fill the shelves of bookstores, a reader seeking a scholarly approach to the subject is no longer reliant on Amy Kelly for an introduction to Eleanor.

These developments in Eleanor scholarship have coincided (as outlined in the introduction) with the rise of the serious, scholarly study of queens and queenship. I have frequently described works such as Kelly's and Meade's as 'feminist' in quotation marks, to convey a sense that I find the term problematic when applied to the Golden Myth of Eleanor. Is it really feminist to replace a Great Man view of history with one centred on Great Women, or to fall back on nineteenth-century portrayals of Eleanor as motivated by excitement, romance or sex? Fortunately, a more serious feminist scholarship has been applied to queens and queenship since the 1970s, as '[f]eminist thought challenged the premises of political history and galvanized a generation of graduate students' to study the history of medieval women.[7] Many contemporary scholars in this field, such as Lois Huneycutt, Miriam Shadis, Theresa Earenfight and Eleanor Woodacre, are associated with the Society for Medieval Feminist Scholarship. There is certainly hope for a more 'realistic image of Eleanor of Aquitaine' that is shaped by women scholars with a nuanced understanding of medieval women's authority.

In the world of the arts, the Black Legend and the Golden Myth still hold sway, as seen in novels, such as Alison Weir's (discussed in Chapter 6), which seek to portray both the scandalous adulterous queen of legend and the powerful female ruler.[8] Historians may shake their heads at the perpetuation of such myths, but many historical novelists such as Sharon Kay Penman and Elizabeth Chadwick are seeking to apply modern scholarship to their fiction, and consequently avoid the most egregious of the legends that surround Eleanor. Indeed, there is a concern among both authors and readers for 'historical accuracy', as can be seen in the sometimes bitter arguments among readers on websites, blogs and social media pages. However, the artistic-license-versus-historical-accuracy argument is a somewhat sterile one, given the paucity of clear evidence for Eleanor's life, and the post-modern awareness of the uncertain and contingent nature of historical 'fact'. In fiction and drama, maybe the future lies with more playful treatments such as Group Anamorphose's stage play that dramatizes (and makes fun of) the scholarly debates surrounding Eleanor, or David Scaer's unpublished (at least at the time of going to press) 'analytical novel' of Eleanor, which combines music, poetry and history.[9]

Why Eleanor?

Yet despite recent developments in the study of medieval queenship in general that suggest Eleanor was far from unique, she continues to capture the popular imagination in a way that comparable figures, such as Berenguela of Castile, do not. I will tentatively suggest some possible explanations for this. One of these is Eleanor's unique position as queen of both France and England, whose divorce and remarriage played a crucial role in the power-politics of both. She was therefore a key figure in two of the most influential nation states (and the leading colonial powers) when modern academic history and historical fiction were developing in the nineteenth century. Berenguela and Spanish queens, by contrast, suffer from the lack of attention paid to Iberia compared to France and England.[10] It may be true that Berenguela is little known outside the circles of scholars of medieval Spain,[11] but the same could be said of the knowledge (outside Spain at least) of, say, Pedro the Cruel or Alfonso the Wise.

However, simple geography does not explain her appeal outside France and Britain (such as the scholarship and historical fiction about Eleanor by US authors), or her prominence in the popular imagination when compared to equally striking women from English medieval history, such as the Empress Matilda (the last biography of whom appeared in 1991, since which time four Eleanor biographies have been published).[12] Eleanor's association not only with Louis VII and Henry II but also with her sons Richard I and John is certainly a factor as shown in the title of Amy Kelly's *Eleanor of Aquitaine and the Four Kings*. The association in early-modern and modern culture of the latter two with the Robin Hood legend has also indirectly helped keep Eleanor in the public eye, as seen by her cameo appearances as a character in several TV and film treatments of the legend, and in the 1997 television adaptation of *Ivanhoe*.

It must also be said that Eleanor's notoriety – however ill-founded – has made her an attractive subject for writers and artists. The medieval rumours of her adultery were, as we have seen, alluded to in *The Lion in Winter* and in many modern novels, while the Fair Rosamond legend became the subject of plays, operas and paintings in the nineteenth century. Of course, this in itself does not fully account for the longevity of Eleanorian exceptionalism, as it begs the question of why Eleanor in particular attracted these sorts of legends (as opposed to Isabella of France (wife of Edward II), who was accused on much more plausible grounds than Eleanor of being an adulteress and murderer, or Eleanor of Provence, who suffered from something of a Black Legend of her own before elements of it attached themselves to her namesake of Aquitaine).

If the notorious Eleanor of the Black Legend explains our fascination with her, so too does the Golden Myth of the queen of the troubadours, who, as conceived of by Kelly and Meade, was responsible for practically every major cultural and intellectual development of her age. Again, there is a risk of making a circular argument here – that legends grew up around Eleanor because she had attracted legends to her – but the Golden Myth is explicable by the unusual combination of circumstances that surrounded Eleanor's life. She may have been a less significant literary patron than, for example, Ermengarde of Narbonne; however, she was in precisely the right places at the right time to be connected (with sufficient imagination) to the great cultural trends of her day. She was the granddaughter of the 'First Troubadour', connecting her (if indirectly) to the emergence of Occitan song. She was in the Paris of the 'wandering scholars'[13] at the height of the 'twelfth-century renaissance'. She was at the court of Henry II at precisely the moment that the Arthurian legend entered French and English literature through the works of Wace and Layamon (and there is actually evidence to connect her to the former); and she appeared, alongside her daughter Marie de Champagne, in Andreas Capellanus's work that was once believed to have codified the idea of courtly love. As we have seen, much of the evidence for these connections is circumstantial at best, but once established in the imagination as a uniquely cultured queen, that image has proved enduring despite scholarly scepticism.

Much the same could be said of another element of her mythos, the feminist icon of a supposed uniquely powerful woman. As we have seen, she was in reality far from unique in this sense, and generally the idea of female powerlessness in the twelfth century has been exaggerated. So why was Eleanor, rather than, say, the Empress Matilda, Berenguela of Castile, or Adela of Blois, adopted to fulfil this role? The glamour of her historical context discussed above certainly added lustre to her image, but contingent factors may also play a part. Amy Kelly's biography of Eleanor – which was accessible, readable, but also scholarly for its day – was *the* Eleanor biography available to readers in the 1960s and

1970s, when Second-Wave Feminism was developing, and when women within the academy (including medievalists) were starting to challenge male-centred histories. The portrayal of Eleanor by Katharine Hepburn, who was a feminist icon in her own right, in 1968 certainly did no harm to her image as a strong woman role-model.

A 'realistic image of Eleanor of Aquitaine' may never be attainable; the discrepancy between what we actually know about her from the medieval sources and the vast amount written about her in both history and imaginative literature suggests that anything to be discovered about her in a documentary sense has probably already been discovered. However, as new critical approaches are applied to her life, we can be hopeful that more nuanced interpretations of Eleanor will continue to be developed as the twenty-first century progresses. A better understanding of Eleanor, not as a proto-modern exception but in the context of other authoritative and cultured medieval women, can help illuminate a world still too-often stigmatized in popular culture as the 'Dark Ages', and maybe encourage us to view our own age, in which women's voices are too often excluded, with a little more self-awareness and humility. It's 2014 and we're all barbarians.

Notes

Introduction

1 Earenfight, 2013, p. 137.
2 DeAragon, 2004.
3 Duby, 1995, pp. 15–17.
4 Wheeler and Parsons, 2002, p. xxix.
5 Barber, 2005, p. 13.
6 A term used, for example, by Martin Aurell. Aurell, 2004, p. 10.
7 Owen, 1993, p. 148.
8 Aurell and Armengaud, 2004, p. 21; 'a été à la fois victime d'une legende noire et bénéficiaire d'un mythe doré'.
9 See, for example, Chapman, 1955, p. 394. 'Eleanor was the kind of person who would attract legend in any age. She had an uncanny ability to get and keep the upper hand … Yet she was full of beauty and grace, the patroness of the troubadours.'
10 Konigsburg, 2001, back matter.
11 Flori, 2004a, p. 53.
12 Vincent, 2004, p. 59.
13 Vincent, 2006, p. 17.
14 Aurell, 2004a, p. 12.
15 John of Salisbury, 1986, p. 3.
16 Boyd, 2004, p. 1.
17 Boyd, 2004, p. 2.
18 Weir, 1999, p. 355.
19 Cook, 1993, p. 29.
20 Meade, 1977, p. x.
21 Kelly, 1950, p. v.
22 Duby, 1995, p. 15.
23 Wemple, S. and McNamara, J., cited in Evergates, 1999, p. 1.
24 Bianchini, 2012, p. 3.
25 Bianchini, 2012, p. 1.
26 Kelly, 1950; Walker, 1950; Pernoud, 1965.
27 See, for example, Benton, 1961.

28 Owen, 1993.

29 Notable examples of the study of queenship include Parsons, 1994; Duggan, 1997; Earenfight, 2013. Examples of studies of specific queens or dynasties include Facinger, 1968; Huneycutt, 2003; Shadis, 2009; Bianchini, 2012.

30 Bianchini, 2012, p. 3.

31 Facinger, 1968, pp. 3–47; Earenfight, 2013, pp. 19, 129.

32 Facinger, 1968; Earenfight, 2013, p. 151.

33 Damon, 2006, pp. 127–8.

34 Shadis, 2003.

35 Earenfight, 2013, p. 129.

36 Earenfight, 2013, p. 6.

37 Turner, 2009, pp. 175–204, 248; Earenfight, 2013, p. 139.

38 Hivergneaux, 2006, p. 72; Turner, 2009, pp. 152, 259.

39 Facinger, 1968, pp. 7–8. It should be noted that Marion Facinger is *not* the same person as Eleanor's biographer Marion Meade, although they are identified as such by Wheeler and Parsons in the bibliography of their *Eleanor of Aquitaine, Lord and Lady*, pp. 478, 493. Marion Meade, pers. comm., 1 November 2007.

40 Geaman, 2010, pp. 10–33.

41 Earenfight, 2013, p. 138.

42 Hivergneaux, 2006, p. 62; 'Elle est donc loin d'agir seule dans ce duché dont elle est l'héritière.'

43 Hivergneaux, 2006, p. 64.

44 Turner, 2009, pp. 46, 56–7.

45 Flori, 2004, p. 37.

46 Facinger, 1968, pp. 7–8.

47 Vincent, 2004, p. 59.

48 Kelly, 1937, pp. 18–19.

49 Owen, 1993, p. 49.

50 Barber, 2005, pp. 15–6.

51 Hivergneaux, 2006, pp. 61–73; Hivergneaux, 2000, pp. 63–88; Hivergneaux, 2002, pp. 55–76; Vincent, 2004, pp. 58–63; Vincent, 2000, pp. 103–35; Vincent, 2006, pp. 17–60.

52 Turner, 2009, p. 124.

53 For example, Kelly, 1950, p. 155, sees Eleanor's departure for Poitou as 'a resolution to cut herself away from feudal kings'.

54 Turner, 2009, pp. 188–9.

55 Volrath, 2006, p. 119.

56 Turner, 2009, p. 151.

57 Turner, 2009, p. 152.

58 Vincent, 2004, pp. 59–60.

59 Turner, 2009, p. 184.

60 Turner, 2009, p. 186.

61 Hivergneaux, 2006, p. 72.

62 Vincent, 2006, p. 50.

63 Vincent, 2006, p. 52.

64 Vincent, 2006, p. 31.

65 Turner, 2009, p. 259.

66 Turner, 2009, pp. 264, 273.

67 Turner, 2009, pp. 269–73.

68 Turner, 2009, p. 278; Gillingham, 1999, pp. 321–32.

69 Turner, 2009, pp. 282–92.

70 Earenfight, 2013, p. 11.

71 Strohm, 1992, p. 95.

72 Earenfight, 2013, p. 7.

73 Richard of Devizes, 1963, pp. 59–60.

74 The mediatory role of queens' intercession is often viewed as a female one 'softening' male authority: 'Queenly intercession was part of the masculine-feminine division of labor … intercession was seen as feminine pleading that made it possible for the king to change his mind' (Earenfight, 2013, p. 12).

75 Cited in Turner, 2009, p. 269.

76 Martindale, 1992, pp. 17–50.

77 Martindale, 1992, p. 50.

78 Earenfight, 2013, p. 137.

79 Earenfight, 2013, p. 139.

80 Earenfight, 2013, p. 3.

81 Earenfight, 2009; Shadis, 2009; Bianchini, 2012.

82 Chibnall, 1991.

83 For a good discussion of Eleanor in this context, see DeAragon, 2002, pp. 97–114; Huneycutt, 2002, pp. 115–32.

84 Earenfight, 2013, p. 132.

85 Huneycutt, 2003.

86 Tanner, 2002, pp. 133–58; Earenfight, 2013, pp. 133–4.

87 Orderic Vitalis, 1969–80, vi, pp. 212–15.

88 Stuard, 1987a, pp. 72–3.

89 LoPrete, 1999, p. 7.

90 LoPrete, 1999, p. 19

91 LoPrete, 1999, pp. 25–6.

92 Parsons, 1997, pp. 26–8.

93 Earenfight, 2013, pp. 123–5.

94 Damon, 2004, p. 50.

95 Kelly, p. 14.

96   McCash, 1996, p. 6.

97   LoPrete, 1999, p. 15.

98   van Houts, 2006, p. 104.

99   Richard of Devizes, 1963, p. 59; Parsons, 2002, p. 296, n. 72.

100   Map, 1983, pp. v–vi. The exact meaning of his claim has been disputed; given that forms of northern French were spoken by the rulers of England, southern Italy and Outremer, it may simply mean that he spoke different dialects of the *langue d'oïl.*

101   Paterson, 1993, p. 222.

102   Paterson, 1993, p. 257.

103   Earenfight, 2013, p. 128.

104   Paterson, 1993, p. 244; Vincent, 2006, p. 24; Turner, 2009, pp. 113–14.

Chapter 1

1   Earenfight, 2013, p. 27.

2   Earenfight, 2013, p. 3.

3   Gibbons, 1996, p. 57.

4   Gibbons, 1996, p. 72.

5   Earenfight, 2013, pp. 7, 23.

6   Earenfight, 2013, p. 22

7   Flori, 2004, pp. 305–6.

8   Aurell, 2007, pp. 139–40.

9   William of Tyre, 1943, ii, p. 180, n. 53.

10   Duby, 1995, p. 32; 'sinon sexuel, du moins politique'.

11   Bull and Léglu, 2005, p. 5.

12   William of Tyre, 1943, ii, p. 180, n. 53.

13   Barber, 2005, p. 26.

14   Aurell, 2007, p. 78. Map, 1983, p. xv. Gerald of Wales, 1978, p. 12.

15   Parsons, 2002, p. 271.

16   Becket, 2000–1, i, pp. 216–7.

17   Becket, 2000–1, i, p. 216, n. 9.

18   Vincent, 2006, p. 48; Hivergneaux, 2006, p. 66.

19   Map, 1983, p. xxxi.

20   Map, 1983, p. xxxvi.

21   Map, 1983, p. 453.

22   Map, 1983, pp. 474–7.

23   Gerald of Wales, 1861–91, viii, pp. 288–301; Flori, 2007, p. 217.

24   Richard of Devizes, 1963, p. 3.

25   Gerald of Wales, 1978, pp. 198–99; Gerald of Wales, 1861–91, viii, p. 300.

26 Aurell, 2007, p. 239.
27 John of Salisbury, 1986, p. xiii.
28 John of Salisbury, 1986, p. xxviii.
29 John of Salisbury, 1986, pp. 52–3.
30 Reichersberg, 1858, p. 34.
31 Flori, 2007, p. 231.
32 William of Tyre, 1943, pp. 180–1.
33 Flori, 2007, p. 230.
34 Kelly, 1950, p. 20; Meade, 1977, p. 78.
35 William of Newburgh, 1988–2007, i, p. 128.
36 William of Newburgh, 1988–2007, i, p. 93.
37 William of Newburgh, 1988–2007, i, p. 97.
38 Richard of Devizes, 1963, p. xv.
39 Richard of Devizes, 1963, pp. 25–6.
40 Gervase of Canterbury, 1879–80, i, p. 149.
41 Cited in Sassier, 1991, p. 231.
42 Bouchard, 2002, pp. 230–1.
43 William of Newburgh, 1988–2007, ii, pp. 128–31, 281.
44 Cited in Flori, 2007, p. 61.
45 Turner, 2009, p. 89; Flori, 2007, pp. 297–8.
46 Turner, 2009, p. 104.
47 Aurell and Armengaud, 2004, p. 21.
48 McCracken, 2002, p. 255.
49 Archibald, 2001, p. 223.
50 William of Tyre, 1943, ii, pp. 180–1.
51 Flori, 2007, p. 211.
52 John of Salisbury, 1986, pp. 52–3.
53 John of Salisbury, 1986, pp. 61–2.
54 William of Newburgh, 1988–2007, pp. 128–9.
55 Gervase of Canterbury, 1879–80, i, p. 242. English translation from Flori, 2007, p. 109.
56 Bullough, 1996, pp. 223–42.
57 Bullough, 1996, p. 225.
58 Flori, 2007, p. 109.
59 Flori, 2007, p. 149.
60 Friedman, 2000, pp. 10–15.
61 Friedman, 2000, pp. 94–107.
62 William of Tyre, 1943, i, p. 362.
63 Cited in Coss, 1998, p. 31.
64 Henry of Huntingdon, 1996, p. 81.
65 Power, 2005, pp. 115–35.

66   Power, 2005, p. 126.

67   Power, 2005, p. 129.

68   Gerald of Wales, 1861–91, viii, pp. 301, 309.

69   Power, 2005, pp. 129–33; Chapman, 1955, pp. 393–4.

70   Ménestral de Reims, 1990, p. 1.

71   Ménestral de Reims, 1990, pp. 12–13

72   Ménestral de Reims, 1990, p. 12.

73   Ménestral de Reims, 1990, p. 3.

74   Ménestral de Reims, 1990, p. 12.

75   Ménestral de Reims, 1990, p. 12.

76   Ménestral de Reims, 1990, p. 13.

77   Turner, 2009, p. 302.

78   Paris, 1866–9, i, p. 289.

79   Parsons, 2002, p. 281.

80   Turner, 2009, p. 311.

81   Flori, 2006, pp. 404–5.

82   Williams, 1995, p. 27.

83   Michelet, 1833–42, ii, p. 380; 'La veritable Mellusine, melée de natures contradictoires, mère et fille d'une generation diabolique, c'est Eléonore de Guyenne'.

84   For example, in Oldenbourg, 1992.

85   Ventadorn, 1999, pp. 280–9.

86   Ventadorn, 1999, pp. 214–5.

87   Ventadorn, 1999, p. 30.

88   Ventadorn, 1999, p. 13.

89   Flori, 2007, p. 223.

90   Verger, 2004, p. 138.

91   Gerald of Wales, 1861–91, viii, p. 163.

92   Howden, 1867, ii, pp. 231–2.

93   Chambers, 1941, p. 463.

94   Higden, 1865–6, viii, pp. 53–5; Chambers, 1941, p. 463.

95   Chambers, 1941, p. 464; Owen, 1993, p. 117.

96   Tudor, 2005, p. 370.

97   Chambers, 1941, p. 464; Owen, 1993, pp. 118–9.

98   Chambers, 1941, p. 464; Owen, 1993, pp. 121–4, 156–60.

99   Holinshed, 1577, iv, p. 472.

100 Hammond, 2006, p. 610.

101 Howell, 2001, p. 196.

102 Mayor, 2000, pp. 575–6.

103 Mayor, 2000, p. 575.

104 Ashliman, 1998–2013; Aarne and Thompson, 1961, pp. 245–6.

105 Chapman, 1995, p. 394; Owen, 1993, pp. 156–61; Carney, 1984, pp. 167–70.

106 Carney, 1984, p. 167.

107 Mulally, 2002, pp. 237–45.

108 Carney, 1984, pp. 167–8.

109 Barber, 1990, p. 18.

110 Le Fur, 2004, p. 205.

111 Bouchet, 1535. The reference to the kings of Naples in the title may refer not just generally to the French kings' claim to the throne, but specifically to the La Trémoille family who were Bouchet's patrons (Le Fur, 2004, p. 206), who had recently acquired a claim to the throne by marriage.

112 Turner, 2009, p. 303.

113 Le Fur, 2004, p. 206; 'rétablir un souvenir plus honorable de son ancienne duchesse'.

114 Bouchet, 1535, p. 5.

115 William of Tyre, 1943, ii, p. 180.

116 For example, Turner, 2009, p. 106.

117 Le Fur, 2004, p. 206.

118 Besly, 1647.

119 Archives de la Vendée, n.d.

120 Omont, 1882, pp. 379–80.

121 Besly, 1647, pp. 477–95.

122 Besly, 1647, p. 143.

123 Besly, 1647, pp. 144–5; 'les impostures qui ont esté inventées & escrites sure ce divorce au prejudice de cette illustre Princesse...'

124 Besly, 1647, p. 145.

125 de Larrey, 1788; Turner, 2009, pp. 303–4.

126 de Larrey, 1788, pp. iv–v; 'Les faiseurs de romans ont ajoutés aux relations des historiens qui ne lui sont avantageuses, des fictions qui le sont encore moins ... Il y a du plaisir à protéger l'innocence opprimée...'

127 de Larrey, 1788, p. 71.

128 de Larrey, 1788, p. 59.

129 de Larrey, 1788, p. 59; 'Les femmes elles-mêmes ne voulant pas s'exempter de cette milice sacrée, formerent des escadrons, renouvellant l'histoire des Amazônes: & la reine Eléonore à leur exemple voulut aussi être du voyage; soit qu'elle crût trouver plus de divertissement...'

130 Choniates, 1984, p. 35; Choniates, 1975, ii, p. 60. The appellation 'Chrysópous' is mysterious. In light of it being applied to a mounted person, it may be relevant that George Akropolites (1217–82) gives this as a name for Manuel Laskaris's horse. Akropolites, 2007, p. 301.

131 Runciman, 1951–4, ii, p. 262, n. 4. Niketas's contemporary John Kinnamos used *Germanoi* to mean French, but *Alemanoi* to mean Germans.

132   Runciman, 1951–4, p. 376, n. 153.

133   Runciman, 1951–4, ii, p. 262, n. 1.

134   Choniates, 1975, ii, p. 87.

135   Kelly, 1950, p. 35.

136   Kelly, 1950, p. 38.

137   Owen, 1993, p. 149.

138   Weir, 1999, p. 51.

139   Flori, 2004, p. 65.

140   Flori, 2007, p. 45; 'a excité l'imagination de plusieurs historiens, qui les relient un peu trop rapidement aux jugements des chroniqueurs imputant l'échec de la deuxième croisade à la présence de trop nombreuses femmes au sein des armées chrétiennes'. Flori, 2004, p. 66.

141   Flori, 2007, p. 45; 'Au XXᵉ siècle encore, certains auteurs accréditent cette version romancée'. Flori, 2004, p. 66.

142   Flori, 2007, pp. 43–4; 'la reine à laquelle il [Niketas] fait allusion semble bien être Aliénor, dont la présence ne passait évidement pas inaperçue'. Flori, 2004, pp. 65–6.

143   Chambers, 1941, 460.

144   Strickland and Strickland, 1840–7, i, p. 313.

145   Strickland and Strickland, 1840–7, i, p. 313.

146   Cited in Owen, 1993, p. 150.

147   *Itinerarium Peregrinorum*, 1997, p. 48.

148   de Larrey, p. 59.

149   François A. Gervaise, cited in Kelly, 1950, p. 35.

150   Walker, 1949–50, pp. 857–61.

151   Walter of Coventry, 1873, ii, p. xxix, n. 1; Walker, 1949–50, p. 857.

152   Strickland, 1840–7, i, p. 314.

153   Walker, 1949–50, p. 857, n. 1.

154   Walker, 1949–50, pp. 859–60.

Chapter 2

1   Abernethy, 2013.

2   Sigu, 2013, pp. 1–2; 'l'indifférence dédaigneuse des philosophes'.

3   Hanawalt, 1987, p. 3.

4   Cited in Hanawalt, 1987, p. 3.

5   Keralio Robert, 1791.

6   Parsons, 2002, pp. 265–300.

7 Stuard, 1987a, pp. 64–5.

8 Keralio Robert, 1791, p. vii; 'semblable à l'une des maîtresses de Jupiter, une reine est jalouse de lancer elle-même la foudre, au risque d'en être consumée la première… Une femme qui peut tout et capable de tout; une femme, devenue reine, change de sexe, se croit tout permis, et ne doute de rien…'

9 Keralio Robert, 1791, p. 85.

10 Keralio Robert, 1791, p. 90.

11 Keralio Robert, 1791, pp. 91–2.

12 Keralio Robert, 1791, p. 94:

> Lorsque les Iles Britanniques parviendront comme nous à la liberté, lorsqu'elles reconnoîtront, comme nous, qu'il n'exista jamais de rois dans les pays libres, lorsqu'ils voudront connoître les crimes des leurs têtes couronnées, Eléonor de Guyenne figurera dans le tableau, et seule, entre toutes les princesses de France, elle aura rempli la fatale destinée de porter chez deux nations le flambeau de la discord, la germe des guerres intestines, et de fomenter avec soin un long et opiniâtre combat entre le pays qu'elle quittoit, et celui où elle venoit s'introduire.

13 Stuard, 1987a, p. 66.

14 Earenfight, 2013, p. 4.

15 Stuard, 1987a, p. 67.

16 Stuard, 1987a, p. 63.

17 Earenfight, 2013, p. 2.

18 Hutton, 1999, p. 138.

19 Rejai and Enloe, 1969, p. 146.

20 Gildea, 1994, p. 35.

21 Michelet, 1864, p. 22.

22 Michelet, 1864, pp. 23–4, 26.

23 Michelet, 1864, p. 27.

24 Michelet, 1864, p. 63.

25 Michelet, 1864, p. 65.

26 Michelet, 1833–42, ii, p. 309; 'Il y a dans cette pale et mediocre figure une force immense qui doit se developer. C'est le roi de l'église et de la bourgeoisie, le roi du peuple et de la loi… La personnalité est faible en lui; c'est moins un homme qu'une idée; être impersonnel, il vit dans l'universalité, dans le peuple, dans l'église, fille du peuple…'

27 Michelet, 1833–42, ii, p. 319.

28 Michelet, 1833–42, ii, pp. 301–2:

> La femme régna dans le ciel, elle régna sur la terre… Bertrade de Monfort gouverne à la fois son premier époux Foulques d'Anjou, et le second Philippe Ier, roi de France… Louis VII date ses actes du couronnement de sa femme Adèle. Les femmes, juges naturels des combats de poésie et des cours d'amour, siégent aussi comme juges, à l'égal de leurs maris, dans les affaires sérieuses.

29 Michelet, 1833–42, ii, p. 302; 'la rapide extinction des mâles, l'adoucissement des moeurs et le progres de l'équité, rouvrent les heritages aux femmes'.

30 Michelet, 1833–42, ii, p. 380.

31 Guizot, 1882, i, p. 171.

32 Cited in Stuard, 1987a, pp. 63–4. Heta Aali directed me to the frequent use of *vindictive* as a descriptor for Merovingian queens in nineteenth-century French historiography.

33 Hutton, 1999, p. 138.

34 Orr, 1976, p. 95.

35 Orr, 1976, p. 139.

36 Orr, 1976, p. 139.

37 Michelet, 1939, pp. 108, 143.

38 Michelet, 1939, p. 108.

39 Earenfight, 2013, p. 4.

40 Aali, 2012.

41 Prus, 1846.

42 Prus, 1852, p. 1.

43 Prus, 1846, ii, pp. 188–90.

44 Prus, 1846, ii, pp. 186, 189–90.

45 Prus, 1846, ii, p. 197.

46 Strickland, 1840–7.

47 Strickland, 1840–7, i, p. 378.

48 Delorme, 1988, pp. 45–50.

49 Strickland, 1840–7, i, p. 378.

50 Strickland, 1840–7, i, p. 313. For myths about Eleanor on crusade, see Chambers, 1941, pp. 459–68.

51 Strickland, 1840–7, i, pp. 316–17.

52 Delorme, 1988, p. 49.

53 Delorme, 1988, p. 45.

54 Delorme, 1988, p. 46.

55 Geary, 2003, p. 15.

56 Geary, 2003, discusses the supposed early-medieval origins of European nations, but the twelfth century was an equally fertile time period to be mined for medieval forebears.

57 Aurell, 2007, pp. 1–4.

58 Aurell, 2007, p. 263.

59 Michelet, 1833–42, ii, p. 320; 'Voilà le midi de la France encore une fois isolé du nord. Une femme va porter à qui elle voudra le prépondérance de l'Occident'.

60 Aurell, 2007, p. 8

61 Michelet, 1833–42, ii, p.122; 'Le génie parisien est la forme la plus complexe à la fois et la plus haute de la France'.

62 Michelet, 1833–42, ii, p. 26.

63 Gras, 1975, p. 104.

64 Michelet, 1833–42, ii, p. 128.

65 Michelet, 1833–42, ii, p. 52.

66 Michelet, 1833–42, ii, p. 127.

67 Michelet, 1833–42, ii, pp. 378–9; 'La jalouse Eléonore, passionée et vindictive comme une femme du Midi...'

68 Michelet, 1833–42, ii, pp. 27–8; 'Le Poitou est la bataille du midi et du nord... le Poitou est lui-même comme sa Mellusine, assemblage de natures diverses, moitié femme et moitié serpent'.

69 Michelet, 1833–42, ii, p. 377.

70 Richard, 1903.

71 Brunel, 1914, p. 449.

72 Richard, 1903, ii, pp. 107, 110.

73 Richard, 1903, ii, pp. 78–94.

74 Richard, 1903, ii, p. 91.

> Le voyage jusqu'à Constantinople ne fut qu'une partie de plaisir, pendant laquelle Aliénor, soustraite à la surveillance jalouse de son mari et à l'oeil vigilante de Suger, entourée de dames de l'Aquitaine qui initiaient aux mystères du jeu de la galanterie avec les troubadours et aux débats des cours d'amour, sentit revivre en elle le sang de Maubergeonne et de Guillaume VII.

75 Richard, 1903, ii, pp. 93–4;

76 Richard, 1903, ii, p. 110; 'Elle voulait être dominée, et comme le dit crûment le peuple, elle était de celles-là qui aiment à être battues'.

77 Chaban-Delmas, 1987, p. 192.

78 Chaban-Delmas, 1987, p. 192; 'Devenue française par son mariage (n'était-ce pas plutôt franque?) elle avait cessé de l'être par son divorce. Devenue anglaise (n'était-ce pas plutôt anglo-normande?) par son remariage, elle s'est conduite en reine comme elle l'avait fait aux côtés de Louis VII mais sans jamais ... cesser de sentir et de se comporter d'abord en fille et maîtresse d'Aquitaine'.

79 Chaban-Delmas, 1987, p. 182; 'pour Aliénor, sauvegarder l'héritage de ses pères ... pour Charles de Gaulle, libérer la Patrie, puis elever la France et sauver la République ...' Born Jacques Delmas, Chaban was the author's Resistance *nom de guerre*, and he took the name Chaban-Delmas after the war.

80 Chaban-Delmas, 1987, p. 23.

81 Chaban-Delmas, 1987, p, 197.

82 Chaban-Delmas, 1987, p. 193.

83 Aurell, 2007, p. 10.

84 Cited in Gillingham, 2001, pp. 2–3.

85 Norgate, 1887, ii, p. 491; Gillingham, 2001, p. 2.

86 Norgate, 1887, i, p. 457.

87 Norgate, 1887, i, pp. 491–2.

88 Stubbs, 1903, i, pp. 482–533.

89 Stubbs, 1903, i, pp. 486, 556.

90 Stubbs, 1903, i, p. 604.

91 Stubbs, 1903, i, p. 686.

92 Stubbs, 1903, i, pp. 514–15.

93 Cited in Meade, 1977, p. vii.

94 Joliffe, 1955, p. 308.

95 Vincent, 2004, p. 59.

96 Weir is also influenced by Pernoud, for example, in an (unsourced) claim that Louis VII expelled the troubadour Marcabru from his court out of jealousy. Weir, 1999, p. 48.

97 Kelly, 1927, p. 32.

98 Kelly, 1927, p. 33.

99 Kelly, 1927, pp. 3–4.

100 Turner, 2009, p. 312.

101 Kelly, 1950, p. 38.

102 Kelly, 1950, p. 20.

103 Weir, 1999, pp. 35–6.

104 Meade, 1977, p. 78.

105 Wheeler and Parsons, 2002, p. xvi.

106 Flori, 2004, pp. 337–83.

107 Kelly, 1937, pp. 3–19.

108 Kelly, 1937, p. 8.

109 Kelly, 1937, pp. 5–10, 15–17. A similar reconstruction can be found in Kelly, 1950, pp. 165–7.

110 Kelly, 1937, pp. 4–5. These incorrect dates are those given by Kelly.

111 Kelly, 1937, p. 12.

112 Diez, 1842.

113 Moore, 1978, p. 148.

114 McCash, 1979, p. 698, n. 2.

115 Meade, 1977, p. x.

116 Meade, 1979; 1983; 1989; 1973.

117 Wheeler and Parsons, 2002, p. xvii.

118 Meade, 1977, p. xi.

119 Meade, 1977, p. ix.

120 Meade, 1977, p. 26. Or five years old, if we accept the dating of Eleanor's birth to 1124. See Flori, 2004, p. 31.

121 Meade, 1977, p. 437, n. 24, 34, 35.

122 Meade, 1977, p. 62.

123　Meade, 1977, pp. 44–6.

124　Meade, 1977, pp. 88–9.

125　Meade, 1977, pp. 99–100, 105.

126　Meade, 1977, pp. 27, 34–5.

127　Pernoud, 1965. Quotations in the text are from Wiles's English translation (Pernoud, 1968), to which the page citations refer.

128　Pernoud, 1980.

129　Pernoud, 1968, p. 272.

130　Pernoud, 1949; Pernoud, 1966.

131　Pernoud, 1949, p. 31.

132　Pernoud, 1968, p. 11.

133　Pernoud, 1968, p. 12.

134　Pernoud, 1968, p. 271; Stuard, 1987a, p. 74.

135　Pernoud, 1968, p. 13.

136　Pernoud, 1968, p. 32.

137　Aurell and Armengaud, 2004, p. 22.

138　Pernoud, 1968, p. 12.

139　Pernoud, 1968, p. 33.

140　Pernoud, 1968, p. 36.

141　Pernoud, 1968, p. 50.

142　Pernoud, 1968, p. 90.

143　Pernoud, 1968, p. 11.

144　Pernoud, 1968, p. 20.

145　Pernoud, 1968, p. 41.

146　Pernoud, 1968, p. 73.

147　Pernoud, 1968, p. 109.

148　Pernoud, 1968, pp. 112–3.

149　Earenfight, 2013, p. 4.

150　Markale, 2009.

151　Markale, 1979.

152　Flori, 2004.

153　Markale, 2007.

154　Guyonvarc'h, 1978, p. 39; 'M. Jean Bertrand, dit Jean Markale, se fait parfois passer pour professeur de lettres classiques. Il ne dit jamais où il enseigne … il ne sait pas accentuer le grec, ignore tout du latin … il ne sait pas combien de cas comporte la déclinaison irlandaise (tantôt deux, tantôt trois) … Tout cela est, au mieux, une plaisanterie'.

155　Brundage, 2002, pp. 218, 221 n. 35.

156　Markale, 2007, p. 138.

157　Markale, 2007, p. 3.

158 Markale, 2007, p. 5.

159 Pappano, 2004, pp. 151–5; Pappano, 2002, pp. 337–68.

160 Flori, 2004.

161 Martindale, 2002, p. 436, n. 12.

162 Markale, 2007, p. 215.

163 Markale, 1997; English translation, Markale, 1999.

164 Trudeau, 2008.

165 Labande, 2005.

166 Duby, 1997, p. 6; 'je connais même des historiens très sérieux dont elle continue d'enflammer l'imagination et de la dévoyer'. Duby, 1995, p. 15.

167 Aurell, 2000, pp. 45–6.

168 Cited in Aurell, 2007, p. 286, n. 72.

169 Cited in Aurell, 2007, p. 286, n. 72.

Chapter 3

1   Boyd, 2004.

2   Turner, 2009, p. 13. On traditions of a Poitevin birthplace for Eleanor, see Boureau et al., 2004, p. 129.

3   Vincent, 2006, p. 51.

4   Hivergneaux, 2006, p. 73; 'un Poitou élargi à l'Aunis et à la Saintonge…'

5   Turner, 2009, p. 11.

6   Hivergneaux, 2006, pp. 71–2.

7   Gillingham, 2005, pp. 57–81.

8   Aurell, 2007, p. 191.

9   Paterson, 1993, pp. 7–8.

10 Turner, 2009, p. 113.

11 Paterson, 1993, p. 244.

12 Vincent, 2006, p. 24.

13 Weir, 1999, p. 34.

14 Flori, 2004, p. 34.

15 Bull and Léglu, 2005, p. 3.

16 Cerquiglini-Toulet, 2011, p. 9.

17 Truong, 2003, 63.

18 Vincent, 2006, p. 44.

19 Swabey, 2004; Markale, 1979.

20 See, for example, the recording by Sinfonye, 1993. As an example of internet veneration of Eleanor as patroness of the troubadours, see Amendola, 2013: 'Eleanor of Aquitaine saw something in her world that needed improvement and

she decided to make it better. She had a dream and the Troubadours shared it with her. Together they created a new blueprint for society through poetry and song, with matters of the heart at its core.'

21 Brown, 2002, p. 2.
22 Moore, 1979, p. 621.
23 Moore, 1979, pp. 622–3.
24 Moore, 1979, p. 624.
25 Turner, 2009, p. 199.
26 Diez, 1842.
27 Moore, 1979, pp. 621–2, 625–6.
28 Moore, 1979, p. 624.
29 Moore, 1979, pp. 626–8.
30 Benton, 1961, p. 589. McCash, 1979, pp. 698–711, offers a more moderate position, arguing that we cannot discount the possibility of a literary connection between Eleanor and Marie, but accepts that there is no firm evidence linking them in Marie's adult lifetime.
31 Moore, 1979, p. 631.
32 Benton, 1962, pp. 471–8.
33 O'Callaghan, 2002, p. 301.
34 Lejeune, 1954, pp. 5–57.
35 Moulinier-Brogi, 2004, p. 146; 'Après son mariage avec Louis VII, elle aurait tenté de s'entourer de gens parlant sa langue maternelle, la langue d'oc, et essayer de recréer, dans la morose cour parisienne, quelque chose lui rappelant le cour d'Aquitaine'.
36 Duby, 1995, p. 16.
37 Pappano, 2004, pp. 151–5; Pappano, 2002, pp. 337–67.
38 Pappano, 2004, p. 151. Pappano wrongly dates Eleanor's escape from Henry while dressed in men's clothes to 1158 (*recte* 1174).
39 Milland-Bove, 2004, p. 158.
40 Milland-Bove, 2004, p. 158.
41 Moulinier-Brogi, 2004, p. 146.
42 O'Callaghan, 2002, p. 304.
43 O'Callaghan, 2002, p. 303.
44 Milland-Bove, 2004, pp. 160–1; Aurell, 2007, p. 139.
45 O'Callaghan, 2002, pp. 301–17.
46 Owen, 1993, p. 148.
47 Aurell, 2007, p. 139.
48 Moulinier-Brogi, 2004, p. 145.
49 Cited in Aurell, 2007, p. 95.
50 Milland-Bove, 2004, p. 158.
51 Harvey, 2005, p. 101.

52 Harvey, 2005, p. 102.
53 Harvey, 2005, p. 104.
54 Harvey, 2005, pp. 104, 109–10.
55 Harvey, 2005, pp. 108–9.
56 Harvey, 2005, pp. 110–11.
57 Cited by Paden, 2005, pp. 162–3.
58 Harvey, 2005, pp. 105–7.
59 Paterson, 1993, p. 328.
60 Volk, 2004, pp. 195–203.
61 Volk, 2004, p. 195.
62 Volk, 2004, p. 202.
63 Hasty, 2000, pp. 142–3.
64 Waddell, 1927, p. 237; 'Were diu werlt alle min/von dem mere unze an den Rin,/des wolt ih mih darben/daz diu chunegin von Engellant/lege an minen armen'.
65 Dronke, 1996, p. 83.
66 Parsons, 2002, p. 279.
67 Bernart de Ventadorn, 1999, pp. 29, 214–5.
68 Turner, 2009, p. 196.
69 Flori, 2004, p. 111.
70 Vincent, 2004, pp. 58–63.
71 Vincent, 2006, p. 29.
72 Hivergneaux, 2000, p. 66; 'il apparaît assez clairement que le pouvoir d'Aliénor s'appuie sur les même bases, essentiellement poitevines, que celui de ses prédécesseurs...'
73 Hivergneaux, 2000, pp. 66–7.
74 Hivergneaux, 2000, pp. 71–2.
75 Vincent, 2004, p. 60.
76 Vincent, 2004, p. 62.
77 Hivergneaux, 2000, pp. 81–2.
78 Hivergneaux, 2000, p. 82; 'l'implantation la plus probante du pouvoir ducal demeure toujours circonscrite à ces regions'.
79 Hivergneaux, 2000, p. 82.
80 Vincent, 2000, pp. 109–10.
81 Hivergneaux, 2000, p. 82.
82 Aurell, 2007, p. 195. Charter of Alphonse of Poitiers (1227) confirming Eleanor's granting of privileges, cited in Besly, 1647, pp. 499–501.
83 Hivergneaux, 2000, p. 83.
84 Aurell, 2007, p. 191.
85 Gillingham, 2001, p. 4.
86 Vincent, 2000, pp. 103–35.
87 Vincent, 2000, pp. 111, 109.

88   Vincent, 2000, pp. 109–10.

89   Vincent, 2000, p. 114.

90   Meade, 1977, p. 4.

91   Paterson, 1993, p. 222.

92   Cited in Pappano, 2002, pp. 342–3.

93   Paterson, 1993, p. 344.

94   Duby, 1995, p. 30.

95   Gildea, 1994, p. 208.

96   Gildea, 1994, p. 211.

97   Gildea, 1994, p. 208.

98   Paterson, p. 3.

99   Gildea, 1994, pp. 208–9.

100   Gildea, 1994, p. 180.

101   Gildea, 1994, p. 209.

102   Gildea, 1994, p. 210.

103   Abley, 2003, pp. 135–41.

104   Abley, 2003, p. 143.

105   Aragon, 1946, pp. 241–3.

106   Pernoud, 1965, p. 5; 'À André Chamson, qui sait encore parler dans la langue d'Aliénor, cette évocation de la Reine des Troubadours'. Chamson (1900–83) was a novelist and essayist from the Cévennes, and member of the Académie Française.

107   Pernoud, 1965, p. 20;

> Louis, comme les chevaliers qui l'entouraient, se sentait un peu déconcerté par l'entourage; l'exubérance de la foule, plus hardie, plus court-vêtue que celle qui peuplait le domaine de l'Ile-de-France ou de Champagne, le parler de langue d'oc qu'ils comprenaient mal, les manières plus bruyantes, les exclamations plus chaleureuses – tout cela les laissait un peu interdits, et ce n'est que lentement, au cours du banquet, dans l'atmosphère de joie générale, que se comblait la distance entre gens du Nord et gens du Midi.

108   Collège Aliénor d'Aquitaine, Salles (Gironde); Collège Aliénor d'Aquitaine, Bordeaux (Gironde); Collège Aliénor d'Aquitaine, Matignas-sur-Jalle (Gironde); Collège Aliénor d'Aquitaine, Castillon-la-Bataille (Gironde); Collège mixte Aliénor d'Aquitaine, Bordeaux (Gironde); École primaire publique Aliénor d'Aquitaine, Cadaujac (Gironde).

109   Le Lycée Aliénor-d'Aquitaine.

110   Collège Aliénor d'Aquitaine.

111   Collège Aliénor d'Aquitaine Château d'Oléron.

112   École maternelle Aliénor d'Aquitaine, Labenne (Landes).

113 Loge Maçonnique Aliénor d'Aquitaine, n.d.; 'Aliénor et son père ont fait de La Rochelle une ville **libre** pour des Hommes **libres**. Il est normal qu'une Loge rochelaise **libre** prenne pour titre distinctif le nom de cette Dame'.

114 Hivergneaux, 2002, p. 58.

115 Aliénor d'Aquitaine ou a l'entrada del tems clar, 2009.

116 Garrouty, 2008; 'les Britanniques ne s'établissent pas seulement dans la petite Aquitaine d'aujourd'hui, mais à travers la grande "Guienne" qu'ils occupaient jadis. l'Aquitaine d'Aliénor. Ils sont 8000 en Poitou-Charentes, 6000 en Midi-Pyrénées, et 4000 en Languedoc-Roussillon'.

117 Baldit, 2012.

118 La Ligue du Midi, 2012a.

119 La Ligue du Midi, 2012b.

120 Paterson, 1993, p. 333.

121 The title derives from the sum of the official numbers of the *départements* which make up the region.

122 Labande, 2005; it was originally published in the *Bulletin de la Société des Antiquaires de l'Ouest* in 1952.

123 Chauou, 2005.

124 The Eleanor of Aquitaine Tour, n.d.

125 Aliénor d'Aquitaine, 2006.

126 Guillaume, 1994, p. 99; '[L]'Aquitaine n'est pas la seule région française à être un construit administratif et planificateur, sans justification culturel possible … Aliénor, dite d'Aquitaine, était beaucoup plus poitevine que bordelaise…'

127 Taliano-des Garets, 1991, pp. 44–55.

128 Chaban-Delmas, 1987.

129 Chaban-Delmas, 1987, p. 22.

130 Chaban-Delmas, 1987, p. 23.

131 Aliénor. Autoroute de Gascogne, n.d.; Darrioumerle, n.d.

132 La Bataille de Castillon, n.d.

Chapter 4

1 Furnivall and Munro, 1913.

2 Bale, 1969.

3 On the dating and sources of the two plays see, for example, Shakespeare, 1954, pp. xi–xxxiii; Shakespeare, 1989, pp. 2–19; Thomas, 1986, 98–100.

4 Waith, 1978, pp. 192–211.

5 Shakespeare, 1989, pp. 59–60.

6 Shakespeare, 1989, p. 38.

7   *King John*, IV. ii, lines 119–23; Shakespeare, 1954, p. xxxi.

8   Shakespeare, 1989, p. 61.

9   *King John*, II. i, lines 124–31.

10 *King John*, II. i, lines 168–70.

11 *King John*, II. i, lines 179–82.

12 *King John*, II. i, lines 195.

13 *King John*, III. i, line 43; pp. 48–51; Shakespeare, 1989, p. 43.

14 *King John*, II. i, line 63.

15 *King John*, I. i, line 150.

16 Shakespeare, 1989, p. 64.

17 Furnivall and Munro, 1913, i, pp. 6–7.

18 *King John*, I. i, line 4.

19 Furnivall and Munro, 1913, i, pp. 55–7.

20 Furnivall and Munro, 1913, ii, p. 101.

21 Furnivall and Munro, 1913, ii, pp. 115–6.

22 Furnivall and Munro, 1913, i, pp. 304–5.

23 Knight, 2003, pp. 53–8.

24 Robin and Marion originated in pastoral poetry and became figures in the May Games. Robin Hood ballads have a longer and possibly independent tradition, dating back at least to the 'rymes of Robyn Hood' alluded to by William Langland in the 1370s. Knight, 2003, pp. 1–43.

25 Knight, 2003, pp. 45–6.

26 Knight, 2003, p. 59.

27 Knight, 2003, pp. 53–4.

28 Knight, 2003, p. 60.

29 Knight, 2003, pp. 60–1.

30 Knight, 2003, pp. 79–82.

31 Knight, 2003, p. 83.

32 Knight, 2003, pp. 84–5, 87–9. Waith, pp. 192–211.

33 Holinshed, 1587, vi, p. 158.

34 Holinshed, 1587, v, p. 472.

35 Stoudemire, 1931, p. 858; Carney, 1984, pp. 167–8.

36 Addison, 1707; Stoudemire, 1931, p. 858.

37 Addison, 1707, pp. 3–4.

38 Addison, 1707, p. 4.

39 Addison, 1707, p. 10.

40 Addison, 1707, p. 33.

41 Addison, 1707, pp. 35–6.

42 Addison, 1707, p. 22.

43 Hammond, 2006, pp. 601–3.

44 Hammond, 2006, p. 604.

45 Hammond, 2006, pp. 606–8.

46 Hammond, 2006, p. 621.

47 Hammond, 2006, p. 617.

48 Hammond, 2006, p. 622.

49 Hull, 1774.

50 Stoudemire, 1931, p. 859.

51 Hull, 1774, p. i.

52 Kahan, 2004, p. 309.

53 Kahan, 2004, p. 311.

54 Hull, 1774, pp. 4–5.

55 Hull, 1774, p. 6.

56 Hull, 1774, p. 6.

57 Kahan, 2004, pp. 310–11.

58 Bonnechose, 1826; Stoudemire, 1931, p. 859.

59 Weatherson, 1988, pp. 107–8.

60 Weatherson, 1988, p. 108.

61 Bonnechose, 1826, p. 3; 'Étranger, sans appui sous le ciel des Anglais'.

62 Weatherson, 1988, p. 108.

63 Weatherson, 1988, p. 112.

64 Bonnechose, 1826, pp. 97–105; Weatherson, 1988, p. 114.

65 Stroudemire, 1931, p. 859.

66 Romani, 1840.

67 Ashbrook, 1987, p. 624.

68 Weatherson, 1988, p. 109.

69 Tambling, 2006, p. 286. Donizetti turned to a non-medieval novel of Scott's in 1835 with *Lucia di Lammermoor*.

70 Ashbrook, 1987, p. 616.

71 Ashbrook, 1984, p. 83.

72 Ashbrook, 1984, p. 357.

73 Weinstock, 1963, p. 343

74 Turner, 2009, pp. 307–8.

75 *New York Times*, 7 February 1893.

76 Furst, 1901, p. 105.

77 Harrison, 1903, p. 864.

78 Smith, 1997, p. 80.

79 Tennyson, 1894, pp. 9–10.

80 Tennyson, 1894, p. 11.

81 Tennyson, 1894, p. 13.

82 Tennyson, 1894, p. 17.

83 Cited in Smith, 1997, pp. 80–1.

84 Tennyson, 1894, p. 18.

85   Tennyson, 1894, p. 19.
86   Tennyson, 1894, p. 135.
87   Tennyson, 1894, p. 144.
88   Tennyson, 1894, p. 84.
89   Tennyson, 1894, pp. 22, 24.
90   Tennyson, 1894, p. 76.
91   Tennyson, 1894, p. 156.
92   Tennyson, 1894, pp. 185–7; Smith, 1997, p. 87.
93   Tennyson, 1894, p. 23.
94   Tennyson, 1894, pp. 33, 143.
95   Tennyson, 1894, p. 35.
96   Tennyson, 1894, p. 43.
97   Tennyson, 1894, p. 141.
98   Tennyson, 1894, pp. 19–24.
99   Tennyson, 1894, p. 139.
100   Tennyson, 1894, p. 11.
101   Tennyson, 1894, pp. 105, 107.
102   Tennyson, 1894, p. 133.
103   Tennyson, 1894, pp. 136–7.
104   Smith, 1997, p. 87.

Chapter 5

1   Wheeler and Parsons, 2002, p. xvii.
2   Ridgwell, 1923.
3   Harrison, 1952; Glenville, 1964; Harvey, 1968; Giles, 1984; Konchalovskiy, 2003.
4   Cooke et al., 1978.
5   Stock, 2009, p. 108.
6   Nash and Jeffrey, 2009, ii, p. 654.
7   Knight, 1994, p. 235.
8   Prime, 2008, p. 475.
9   Knight, 2003, p. 161.
10   Burt, 1955.
11   Curtiz, 1938.
12   Knight, 2003, p. 159.
13   Levin and Sherman, 1946.
14   Weintraub et al., 1997–9.
15   Knight, 2003, pp. 172–3.
16   Minghella and Allan, 2006–9.

17 Knight, 2003, p. 167.

18 Aberth, 2003, p. 180.

19 Scott, 2010; Reitherman, 1973.

20 Anouilh, 1995, p. xx.

21 Finke and Shichtman, 2010, p. 97.

22 Finke and Shichtman, 2010, p. 97.

23 Finke and Shichtman, 2010, pp. 98–9.

24 Anouilh, 1995, pp. 75–6, 91–2.

25 Turner, 2009, p. 3.

26 Goldman, 1966.

27 Goldman, 1966, p. iii.

28 Finke and Shichtman, 2010, p. 98.

29 Goldman, 1981, p. 11.

30 Cited in Dickens, 1971, p. 193.

31 Higham, 1975, p. 210.

32 Britton, 1995, p. 22.

33 Higham, 1975, pp. 207–8.

34 Higham, 1975, p. 4.

35 Roger of Howden, 1867, i, p. 305.

36 Finke and Shichtman, 2010, pp. 98–9. It is not always obvious which anachronisms are deliberate. Finke and Shichtman describe Henry's reference to 'a king named Lear' as 'wildly anachronistic…', even though he would have been familiar with the figure of Lear in Geoffrey of Monmouth's *History of the Kings of Britain*.

37 Harty, 1999, p. 5.

38 Finke and Shichtman, 2010, p. 99.

39 Hapogian, n.d.

40 Finke and Shichtman, 2010, p. 48.

41 Higham, 1975, pp. 208–9.

42 Sobchak, 1997, p. 5.

43 Cited in Sobchak, 1997, p. 6.

44 Ebert, 1968.

45 Tolhurst, 2004, pp. 9–13.

46 See, for example, her supportive review of a publication advocating birth control; Hepburn, 1934, pp. 762–3.

47 Britton, 1995, pp. 19–22.

48 Thumim, 1986, pp. 72–3.

49 Thumim, 1986, p. 77.

50 Britton, 1995, pp. 233–4.

51 This interpretation is emphasized more clearly in the 2003 film production of *Lion*, in which Glenn Close delivers the 'I rode bare-breasted half-way to Damascus' with wistful nostalgia in place of Hepburn's proud defiance.

52   Anouilh, 1995, p. 92.

53   Lowry, 2004.

54   Some recent examples include Houston, TX, January–February 2013; Midvale, UT; Staunton, VA, January 2013.

55   Fricker, 2011.

56   Austin, 1984; Knight, 2003, p. 170.

57   *The Devil's Crown*, n.d.; Zoe Wanamaker played the role of Berengaria of Navarre.

58   Finke and Shichtman, 2010, pp. 24–9.

59   Finke and Shichtman, 2010, p. 25.

60   Barber, 1978. Barber has written scholarly papers on Eleanor, for example Barber, 2005.

61   Orme, 1997.

62   Eleanor had earlier featured in two episodes of the ITV children television series *Ivanhoe* (Smith and Coote, 1958–9), played by Phyllis Neilsen-Terry.

63   A clip of the scene can be viewed online at http://www.youtube.com/watch?v=kwRu2QRR6CE [3 July 2012].

64   Oldenbourg, 1992.

65   Oldenbourg, 1965; Oldenbourg, 1959.

66   http://books.google.com/ngrams/graph?content=b%C3%BBcher+de+Monts%C3%A9gur&year_start=1800&year_end=2000&corpus=19&smoothing=0&share= [10 January 2013].

67   Oldenbourg, 1946.

68   Oldenbourg, 1992, p. 15.

69   'J.S.', 1960, pp. 200–1.

70   Oldenbourg, 1992, p. 22.

71   Oldenbourg, 1992, p. 25.

72   Oldenbourg, 1992, p. 19.

73   Oldenbourg, 1992, p. 32.

74   Oldenbourg, 1965, p. 646.

75   Oldenbourg, 1992, p. 14.

76   Oldenbourg, 1992, p. 15.

77   Rogero, 2006; 'Conférence spectacle animée par trois historiens-comédiens et un modérateur, sur le thème de la véritable personnalité d'Aliénor d'Aquitaine'; Aliénor Exagère, n.d.

78   http://www.youtube.com/watch?v=ChpF3tcCkVc&list=UUvQyRl2gMks7UEElLjXPwow&index=4 [5 January 2013].

79   http://www.youtube.com/watch?v=69lJI2k5YW0&NR=1&feature=endscreen [5 January 2013].

80   http://www.youtube.com/watch?v=UpMunIYxHSg&list=UUvQyRl2gMks7UEElLjXPwow [5 January 2013].

81 'L'arbre qui cache la forêt'. https://www.youtube.com/watch?v=qn6EyeO_rVg [5 January 2013].

82 'Aliénor exagère!', n.d.;

> Pour concevoir ce spectacle, nous nous servons d'abord du mouvement dramatique qui anime les livres d'historiens eux-mêmes: la plupart prétendent à l'objectivité et soupçonnent leurs collègues de se laisser emporter par leur sensibilité. Cette pluralité des analyses historiennes nous conduit aujourd'hui aux controverses au sujet de la « vraie » Aliénor. Parmi elles: Aliénor a-t-elle eu ou non les amants qu'on lui prête? Aliénor a-t-elle exercé ou non un pouvoir réel sur ses royaumes? Aliénor a-t-elle divisé ou unifié sa famille? Partant des faits historiques, nous glissons vers leur interprétation incertaine, et débouchons sur la dispute collective;
>
> Ce qui nous fascine chez elle, c'est sa position singulière d'épouse, de mère, et de femme de pouvoir. A y regarder de plus près, on s'apercevra que l'extraordinaire n'est pas tant l'action d'Aliénor en soi, mais l'action d'Aliénor dans le contexte spécifique de cette société médiévale régie par les hommes, et où la femme n'est sensée avoir qu'un rôle de second plan.

83 Aberth, for example, notes that Disney's live-action movie *The Story of Robin Hood and his Merrie Men* (1952) includes 'some historically accurate details', citing Eleanor's role as regent in Richard's absence. Aberth, 2003, p. 176.

Chapter 6

1 Lukács, 1962, p. 15.

2 Mitchell and Parsons, 2013, p. 3.

3 Stevens, 2013, pp. 20–1.

4 Stevens, 2013, p. 30.

5 'Amours d'Éléonore d'Aquitaine', 1779, pp. 61–90. A valuable overview of this and other fictional portrayals of Eleanor is provided by de Mascureau, 2004a.

6 'Amours d'Éléonore d'Aquitaine', 1779, p. 65.

7 Mayer, 1779, pp. 91–116.

8 Sigu, 2013, p. 2.

9 Sigu, 2013, pp. 3–4.

10 Wells, 1986, p. 9.

11 Sigu, 2013, pp. 5–6.

12 Sigu, 2013, pp. 9–10.

13 Sigu, 2013, p. 7.

14 '[L]a censure de son siècle & de la Postérité'. 'Amours d'Éléonore d'Aquitaine', 1779, p. 62.

15 Sigu, 2013, p. 11.

16 'jeune, belle, & vive … Elle avoit pour les plaisirs un penchant décidé.' 'Amours d'Éléonore d'Aquitaine', 1779, p. 63.

17 '*moins en reine qu'en femme prostituée*'; 'reçut des présens d'un jeune Turc, nommé Saladin.' 'Amours d'Éléonore d'Aquitaine', 1779, pp. 64–5, note.

18 'étoit doux, mais froid; sage, mais modeste; trop ennemi des plaisirs, recherchant trop les Moines…'. 'Amours d'Éléonore d'Aquitaine', 1779, p. 64.

19 'Amours d'Éléonore d'Aquitaine', 1779, p. 65.

20 Besly, 1647, p. 144.

21 'Amours d'Éléonore d'Aquitaine', 1779, pp. 79–84.

22 De Larrey, 1788, p. 139. De Larrey, who set out to defend Eleanor, does not claim that she poisoned Rosamond, but nevertheless maintains that she would have killed her had Rosamond not died first!

23 'Amours d'Éléonore d'Aquitaine', 1779, pp. 85–6.

24 'Amours d'Éléonore d'Aquitaine', 1779, pp. 87–9; 'une femme méchante'.

25 Mayer, 1779, pp. 91–116.

26 Mayer, 1779, pp. 91–3. Mayer identifies Guillaume with a different count of Ponthieu, William IV, who he points out would only have been twelve years old at the time.

27 Mayer, 1779, p. 94.

28 Mayer, 1779, pp. 98–9.

29 Mayer, 1779, pp. 93, 96.

30 Mayer, 1779, p. 99; 'La Cour de Rome exerçoit sur la Cour de France une suprématie étonnante … l'aveugle devotion avoit mis les Croisades à la mode…'

31 Mayer, 1779, pp. 101–14.

32 Mayer, 1779, p. 101.

33 Simeone, 1961, pp. 230–4.

34 Simeone, 1961, p. 230.

35 Keralio Robert, 1791; Parsons, 2002.

36 Macheco, 1823.

37 'The family tree of Guillaume de Tournemire', n.d.; 'Claude, Palamède, Louis Macheco de Premaux (1773–1848)', n.d.; Malègue, 1866, pp. 493–4.

38 Macheco, 1823, i, p. 284.

39 Macheco, 1823, i, p. i.

40 Macheco, 1823, i, pp. 9–11.

41 Macheco, 1823, i, p. 13.

42 Macheco, 1823, i, pp. 11, 32; 'Appelée au premier trône du monde, soyez à la fois la souveraine et le modèle de vos peuples; devenez par vos vertus l'orgueil de la France…'

43 Macheco, 1823, i, pp. 79–82.

44 Macheco, 1823, i, pp. 1–4.

45 Macheco, 1823, i, p. 5.

46 Macheco, 1823, i, pp. 260–96.

47 Macheco, 1823, i, p. 1; 'Toutes les passions dont l'âme d'une femme est capable, l'amour, la coquetterie, la légèreté, la jalousie, l'ambition…'

48 Macheco, 1823, i, p. 48; 'un mélange de coquetterie et de la légèreté avec des idées profondes; de la politique, avec les plus frivoles occupations…'

49 Macheco, 1823, i, p. 2; 'Il y a une grande moralité à montrer après des erreurs et des crimes, le malheur et le repentir…'

50 Strickland and Strickland, 1840–7, i, p. 378.

51 Macheco, 1823, i, p. 19.

52 Macheco, 1823, i, p. 31.

53 Macheco, 1823, i, p. 5.

54 Macheco, 1823, i, pp. 238–9, 292; 'Le caractère de la reine, jaloux et altier, rend cette histoire vraisemblable'.

55 Macheco, 1823, i, pp. 76–7.

56 Macheco, 1823, i, pp. 109–10, 263.

57 *Itinerarium Peregrinorum*, 1997, p. 120.

58 Bloss, 1853.

59 Bloss, 1853, p. 6.

60 Zinn, 1996, p. 117.

61 Lanphear, 2007, p. 8. My thanks are due to Ms Lanphear for allowing me to read her paper.

62 Lanphear, 2007, p. 1.

63 Lanphear, 2007, p. 8.

64 Bloss, 1853, p. 457.

65 Bloss, 1853, p. x.

66 Bloss, 1853, p. ix.

67 Bloss, 1853, p. 133.

68 Bloss, 1853, pp. 140–5.

69 Bloss, 1853, pp. 183–4.

70 Bloss, 1853, p. 167.

71 Bloss, 1853, p. xi.

72 'University of Rochester History', n.d.

73 Sutherland, 2010.

74 Light, 1989, p. 60.

75 Cited in Napier, 1992, p. 14.

76 Leveen, 2012.

77 Tod, 2012, p. 1. It should be noted that Tod's survey sample was self-selecting, by her own admission: 'some might suggest a built-in bias since the survey was initially posted at places that attract historical fiction readers' (Tod, 2012, p. 9).

78 Tod, 2012, p. 4.
79 'Member Directory', 2013. Out of 821 listed members, 552 were women, 206 were men, 44 undetermined (e.g. used initials or pseudonyms, or have gender-neutral given names), 19 were institutional or non-author members.
80 Cited by Hu, 2012.
81 Massie, 2012.
82 Plaidy, 1987.
83 Plaidy, 1976, covers Eleanor's marriage to Louis VII and the early half of Henry II's reign; Plaidy, 1977b, the rebellion of the Young king and its consequences; Plaidy, 1977a, the reign of Richard I; and Plaidy, 1978, that of John.
84 Lambert, 1993.
85 Plaidy, 2007.
86 Plaidy, 2007, p. 95.
87 Plaidy, 2007, p. 72.
88 Plaidy, 2007, p. 38.
89 Penman, 1995, covers the reign of Stephen and Henry's marriage to Eleanor; Penman, 2002, is concerned with the early part of Henry II's reign to the death of Becket; Penman, 2008, focuses on the latter part of Henry's reign, including the revolts of his sons and Eleanor's imprisonment; Penman, 2011, tells the story of Richard I's reign up to his involvement in the Third Crusade.
90 Penman, 1996; 1998; 2003; 2006.
91 Penman, 2008, p. 36.
92 Penman, 2002, p. 353. In fairness to Penman, arranged royal or aristocratic marriage is often presented in romantic terms in her novels, as in the case of Geoffrey and Constance of Brittany in *The Devil's Brood*, and Richard and Berengeria of Navarre in *Lionheart*.
93 Penman, 2008, p. 41.
94 Light, 1989, p. 60.
95 Plaidy, 2007, pp. 551–2.
96 Penman, n.d.b.
97 Penman, 2008, p. 737.
98 Penman, 2008, pp. 737–42.
99 Penman, n.d.b.
100 Plaidy, 2007, p. 559.
101 Light, 1989, p. 60.
102 Tod, 2012, p. 3.
103 Light, 1989, p. 60.
104 Pers. comm., 21 June 2013.
105 Konigsburg, 2001, back matter.
106 Konigsburg refers to it as Hell, but it is clearly modelled on Purgatory, as its denizens are able to escape from it.

107 Konigsburg, 2001, p. 6.

108 Hendershot et al., 1998, p. 678.

109 Konigsburg, 2001, p. 200.

110 Napier, 1992, p. 14.

111 Konigsburg, 2001, back matter.

112 Jones and Konigsburg, 1986, p. 182.

113 Konigsburg, 2001, p. 134.

114 Gregory, 2002.

115 Gregory, 2002, pp. 161–84.

116 Gregory, 2002, p. 185.

117 Finke and Shichtman, 2010, p. 48. Finke and Shichtman are writing about film, but their observation about 'signs of the medieval' for a modern audience can reasonably be applied to text and image.

118 Gregory, 2002, p. 3.

119 Gregory, 2002, pp. 4, 50.

120 Coppin, 1999.

121 Coppin, 1999, back matter.

122 De Gélannes, 1955.

123 Brux, 1957.

124 Calmel, 2001; 2011; 2012.

125 García, n.d. Calmel's website includes press features on her novel from Spain, Germany, the Netherlands and Poland.

126 'Le Lit d'Aliénor', n.d.

127 Calmel, 2011, p. 1

128 Calmel, 2011, p. 1.

129 Fripp, 2008.

130 Fripp, 2009.

131 Markale, 2007, p. 139.

132 Review of *Duchess of Aquitaine* (2007).

133 For example, McCaffrey and Ball, 1997.

134 Ball, 2006, pp. 1–4.

135 Ball, 2006, p. 14.

136 Delalande et al., 2012.

137 'BD les Reines de sang', n.d.

138 Delalande et al., 2012, p. 4; 'en cette nuit, ton âme s'est perdue ... et pourquoi, mon jeune roi? Pour qui? Tu sais pour qui, Louis de France! Elle t'a ensorcelé'.

139 Gloris et al., 2012.

140 www.amazon.fr, n.d.

141 www.amazon.com, n.d.

142 www.amazon.co.uk, n.d.

143 De Groot, 2009, pp. 32–3.

144 Weir, n.d.

145 Tod, 2012, p. 4.

146 Forrester, 2010.

147 Meslow, 2013.

148 Wilmore, 2013.

149 Christian and Lindsay, 1991, p. 241.

150 Aberth, 2003, p. 167.

151 Slotkin, 2005, p. 229.

152 Carr, 1962, p. 9.

153 Slotkin, 2005, p. 222.

154 Weir, 2010.

155 Weir, 2010, pp. 4–6.

156 Cited in Brown, 2002, p. 35, n. 20.

157 Weir, 1999, p. 31.

158 Weir, 2010, p. 6

159 Godard, 2002.

160 'Jocelyne Godard', n.d.

161 Interview by N. A. Kay, *Le Journal Délirium*, reproduced in 'Interviews', n.d.; http://www.jocelynegodard.com/pages/interview.htm;

> C'est vrai que c'est un parti pris depuis le premier livre que j'ai écrit sur Dhuoda, la première femme écrivain carolingienne au temps de Charlemagne. En écrivant ce premier livre j'ai pris le parti de faire connaître toutes les femmes qui avaient une vie intéressante, marquante et enrichissante mais qui ont été occultées au fil des années. J'ai choisi de faire revivre ces femmes qui ont marqué leur époque mais que l'on a tendance à ignorer aujourd'hui.

162 Interview by Géraldine Baraud, *La Renaissance*, reproduced in 'Interviews' n.d.; 'Cette vaste période qui s'étend de l'an mille à 1,400 gagne à être davantage connue, à travers la littérature'.

Chapter 7

1 Weir, 1999, p. 1.

2 Norgate, 1887, i, p. 392.

3 Chadwick, 2013.

4 Meade, 1977, p. 437 n. 34, 35.

5 Richard of Devizes, 1963, pp. 25–6.

6 Meade, 1977, p. 78.

7 Bernard of Clairvaux, 1953, p. 175; Meade, 1977, p. 79.

8 Bull and Léglu, 2005, p. 5.

9   Gibbons, 1996, p. 57.

10   Lutan, 2004, p. 111.

11   Nolan, 2009, pp. 77–86.

12   Brown, 2002, p. 22. Eleanor's seal as queen of England is used as a cover image for Wheeler and Parsons's book, perhaps as a reaction against the common use of romanticized or disputed images of Eleanor as book covers.

13   Nolan, 2009, pp. 82, 84–5.

14   Brown, 2002, p. 23.

15   Brown, 2002, pp. 23–4.

16   Nolan, 2009, p. 82.

17   Brown, 2002, p. 23.

18   Nolan, 2009, p. 84.

19   Nolan, 2009, p. 85.

20   Nolan, 2009, p. 84.

21   Nolan, 2009, p. 83.

22   Voyer, 2004, p. 187.

23   Kenaan-Kedar, 2004, p. 85.

24   Voyer, 2004, p. 188.

25   Nolan, 2009, pp. 82–3.

26   Voyer, 2004, p. 187.

27   Voyer, 2004, pp. 188–9.

28   Voyer, 2004, p. 192.

29   Petzhold, 1995, p. 36; Caviness, 1996, p. 129.

30   See Lewis, 2002, pp. 159–75 for 1166 (rather than 1167) as the more likely date for John's birth.

31   Perrot, 2004, pp. 182–4.

32   Perrot, 2004, p. 182.

33   Andrault-Schmitt, 2004, p. 102.

34   Andrault-Schmitt, 2004, p. 102; 'ce type de commande est une opération limitée, sans rapport avec un "programme" architectural…'

35   Perrot, 2004, p. 182.

36   Becket, 2000–1, i, pp. 216–17.

37   Vincent, 2006, p. 25.

38   Kenaan-Kedar, 2004, pp. 86–9.

39   Lutan, 2004, pp. 113–14.

40   Riches, 2000, p. 101.

41   Nolan, 2009, p. 112.

42   Nolan, 2009, p. 111.

43   Nolan, 2009, pp. 111–12.

44   Nolan, 2009, pp. 112–13.

45   Nolan, 2009, pp. 110–11. Erlande-Brandenbourg, 2004, pp. 175–6

46 Nolan, 2009, p. 176.

47 Siberry, 2000, p. 166.

48 Siberry, 2000, p. 170.

49 Siberry, 20009, p. 170.

50 These paintings are reproduced and discussed in Le Fur, 2004, pp. 204–9.

51 Gavard, 1842, p. 64.

52 Bourdin, n.d., p. 40. The online catalogue of Winterhalter's work lists the painting 'present location unknown'. 'Franz Xaver Winterhalter' (2014).

53 Soulié, 2011, p. 90;

> Eléonore de Guyenne, femme hardie et entreprenante, voulut suivre son mari, le roi Louis VII, moins peut-être par enthousiasme religieux que pour satisfaire ses goûts aventureux. Sa conduite légère pendant l'expédition détermina plus tard un divorce impolitique qui fit passer la Guyenne dans la maison des Plantagenets. Des fouilles récentes ont fait découvrir des cuirasses de cette époque dont la forme indiquait suffisamment qu'elles avaient servi à des femmes. On a supposé qu'elles venaient des guerrières parties à la suite d'Eléonore de Guyenne.

54 Siberry, 2000, pp. 165–6; Ganim, 2008, p. 100.

55 Roy Strong, cited in Siberry, 2000, p. 161. Strong bases his statement on a survey of the subject matter of paintings exhibited by the Royal Academy.

56 Rossetti, 1975, p. 107.

57 Siberry, 2000, p. 171.

58 Chapman, 1955, pp. 393–6.

59 De Mascureau, 2004b, p. 24.

60 Favreau, 2003, p. 43.

61 Martin, 1984.

62 Caviness, 1996, p. 129.

63 Strickland and Strickland, 1840–7, i, p. 92.

64 Bloss, 1853, p. 118.

65 Michaud, 1877, facing p. 180.

66 Ridpath, 1885, ii, p. 349.

67 So far has this identification developed that the image was used by the French postal service for a stamp commemorating the 800th anniversary of Eleanor's death in 2004.

68 Pers. comm., 17 March 2010.

69 Van Eyck, 2013.

70 Brux, 1957.

71 Jones, 2013.

72 English, 2011.

73 Gillian, 2013.

74 Schoenberg, 2008.

Conclusion

1   Labande, 2005.
2   Labande, 2005, pp. 119, 81–2.
3   Brown, 1976.
4   Flori, 2004.
5   Turner, 2009.
6   Wheeler and Parsons, 2002; Aurell, 2004a. Aurell had earlier directly addressed the myths surrounding Eleanor in Aurell, 2000.
7   Earenfight, 2013, p. 5.
8   Weir, 2010.
9   Scaer, 2012.
10 Bianchini, p. 5.
11 Bianchini, p. 1.
12 Of Matilda: Chibnall, 1991; of Eleanor: Weir, 1999; Flori, 2004; Boyd, 2004, Turner, 2009.
13 Waddell, 1927.

Select Bibliography

Primary

Akropolites, George. (2007), *The History*, trans. R. Macrides. Oxford: Oxford University Press.

Becket, Thomas. (2000–1), *The Correspondence of Thomas Becket*, 2 vols., ed. A. Duggan. Oxford: Oxford University Press.

Bernard of Clairvaux. (1953), *The Letters of St Bernard of Clairvaux*, ed. and trans. B. S. James. Chicago: Henry Regnery.

Bernart de Ventadorn. (1999), *A Bilingual Edition of the Love Songs of Bernart de Ventadorn in Occitan and English: Sugar and Salt*, ed. and trans. R. Apter. Lewiston: Mellen.

Choniates, Niketas. (1975), *Historia*, ed. I. A. Van Dieten, 2 vols. Berlin: De Gruyter.

———. (1984), *'O City of Byzantium': Annals of Niketas Choniates*, ed. and trans. H. J. Magoulis. Detroit: Wayne State University Press.

Gerald of Wales. (1861–91), *De principis instructione*, in *Giraldi Cambrensis Opera*, 8 vols., Rolls Series [RS] 21, ed. J. S. Brewer, J. F. Dimock, and G. F. Warner. London: Her Majesty's Stationery Office.

———. (1978), *The Journey through Wales and the Description of Wales*, ed. and trans. L. Thorpe. Harmondsworth: Penguin.

Gervase of Canterbury. (1879–80), *Historical Works, the Chronicle of the Reigns of Stephen, Henry II, and Richard I*, Rolls Series [RS] 73, ed. W. Stubbs. London: Her Majesty's Stationery Office.

Henry of Huntingdon. (1996), *The History of the English People, 1000–1154*, ed. and trans. D. Greenway. Oxford: Oxford University Press.

Higden, Ranulf. (1865–6), *Polychronicon Ranulphi Higden, Monachi Cestrensis; Together with the English Translation of John of Trevisa and of an Unknown Writer in the 15th Century*, 9 vols., RS 41, ed. C. Babington and J. R. Lumby. London: Her Majesty's Stationery Office.

Holinshed, Raphael. (1577), *Historie of England*, 4 vols. London: Henry Bynneman.

———. (1587), *Chronicles of England, Scotland, and Ireland*, 2nd edn., 6 vols. London: Henry Denham.

Itinerarium Peregrinorum et Gesta Regis Ricardi. (1997), *Chronicle of the Third Crusade*, ed. and trans. H. J. Nicholson. Aldershot: Ashgate.

John of Salisbury. (1986), *Historia pontificalis*, ed. and trans. M. Chibnall. Oxford: Clarendon Press.

Map, Walter. (1983), *De Nugis Curialium: Courtiers' Trifles*, ed. and trans. M. R. James, C. N. L. Brooke and R. Mynors. Oxford: Clarendon Press.

The Ménestral de Reims. (1990), *A Thirteenth-Century Minstrel's Chronicle (Récits d'un Ménestral de Reims)*, trans. R. Levine. Lampeter: Mellen.

Orderic Vitalis. (1969–80), *The Ecclesiastical History*, ed. and trans. M. Chibnall, 6 vols. Oxford: Oxford University Press.

Paris, Matthew. (1866–9), *Historia Anglorum, sive, ut vulgo dicitur, Historia minor*, 3 vols, RS 44, ed. F. Madden. London: Her Majesty's Stationery Office.

Reichersberg, Gerhoh von. (1858), *De investigatione antichristi*, ed. J. Stültz. Vienna: Archiv für österreichische Geschichte.

Richard of Devizes. (1963), *The Chronicle of Richard of Devizes*, ed. and trans. J. T. Appleby. London: Thomas Nelson.

Roger of Howden. (1867), *Gesta Regis Henrici Secundi Benedicti Abbatis. The Chronicle of the Reigns of Henry II and Richard I, 1169–1192, known Commonly under the Name of Benedict of Peterborough*, 2 vols. RS 49, ed. W. Stubbs. London: Her Majesty's Stationery Office.

Rossetti, William Michael. (1975), *The P. R. B. Journal: William Michael Rossetti's Diary of the Pre-Raphaelite Brotherhood*, ed. William E. Fredeman. Oxford: Clarendon Press.

Walter of Coventry. (1873), *Memoriale Fratris Walteri de Coventria*, RS 58, 2 vols., ed. W. Stubbs. London: Her Majesty's Stationery Office.

William of Newburgh. (1988–2007), *The History of English Affairs*, 2 vols., ed. and trans. P. G. Walsh and M. J. Kennedy. Oxford: Oxford University Press.

William of Tyre. (1943), *History of Deeds Done Beyond the Sea*, ed. and trans. E. A. Babcock and A. C. Krey, 2 vols. New York: Columbia University Press.

Secondary

Aali, H. (2012), 'Early 19th-Century French Medievalism: Merovingian Queens in Historiography and in Historical Literature'. Paper presented at the International Conference on Medievalism, Kent State University-Stark, North Canton, OH.

Aarne, A. and Thompson S. (1961), *The Types of the Folktale: A Classification and Bibliography*. Helsinki: Suomlainen Tiedeakatemia.

Aberth, J. (2003), *A Knight at the Movies*. New York: Routledge.

Abley, M. (2003), *Spoken Here: Travels Among Threatened Languages*. Boston: Mariner Books.

Andrault-Schmitt, C. (2004), 'L'Architecture "Angevine" à l'époque d'Aliénor', in *303*, pp. 99–107.

Archibald, E. (2001), *Incest and the Medieval Imagination*. Oxford: Oxford University Press.

Ashbrook, W. (1984), *Donizetti and His Operas*. Cambridge: Cambridge University Press.

——. (1987), 'Donizetti and Romani'. *Italica*, 64, pp. 606–31.

Aurell, M. (2003a), 'Aliénor d'Aquitaine (1124–1204) et ses historiens: La destruction d'un mythe?' in *Guerre, pouvoir et noblesse au Moyen Âge. Mélanges en l'honneur de Philippe Contamine*, ed. J. Paviot and J. Verger, Paris: Presse de l'Université de Paris-Sorbonne, pp. 43–9.

——. (ed.) (2003b), *La Cour Plantagenêt (1154–1204): Actes du colloque tenu á Thouars de 30 Avril au 2 mai 1999*. Poitiers: Université de Poitiers [*La Cour Plantagenêt*].

——. (ed.) (2004a), *Aliénor d'Aquitaine. Revue 303*, 81. Nantes: Association 303[*303*].

——. (2004b), 'Aliénor d'Aquitaine en son temps', in *303*, pp. 6–17.

——. (2007), *The Plantagenet Empire, 1154–1224*, trans. D. Crouch. Harlow: Pearson.

—— and Armengaud J.-P. (2004), 'Entretien avec Jacques le Goff', in *303*, pp. 20–5.

—— and Tonnerre N.-Y. (eds) (2006), *Plantagenêts et Capétiens: Confrontations et héritages*. Turnhout: Brepols [*Plantagenêts et Capétiens*].

Barber, R. W. (1978), *The Devil's Crown. A History of Henry II and His Sons*. London: BBC Books.

——. (1990), *King Arthur, Hero and Legend*. Woodbridge: Dorset.

——. (2005), 'Eleanor of Aquitaine and the Media', in *The World of Eleanor of Aquitaine*, pp. 13–27.

Benton, J. F. (1961), 'The Court of Champagne as a Literary Centre'. *Speculum*, 36, pp. 551–91.

——. (1962), 'The Evidence for Andreas Capellanus Re-examined Again'. *Studies in Philology*, 59, pp. 471–8.

Besly, J. (1647), *Histoire des comtes de Poictou et ducs de Guyenne*. Paris: Gervais Alliot.

Bianchini, J. (2012), *The Queen's Hand: Power and Authority in the Reign of Berenguela of Castile*. Philadelphia: University of Pennsylvania Press.

Bouchard, C. B. (2002), 'Eleanor's Divorce from Louis VII: The Uses of Consanguinity', in *Lord and Lady*, pp. 223–35.

Bouchet, J. (1535), *Les Annales d'Aquitaine, faictes et gestes en sommaire des roys de France, et d'Angleterre, et païs de Naples et de Milan*, 2nd edn. Poitiers: Jacques Bouchet.

Bourdin, E. (ed.) (n.d.) *Guide du Voyageur à Versailles*. Paris: Ernest Bourdin.

Boureau, J., Levesque, R. and Sachot, I. (2004), 'Sur les Pas d'Aliénor, l'abbaye de Nieul-sur-l'Autise', in *303*, pp. 129–30.

Boyd, D. (2004), *Eleanor, April Queen of Aquitaine*. Stroud: Sutton.

Britton, A. (1995), *Katharine Hepburn: Star as Feminist*. New York: Continuum.

Brown, E. A. R. (1976), 'Eleanor of Aquitaine, Parent, Queen and Duchess', in *Eleanor of Aquitaine: Patron and Politician*, ed. W. W. Kibler, Austin, TX: University of Texas Press, pp. 9–34.

——. (2002), 'Eleanor of Aquitaine Reconsidered: The Woman and Her Seasons', in *Lord and Lady*, pp. 1–54.

Brundage, J. A. (2002), 'The Canon Law of Divorce', in *Lord and Lady*, pp. 213–22.

Brunel, C. (1914), 'Alfred Richard'. *Bibliothèque de l'école des chartes*, 75, p. 449.

Bull, M.and Léglu, C. (eds) (2005), *The World of Eleanor of Aquitaine: Literature and Society in Southern France Between the Eleventh and Thirteenth Centuries*. Woodbridge: Boydell [*The World of Eleanor of Aquitaine*].

Bullough, V. L. (1996), 'Cross Dressing and Gender Role Change in the Middle Ages', in *Handbook of Medieval Sexuality*, ed. V. L. Bullough and J. Brundage, New York: Routledge, pp. 223–42.

Carney, E. (1984), 'Fact and Fiction in "Queen Eleanor's Confession"'. *Folklore*, 95, 67–70.

Carr, E. H. (1962), *What Is History?* New York: Knopf.

Caviness, M. (1996), 'Anchoress, Abbess, Queen', in *The Cultural Patronage of Medieval Women*, ed. J. H. McCash, Athens, GA: University of Georgia Press, pp. 105–54.

Cerquiglini-Toulet, J. (2011), *A New History of French Medieval Literature*, trans. S. Preisig. Baltimore: Johns Hopkins University Press.

Chaban-Delmas, J. (1987), *La Dame d'Aquitaine*. Monte Carlo: DMC Edition.

Chambers, F. M. (1941), 'Some Legends of Eleanor of Aquitaine'. *Speculum*, 16, pp. 459–68.

Chapman, R. L. (1955), 'A Note on the Demon Queen Eleanor'. *Modern Language Notes*, 70, pp. 393–6.

Chauou, A. (2005), *Sur les pas de Aliénor d'Aquitaine*. Rennes: Ouest-France.

Chibnall, M. (1991), *The Empress Matilda: Queen Consort, Queen Mother and Lady of the English*. Oxford: Blackwell.

Christian, E. E. and Lindsay B. (1991), 'Detecting the Medieval World. An Interview with Ellis Peters'. *The Year's Work in Medievalism*, 6, pp. 239–60.

Cook, P. (1993), *Queen Consorts of England: The Power Behind the Throne*. New York: Facts on File.

Coss, P. (1998), *The Lady in Medieval England, 1000–1500*. Stroud: Sutton.

Damon, G. (2004), 'Dames du Poitou au temps d'Aliénor', in *303*, pp. 46–51.

——. (2006), 'La place et le pouvoir des dames dans la société poitevine au temps d'Aliénor d'Aquitaine' in *Plantagenêts et Capétiens*, pp. 125–41.

DeAragon, R. C. (2002), 'Wife, Widow, and Mother: Some Comparisons between Eleanor of Aquitaine and Noblewomen of the Anglo-Norman World', in *Lord and Lady*, pp. 97–114.

——. (2004), 'Do We Know What Think We Know? : Making Assumptions about Eleanor of Aquitaine'. *Medieval Feminist Forum*, 34, pp. 14–20.

De Groot, J. (2009), *Consuming History: Historians and Heritage in Contemporary Popular Culture*. London: Routledge.

De Larrey, I. (1788), *Histoire d'Éléonor de Guienne, duchesse d'Aquitaine*, ed. J. Cussac. Paris: Cussac.

De Mascureau, M.-A. (2004a), 'La légende noire d'Aliénor d'Aquitaine', in *303*, pp. 210–17.

——. (2004b), 'Repères chronologiques sur la vie d'Aliénor'. *L'Actualité Poitou-Charentes*, 65, p. 24.

Delorme, M. (1988), ' "Facts not Opinions" – Agnes Strickland'. *History Today*, 38 (2), pp. 45–50.

Dickens, H. (1971), *The Films of Katharine Hepburn*. New York: Citadel.

Diez, F. C. (1842), *Essai sur les Cours d'Amour*, trans. F. de Roisin. Paris: J. Labitte.

Dronke, P. (1996), *The Medieval Lyric*, 3rd edn. Cambridge: D. S. Brewer.

Duby, G. (1995), *Dames du XIIe Siècle, 1: Héloïse, Aliénor, Iseut et quelques autres*. Paris: Gallimard. English translation: Duby, G. (1997), *Women of the Twelfth Century, Volume 1: Eleanor of Aquitaine and Six Others*, trans. J. Birrell. Chicago: University of Chicago Press.

Duggan, A. J. (ed.) (2002), *Queens and Queenship in Medieval Europe: Proceedings of a Conference held at King's College London, April 1995*. Woodbridge: Boydell.

Earenfight, T. (2009), *The King's Other Body: María of Castile and the Crown of Aragon*. Philadelphia: University of Pennsylvania Press.

———. (2013), *Queenship in Medieval Europe*. New York: Palgrave Macmillan.

Erlande-Brandenbourg, A. (2004), 'Le gisant d'Aliénor d'Aquitaine', in *303*, pp. 174–9.

Evergates, T. (ed.) (1999), *Aristocratic Women in Medieval France*. Philadelphia: University of Pennsylvania Press.

Facinger, M. F. (1968), 'A Study of Medieval Queenship: Capetian France (987–1237)', in *Studies in Medieval and Renaissance History*, 5, ed. W. M. Bowsky, Lincoln, NE: Univeristy of Nebraska Press, pp. 1–47.

Favreau, R. (2003), ' "Bonnes-villes" du Centre-Ouest: Les communes médiévales'. *L'Actualité Poitou-Charentes*, 61, pp. 41–6.

Finke, L. A. and Shichtman, M. B. (2010), *Cinematic Illuminations: The Middle Ages on Film*. Baltimore: Johns Hopkins University Press.

Flori, J. (2004), *Aliénor d'Aquitaine: La reine insoumise*. Paris: Payot. English translation: Flori, J. (2007), *Eleanor of Aquitaine: Queen and Rebel*, trans. O. Classe. Edinburgh: Edinburgh University Press, 2007.

———. (2004a), 'Aliénor l'insoumise: le rôle de la personnalité d'Aliénor dans l'histoire de son temps' in *303*, pp. 52–7.

———. (2006), *Richard the Lionheart: King and Knight*, trans. J. Birrell. Edinburgh: Edinburgh University Press.

Friedman, J. B. (2000), *The Monstrous Races in Medieval Art and Thought*. Syracuse: Syracuse University Press.

Furst, C. (1901), 'Tennyson's "Fair Rosamund" in *Becket*'. *Modern Language Notes*, 16, pp. 105–12.

Ganim, J. M. (2008), *Medievalism and Orientalism: Three Essays on Literature, Architecture and Cultural Identity*. New York: Palgrave Macmillan.

Gavard, C. (1842), *Galeries Historiques du Palais de Versailles*. Paris: Imprimerie Royale.

Geaman, K. (2010), 'Queen's Gold and Intercession: The Case of Eleanor of Aquitaine'. *Medieval Feminist Forum*, 46 (2), pp. 10–33.

Geary, P. (2003), *The Myth of Nations: The Medieval Origins of Europe*. Princeton: Princeton University Press.

Gibbons, R. (1996), 'Isabeau of Bavaria, Queen of France (1385–1422): The Creation of an Historical Villainess: The Alexander Prize Essay'. *Transactions of the Royal Historical Society, 6th series*, 6, pp. 51–73.

Gildea, R. (1994), *The Past in French History*. New Haven, CT: Yale University Press.

Gillingham, J. (1999), *Richard I*. New Haven, CT: Yale University Press.

———. (2001), *The Angevin Empire*, 2nd edn. London: Arnold.

———. (2005), 'Events and Opinions: Norman and English Views of Aquitaine, c. 1152–c.1204', in *The World of Eleanor of Aquitaine*, pp. 57–81.

Gras, C. (1975), 'Le mouvement régionaliste français et l'histoire sociale: Eléments de problématique et de bibliographie'. *Le Mouvement Social*, 92, pp. 103–17.

Guillaume, P. (1994), 'La trace girondine ou la culture politique d'Aquitaine'. *Vingtième Siècle. Revue d'histoire*, 44, pp. 95–102.

Guizot, F. (1882), *The History of England from the Earliest Times to the Accession of Queen Victoria*, ed. Mme de Witt (née Guizot), trans. Moy Thomas, 2 vols. London: S. Low, Marston, Searle, and Rivington.

Guyonvarc'h, C.-J. (1978), *Textes Mythologiques Irlandais*. Rennes: Ogam-Celticum.

Hammond, B. (2006), 'Joseph Addison's Opera "Rosamond": Britishness in the Early Eighteenth Century'. *ELH*, 73, pp. 601–29.

Hanawalt, B. A. (1987), 'Golden Ages for the History of Medieval English Women', in *Women in Medieval History and Historiography*, ed. S. M. Stuard, Philadelphia: University of Pennsylvania Press, pp. 1–24.

Harrison, F. (1903), 'Tennyson: A New Estimate'. *The North American Review*, 176, pp. 856–67.

Harty, K. J. (1999), *The Reel Middle Ages: American, Western and Eastern European, Middle Eastern and Asian Films about Medieval Europe*. McFarland: Jefferson, NC.

Harvey, R. (2005), 'Eleanor of Aquitaine and the Troubadours', in *The World of Eleanor of Aquitaine*, pp. 101–14.

Hasty, W. (2000), 'Love Lyrics', in *German Literature of the High Middle Ages*, ed. W. Hasty, Woodbridge: Camden House, pp. 141–59.

Hendershot, J., Peck, J. and Konigsburg, E. L. (1988), ' "The View from Saturday": A Conversation with E. L. Konigsburg, Winner of the 1997 Newbery Medal'. *The Reading Teacher*, 51, pp. 676–80.

Hepburn, K. H. (1934), 'Review of Marie E. Kopp, *Birth Control in Practice*'. *Social Service Review*, 8, pp. 762–3.

Higham, C. (1975), *Kate: The Life of Katharine Hepburn*. New York: W. W. Norton.

Hivergneaux, M. (2000), 'Aliénor d'Aquitaine: le pouvoir d'une femme à la lumière de ses chartes (1152–1204)', in *La Cour Plantagenêt (1154–1204)*, pp. 63–88.

———. (2002), 'Queen Eleanor and Aquitaine, 1137–1189', in *Lord and Lady*, pp. 55–76.

———. (2006), 'Autour d'Aliénor d'Aquitaine: entourage et pouvoir au prisme des chartes (1137–1189)' in *Plantagenêts et Capétiens*, pp. 61–73.

Howell, M. (2001), *Eleanor of Provence: Queenship in Thirteenth Century England*. Oxford: Blackwell.

Huneycutt, L. L. (2002), '*Alianora Regina Anglorum*: Eleanor of Aquitaine and her Anglo-Norman Predecessors as Queens of England', in *Lord and Lady*, pp. 115–32.

———. (2003), *Matilda of Scotland: A Study in Medieval Queenship*. Woodbridge: Boydell.

Hutton, R. (1999), *The Triumph of the Moon: A History of Modern Pagan Witchcraft*. Oxford: Oxford University Press.

'J. S.' (1960), 'Zoé Oldenbourg, *Le Bûcher de Montségur*'. Review, *Archives de sociologie des religions*, 10, pp. 200–1.

Joliffe, J. E. A. (1955), *Angevin Kingship*. London: Adam and Charles Black.

Jones, L. T. and Konigsburg, E. L. (1986), 'Profile: Elaine Konigsburg'. *Language Arts*, 63, pp. 177–84.

Kahan, J. (2004), *Shakespeare Imitations, Parodies and Forgeries, 1710–1820*. Abingdon: Taylor and Francis.

Kelly, A. (1927), *A Curriculum to Build a Mental World: A Proposal for a College of Liberal Arts for Women*. Baltimore: Bryn Mawr School.

———. (1937), 'Eleanor of Aquitaine and the Courts of Love'. *Speculum*, 12, pp. 3–19.

———. (1950), *Eleanor of Aquitaine and the Four Kings*. Cambridge, MA: Harvard University Press.

Kenaan-Kedar, N. (2004), 'Aliénor d'Aquitaine et les arts visuels', in *303*, pp. 86–9.

Keralio Robert, L. (1791), *Les Crimes des reines de France, depuis le commencement de la monarchie jusqu'à Marie Antoinette*. Paris: L. Prudhomme.

Knight, S. (1994), *Robin Hood. A Complete Study of the English Outlaw*. Oxford: Blackwell.

———. (2003), *Robin Hood. A Mythic Biography*. Ithaca, NY: Cornell University Press.

Labande, E.-R. (1951), 'Pour une image véridique d'Aliénor d'Aquitaine', *Bulletin de la Societé des antiquaires de l'Ouest*, 2nd series 2, pp. 175–234.

———. (2005), *Pour une image véridique d'Aliénor d'Aquitaine*, ed. M. Aurell. La Crèche: Geste éditions.

Lanphear, M. J. (2007), 'Celestia Angenette Bloss'. Paper presented at Susan B. Anthony House, Rochester, NY, 8 January 2007.

Le Fur, D. (2004), 'Le Souvenir d'Aliénor à l'époque moderne' in *303*, pp. 204–9.

Lejeune, R. (1954), 'Rôle littéraire d'Aliénor d'Aquitaine et de sa famille'. *Cultura neo-latina. Bolletino dell'Istituto di Filologia Romanza*, 14, pp. 5–57.

Lerner, Bettina R. (2007), 'Michelet Mythologue'. *Yale French Studies*, 111, pp. 61–72.

Lewis, A. W. (2002), 'The Birth and Childhood of King John: Some Revisions', in *Lord and Lady*, pp. 159–75.

Light, A. (1989), '"Young Bess": Historical Novels and Growing up'. *Feminist Review*, 33, pp. 57–71.

LoPrete, K. (1999), 'Adela of Blois: Familial Alliances and Female Lordship', in *Aristocratic Women in Medieval France*, ed. T. Evergates, Philadelphia: University of Pennsylvania Press, pp. 7–43.

Lukács, G. (1962), *The Historical Novel*, trans. H. and S. Mitchell. Harmondsworth: Penguin.

Lútan, S. (2004), 'L'iconographie royale de Saint-Martin de Candes', in *303*, pp. 108–117.

McCash, J. H. (1979), 'Marie de Champagne and Eleanor of Aquitaine: A Relationship Reexamined'. *Speculum*, 54, pp. 698–711.

———. (ed.) (1996), *The Cultural Patronage of Medieval Women*. Athens, GA: University of Georgia Press.

McCracken, P. (2002), 'Scandalizing Desire: Eleanor of Aquitaine and the Chroniclers', in *Lord and Lady*, pp. 247–63.

Malègue, H. (1866), *Guide de l'étranger dans la Haute Loire*. Le Puy: Marchessou.

Markale, J. (1979), *La vie, l'influence d'Aliénor d'Aquitaine, Comtesse de Poitou, Duchesse d'Aquitaine, Reine de France, puis d'Angleterre, Dame des Troubadours et des Bardes bretons*. Paris: Payot. English translation: Markale, J. (2007), *Eleanor of Aquitaine; Queen of the Troubadours*, trans. J. E. Graham. Rochester, VT: Inner Traditions.

———. (1997), *La Grande déesse : Mythes et sanctuaires. De la Vénus de Lespugue à Notre-Dame de Lourdes*. Paris: Albin Michel. English translation: Markale, J. (1999), *The Great Goddess: Reverence of the Divine Feminine from the Paleolithic to the Present*, trans. J. Gladding. Rochester, VT: Inner Traditions.

———. (2009), *L'énigme du Saint Graal: De Rennes-le-Château à Marie Madeleine*. Paris: J'ai lu.

Martin, B. F. (1984), *The Hypocrisy of Justice in the Belle Époque*. Baton Rouge: Louisiana State University Press.

Martindale, J. (1992), 'Eleanor of Aquitaine', in *Richard Coeur de Lion in History and Myth*, ed. J. L. Nelson, London: King's College Centre for Late Antique and Medieval Studies, pp. 17–50.

———. (2002), 'Eleanor of Aquitaine and a "Queenly Court" ', in *Lord and Lady*, pp. 423–40.

Mayer, C.-J. de (1779), 'Observations et notes historiques sue la règne de Louis VII'. *Bibliothèque universelle des romans*, 33, pp. 91–116.

Mayor, A. (2000), 'Labyrinth', in *Medieval Folklore: An Encyclopedia of Myths, Legends, Tales, Beliefs and Customs*, ed. C. Lindahl, J. McNamar and J. Lindow, Santa Barbara: ABC-CLIO, pp. 575–6.

Meade, M. (1973), *Bitching*. London: Garnstone Press.

———. (1977), *Eleanor of Aquitaine: A Biography*. New York: Hawthorn Books.

———. (1979), *Stealing Heaven: The Love Story of Heloise and Abelard*. New York: W. Morrow.

———. (1989), *Dorothy Parker, What Fresh Hell Is This?* New York: Penguin.

Michaud, J. (1877), *Histoire des croisades, illustrées de 100 grands compositions par Gustave Doré*. Jouvet: Paris: Furne.

Michelet, J. (1833–42), *Histoire de France*, 7 vols. Paris: Hachette.

———. (1864), *Historical View of the French Revolution*, ed. and trans. C. Cocks. London: H. G. Bohn.

———. (1939), *Satanism and Witchcraft: A Study in Medieval Superstition*, trans. A. R. Allison. New York: Citadel.

Milland-Bove, B. (2004), 'Aliénor d'Aquitaine: femme de lettres ou homme d'état?' in *303*, pp. 156–61.

Mitchell, K. and Parsons, N. (2013), 'Reading the Represented Past: History and Fiction from 1700 to the Present', in *Reading Historical Fiction: The Revenant and Remembered Past*, ed. K. Mitchell and N. Parsons, Basingstoke and New York: Palgrave Macmillan, pp. 1–18.

Moore, J. C. (1978), review of *Eleanor of Aquitaine: Patron and Politician*, ed. W. W. Kibler. *Speculum*, 53 (1), pp. 148–9.

———. (1979), '"Courtly Love": A Problem of Terminology'. *Journal of the History of Ideas*, 40, pp. 621–32.

Moulinier-Brogi, L. (2004), 'Aliénor et les femmes savantes du XIIᵉ siècle', in *303*, pp. 142–9.

Mulally, E. (2002), 'The Reciprocal Loyalty of Eleanor of Aquitaine and William Marshal', in *Lord and Lady*, pp. 237–45.

Napier, S. (1992), 'Nuns, Midwives, and Witches: Women's Studies in the Elementary Classroom', *The Radical Teacher*, 41, pp. 11–14.

Nash, G. B. and Jeffrey J. R. (2009), *The American People. Creating a Nation and a Society*, 2 vols. New York: Vango Books.

Nolan, K. D. (ed.) (2003), *Capetian Women*. New York: Palgrave Macmillan.

———. (2009), *Queens in Stone and Silver: The Creation of a Visual Imagery of Queenship in Capetian France*. New York: Palgrave Macmillan.

Norgate, K. (1887), *England under the Angevin Kings*, 2 vols. London: Macmillan.

O'Callaghan, T. F. (2002), 'Tempering Scandal: Eleanor of Aquitaine and Benoît de Sainte-Maure's *Roman de Troie*', in *Lord and Lady*, pp. 301–17.

Oldenbourg, Z. (1959), *Le Bûcher de Montségur. 16 mars 1244*. Paris: Gallimard.

———. (1965), *Les Croisades*. Paris: Gallimard.

Omont, H. (1882), review of *Lettres de Jean Besly (1612–1647)*, ed. Applin Briquet. *Bibliothèque de l'école des chartes*, 43, pp. 379–80.

Orr, L. (1976), *Jules Michelet: Nature, History and Language*. Ithaca, NY: Cornell University Press.

Owen, D. D. R. (1993), *Eleanor of Aquitaine: Queen and Legend*. Oxford: Blackwell.

Paden, W. D. (2005), 'Troubadours and History', in *The World of Eleanor of Aquitaine*, pp. 157–82.

Pappano, M. A. (2002), 'Marie de France, Aliénor d'Aquitaine, and the Alien Queen', in *Lord and Lady*, pp. 337–68.

———. (2004), 'La *regina bisperta*: Aliénor d'Aquitaine et ses relations littéraires au XIIe siècle', in *303*, pp. 151–5.

Paterson, L. M. (1993), *The World of the Troubadours: Medieval Occitan Society, c. 1100 – c. 1300*. Cambridge: Cambridge University Press.

Parsons, J. C. (ed.) (1994), *Medieval Queenship*. Stroud: Sutton.

———. (1997), *Eleanor of Castile: Queen and Society in Thirteenth-Century England*. New York: St Martin's Press.

———. (2002), 'Damned if She Didn't and Damned When She Did: Bodies, Babies, and Bastards in the Lives of Two Queens of France', in *Lord and Lady*, pp. 265–300.

Pernoud, R. (1949), *L'unité française*, 2nd edn. Paris: Que sais-je?

———. (1965), *Aliénor d'Aquitaine*. Paris: Albin Michel. English translation: Pernoud,
R. (1968), *Eleanor of Aquitaine*, trans. P. Wiles. New York: Coward-McCann.

———. (1966), *La formation de la France*. Paris: Que sais-je?

———. (1980), *La Femme au temps des cathédrales*. Paris: Stock.

Perrot, F. (2004), 'Le Portrait d'Aliénor de la *crucifixion* à la cathédrale de Poitiers', in
303, pp. 181–4.

Petzhold, A. (1995), *Romanesque Art*. London: Weidenfeld and Nicolson.

Power, D. (2005) 'The Stripping of a Queen: Eleanor of Aquitaine in Thirteenth-
Century Norman Tradition', in *The World of Eleanor of Aquitaine*, pp. 115–35.

Prime, R. (2008), ' "The Old Bogey": The Hollywood Blacklist in Europe'. *Film History*,
20, pp. 474–86.

Prus, L. (1846), *Histoire des reines de France*, 2 vols. London: Self-published.

———. (1852), *A Residence in Algeria*, trans. Sophia, countess of Zetland. London:
W. Pickering.

Rejai, M. and Enloe C. H. (1969), 'Nation-States and State-Nations'. *International
Studies Quarterly*, 13, pp. 140–58.

Richard, A. (1903), *Histoire des comtes de Poitou, 778–1204*, 2 vols. Paris: A. Picard.

Riches, S. (2000), *St George: Hero, Martyr and Myth*. Stroud: Sutton.

Ridpath, J. C. (1885), *Cyclopedia of Universal History*, 3 Vols. Cincinnati: Jones
Brothers.

Rosenberg, M. V. (1937), *Eleanor of Aquitaine: Queen of the Troubadours and the Courts
of Love*. Boston: Houghton Mifflin.

Rossetti, W. M. (1975), *The P. R. B. Journal: William Michael Rossetti's Diary of the
Pre-Raphaelite Brotherhood*, ed. W. E. Fredeman. Oxford: Clarendon Press.

Runciman, S. (1951–4), *A History of the Crusades*, 3 vols. Cambridge: Cambridge
University Press.

Sassier, Y. (1991), *Louis VII*. Paris: Fayard.

Shadis, M. T. (2003), 'Blanche of Castile and Facinger's "Medieval Queenship", in
Capetian Women.

———. (2009), *Berenguela of Castile (1180–1246) and Political Women in the High
Middle Ages*. New York: Palgrave Macmillan.

Siberry, E. (2000), *The New Crusaders: Images of the Crusades in the Nineteenth and
Early Twentieth Centuries*. Aldershot: Ashgate.

Sigu, V. (2013), *Médiévisme et Lumières. Le moyen âge dans la 'Bibliothèque universelle
des romans'*. Oxford: Voltaire Foundation.

Simeone, W. E. (1961), 'The Robin Hood of Ivanhoe'. *Journal of American Folklore*, 74,
pp. 230–4.

Slotkin, R. (2005), 'Fiction for the Purposes of History'. *Rethinking History*, 9, pp. 221–36.

Smith, E. E. (1997), *Tennyson's 'Epic Drama'*. Lanham, MD: University Press of America.

Sobchak, V. (1997), 'The Insistent Fringe: Moving Images and Historical Consciousness'.
History and Theory, 36, pp. 4–20.

Soulié, E. (2011), *Notice des peintures et sculptures composant le musée impérial de Versailles*, reprint. Paris: Nabu Press.

Stevens, A. H. (2013), 'Learning to Read the Past in the Early Historical Novel', in *Reading Historical Fiction: The Revenant and Remembered Past*, ed. K. Mitchell and N. Parsons, Basingstoke and New York: Palgrave Macmillan, pp. 19–32.

Stock, L. K. (2009), 'Now Starring in the Third Crusade: Depictions of Richard I and Saladin in Films and Television Series', in *Hollywood in the Holy Land. Essays on Film Depictions of the Crusades and Christian-Muslim Clashes*, ed. N. Haydock and E. L. Risden, Jefferson, NC: McFarland, pp. 93–122.

Stoudemire, S. A. (1931), 'A Spanish Play on the Fair Rosamund Legend'. *Studies in Philology*, 28, pp. 857–61.

Strickland, A. and Strickland, E. (1840–7), *Lives of the Queens of England*, 12 vols. London: Bell and Daldy.

Strohm, P. (1992), *Hochon's Arrow: The Social Imagination of Fourteenth-Century Texts*. Princeton: Princeton University Press.

Stuard, S. M. (1987a), 'Fashion's Captives: Medieval Women in French Historiography', in *Women in Medieval History and Historiography*, ed. S. M. Stuard, Philadelphia: University of Pennsylvania Press, pp. 59–80.

———. (ed.) (1987b), *Women in Medieval History and Historiography*. Philadelphia: University of Pennsylvania Press.

Stubbs, W. (1903), *The Constitutional History of England, 6th edition, 3 vols*. Oxford: Clarendon Press.

Swabey, F. (2004), *Eleanor of Aquitaine, Courtly Love, and the Troubadours*. Westport, CT: Greenwood.

Taliano-des Garets, F. (1991), 'Un grand maire et la culture. Le "chabanisme culturel" '. *Vingtième Siècle. Revue d'histoire*, 61, pp. 44–55.

Tambling, J. (2006), 'Scott's "Heyday" in Opera', in *The Reception of Walter Scott in Europe*, ed. M. Pittock, London: Continuum, pp. 285–92.

Tanner, H. J. (2002), 'Queenship: Office, Custom or Ad Hoc? The Case of Queen Matilda III of England (1135–1152)', in *Lord and Lady*, pp. 133–58.

Thomas, S. (1986), ' "Enter the Sheriffe": Shakespeare's *King John* and *The Troublesome Raigne*'. *Shakespeare Quarterly*, 37, pp. 98–100.

Thumim, J. (1986), ' "Miss Hepburn Is Humanized": The Star Persona of Katharine Hepburn'. *Feminist Review*, 24, pp. 71–102.

Tolhurst, F. (2004), 'The Outlandish Lioness: Eleanor of Aquitaine in Literature'. *Medieval Feminist Forum*, 37, pp. 9–13.

Trudeau, S. (2008), 'Review of Jean Markale, *Eleanor of Aquitaine; Queen of the Troubadours*, trans. J. E. Graham, Inner Traditions, Rochester, 2007'. *SageWoman*, p. 74.

Truong, A.-G. (2003), 'Poitevin-saintongeais: Déclin d'oc entre Loire et Gironde'. *L'Actualité Poitou-Charentes*, pp. 61–3.

Tudor, A. (2005), *Tales of Vice and Virtue: The First Old French Vie des Pères*. Amsterdam: Editions Rodopi.

Turner, R. V. (2009), *Eleanor of Aquitaine*. New Haven, CT: Yale University Press.

Van Houts, E. (2006), 'Les Femmes dans le royaume Plantagenêt: gendre, politique et nature', in *Plantagenêts et Capétiens*, pp. 95–112.

Verger, J. (2004), 'Aliénor et la renaissance intellectuelle du XIIᵉ siècle', in *303*, pp. 136–41.

Vincent, N. (2000), 'King Henry II and the Poitevins', in *La Cour Plantagenêt*, pp. 103–35.

———. (2004), 'Aliénor, reine d'Angleterre', in *303*, pp. 58–63.

———. (2006), 'Patronage, Politics and Piety in the Charters of Eleanor of Aquitaine', in *Plantagenêts et Capétiens*, pp. 17–60.

Volk, P. (2004), 'La reine Aliénor et la poésie courtoise Allemande', in *303*, pp. 195–203.

Volrath, H. (2006), 'Aliénor d'Aquitaine et ses enfants: une relation affective?' in *Plantagenêts et Capétiens*, pp. 113–23.

Vones-Liebenstein, Ursula. (2006), 'Aliénor d'Aquitaine, Henri le Jeune et la révolte de 1173: Un prélude à la confrontation entre Plantagenêt et Capétiens?' in *Plantagenêts et Capétiens: Confrontations et héritages*, ed. Martin Aurell and Noël-Yves Tonnerre, Turnhout: Brepols, pp. 75–93.

Voyer, C. (2004), 'Les Plantagenêts et la chapelle de Sainte-Radegonde de Chinon: une image en débat', in *303*, pp. 186–93.

Waddell, H. (1927), *The Wandering Scholars*. London: Constable.

Waith, E. (1978), 'King John and the Drama of History'. *Shakespeare Quarterly*, 29, pp. 192–211.

Walker, C. H. (1949–50), 'Eleanor of Aquitaine and the Disaster at Cadmos Mountain on the Second Crusade'. *American Historical Review*, 55, pp. 857–61.

———. (1950), *Eleanor of Aquitaine*. Chapel Hill, NC: University of North Carolina Press.

Warren, W. L. (1973), *Henry II*. London: Yale University Press.

Weatherson, A. (1988), 'English Legend, French Play, Two Italian Composers'. *Donizetti Society Journal*, 6, pp. 107–21.

Weinstock, H. (1963), *Donizetti and the World of Opera in Italy, Paris, and Vienna in the First Half of the Nineteenth Century*. New York: Pantheon.

Weir, A. (1999), *Eleanor of Aquitaine, by the Wrath of God, Queen of England*. London: Jonathan Cape.

Wells, B. R. (1986), 'Miniature-Caricature: *La Vita di Castruccio Castracani* in the *Bibliothèque universelle des romans*'. *South Atlantic Review*, 51, pp. 9–20.

Wheeler, B. and Parsons J. C. (eds) (2002), *Eleanor of Aquitaine: Lord and Lady*. Basingstoke: Palgrave Macmillan [*Lord and Lady*].

Williams, G. S. (1995), *Defining Dominion: The Discourses of Magic and Witchcraft in Early Modern France and Germany*. Ann Arbor: University of Michigan Press.

Zinn, H. (1996), *A People's History of the United States, 2nd edn*. Harlow: Longman.

Literary works

Addison, J. (1707), *Rosamond: An Opera*. London: Jacob Tonson.

'Amours d'Éléonore d'Aquitaine, reine de la France, et ensuite d'Angleterre, et de Guillaume, comte de Ponthieu, et de Henri, duc de Normandie, manuscrit' (1779), in *Bibliothèque universelle des romans*, 33, pp. 61–90.

Anouilh, J. (1995), *Becket*, trans. L. Hill. New York: Coward-McCann.

Aragon, L. (1946), 'Crusaders', trans. S. Wood. *The Kenyon Review*, 8, pp. 241–3.

Bale, J. (1969), *John Bale's King Johan*, ed. B. B. Adams. San Marino, CA: Huntington Library.

Ball, M. (2006), *Duchess of Aquitaine*. New York: St. Martin's Press.

Bloss, C. A. (1853), *Heroines of the Crusades*. Rochester, NY: Wanzer, Beardsley.

Bonnechose, E. de (1826), *Rosamonde, tragédie en cinq actes*. Paris: Lecaudey.

Brux, E. (1957), *Aliénor d'Aquitaine et les cours d'amour*. La Flèche: Brodard et Taupin.

Calmel, M. (2001), *Le lit d'Aliénor*. Paris: XO Éditions.

———. (2011), *Aliénor. Le règne des Lions*. Paris: XO Éditions.

———. (2012), *Aliénor. L'alliance brisée*. Paris: XO Éditions.

Coppin, B. (1999), *Aliénor d'Aquitaine, une reine à l'aventure*. Paris: Flammarion.

De Gélannes, B. (1955), *La Vie Galante de … Éléonore d'Aquitaine*. Paris: Éditions de l'Arabesque.

Delalande, A., Mogavino, S., Gomez, C. and Chec, C. (2012), *Aliénor: La Légende Noire*, vol. 1. Paris: Delcourt.

English, C. (2011), *To Be Queen: A Novel of the Early Life of Eleanor of Aquitaine*. New York: NAL Trade.

Fripp, R. (2008), *Power of a Woman. Memoirs of a Turbulent Life: Eleanor of Aquitaine*. Toronto: Shillingstone Press.

———. (2009), *Spirit in Health: Spiritual Roots in Modern Healing, or Social and Medical Sciences Enlist Ancient Mind-body Healing Techniques*. Toronto: Shillingstone Press.

Furnivall, F. J. and Munro, J. (eds) (1913), *The Troublesome Reign of King John*. London: Chatto and Windus.

Gloris, T., Gloris, M., Calderon, J. and Corgie, J. (2012), *Isabelle, la Louve de France*, vol. 1. Paris: Delcourt.

Godard, J. (2002), *Les Amours d'Aliénor d'Aquitaine. Prendre cœur et prendre dame*. Paris: Le Semaphore.

Goldman, J. (1966), *The Lion in Winter. A Comedy in Two Acts*. New York: Random House.

———. (1981), *The Lion in Winter*, 2nd edn. New York: Random House.

Gregory, K. (2002), *Eleanor: Crown Jewel of Aquitaine. France, 1136*. New York: Scholastic.

Hull, T. (1774), *Henry the Second, or, The Fall of Rosamond*. London: John Bell.

Jones, E. (2013), *Gilded Cages: The Trials of Eleanor of Aquitaine: a Novel*. Available from: Amazon Digital [1 January 2014].

Konigsburg, E. L. (1973), *A Proud Taste for Scarlet and Miniver*, 1st edn. New York: Atheneum.

———. (2001), *A Proud Taste for Scarlet and Miniver*, 2nd edn. New York: Atheneum.

Macheco, Comtesse P. de (1823), *Éléonore d'Aquitaine*, 2 vols. Paris: Janet et Cotelle.

McCaffrey, A. and Ball M. (1997), *Acorna the Unicorn Girl*. New York: Eos.

Meade, M. (1983), *Sybilie*. New York: W. Morrow.

Oldenbourg, Z. (1946), *Argile et Cendres*. Paris: Gallimard.

———. (1992), *Aliénor: Pièce en quatre tableaux*. Paris: Gallimard.

Penman, S. K. (1995), *When Christ and his Saints Slept*. New York: Holt.

———. (1996), *The Queen's Man*. New York: Holt.

———. (1998), *Cruel as the Grave*. New York: Holt.

———. (2002), *Time and Chance*. New York: Putnam.

———. (2003), *Dragon's Lair*. New York: Putnam.

———. (2005), *Prince of Darkness*. New York: Putnam.

———. (2008), *The Devil's Brood*. New York: Penguin.

———. (2011), *Lionheart*. New York: Penguin.

Plaidy, J. (1976), *The Plantagenet Prelude*. London: Robert Hale.

———. (1977a), *Heart of a Lion*. London: Robert Hale.

———. (1977b), *The Revolt of the Eaglets*. London: Robert Hale.

———. (1978), *The Prince of Darkness*. London: Robert Hale.

———. (1987), *The Courts of Love: The Story of Eleanor of Aquitaine*. London: Robert Hale.

———. (2007), *The Plantagenet Prelude*. London: Arrow Books.

Rogero, L. (2006), *Aliénor exagère!*, unpublished play, performed 2006–12.

Romani, F. (1840), *Éleonora di Guienna: opera seria*. Paris, 1840.

Scaer, D. O. (2012), *Passacaglia: An Analytical Novel*. Unpublished MS.

Shakespeare, W. (1954), *King John*, ed. E. A. J. Honigmann. Cambridge, MA: Harvard University Press.

———. (1974), *King John*, ed. R. L. Smallwood. London: Penguin.

———. (1989), *The Life and Death of King John*, ed. A. R. Braunmuller. Oxford: Oxford University Press.

Tennyson, A. (1894), *Becket*. New York: Dodd, Mead.

Weir, A. (2010), *Captive Queen: A Novel of Eleanor of Aquitaine*. New York: Ballantine.

Film and television

Austin, R. (director) (1984), *The Zany Adventures of Robin Hood*. Charles Fries Productions.

Burt, D. (director) (1955), 'Queen Eleanor' (television episode), 14 November 1955, *The Adventures of Robin Hood*. ITC.

Cooke, A., Howell, J. and Wilson, R. (directors) (1978), *The Devil's Crown* (television series), 30 April–1 July 1978, BBC.

Curtiz, M. (director) (1938), *The Adventures of Robin Hood*. Warner Bros.

Giles, D. (director) (1984), *The BBC Television Shakespeare's The Life and Death of King John* (television play), 24 November 1998, BBC.

Glenville, P. (director) (1964), *Becket*. Paramount.

Harrison, S. (director) (1952), *The Life and Death of King John* (television broadcast), 20 January 1952, BBC.

Harvey, A. (director) (1968), *The Lion in Winter*. AVCO Embassy.

Konchalovskiy, A. (2003). *The Lion in Winter* (television movie), 23 May 2004, Showtime.

Levin, H. and Sherman, G. (directors) (1946), *The Bandit of Sherwood Forest*. Columbia.

Minghella, D. and Allan, F. (producers) (2006–9), *Robin Hood* (television series), 7 October 2006–27 June 2009, Tiger Aspect.

Orme, S. (director) (1997), *Ivanhoe* (television series), 12 January–16 February 1997. BBC.

Reitherman, W. (director) (1973), *Robin Hood*. Disney.

Scott, R. (director) (2010), *Robin Hood*. Universal Pictures.

Smith, H. and Coote B. (producers) (1958–9), *Ivanhoe* (television series), 5 January 1958–4 January 1959. ITV.

Ridgwell, G. (director) (1923), *Becket*, Stoll Picture Productions.

Weintraub, S., Kuhn, T. and Weintraub, F. (producers) (1997–8), *The New Adventures of Robin Hood* (television series), 13 January 1997–13 December 1998, TNT.

Online sources

Abernethy, S. (13 November 2013), Eleanor, 'Queen of France and England and Duchess of Aquitaine', *Medievalists.net*. Available from: http://www.medievalists. net/2013/11/13/eleanor-queen-of-france-and-england-and-duchess-of-aquitaine [25 November 2013].

Aliénor (n.d.), Autoroute de Gascogne. Available from: http://www.a65-alienor.com/ cms [20 December 2012].

Aliénor d'Aquitaine (2006), Conseil régional d'Aquitaine, programme BNSA. Available from: http://www.alienor-aquitaine.org [20 December 2012].

Aliénor d'Aquitaine ou a l'entrada del tems clar (2009), Gargamela Théâtre. Available from: http://s295695177.onlinehome.fr/gargamela/fiche.php?id=46 [2 August 2010].

'Aliénor Exagère' (n.d.), Group Anamorphose. Available from: http://groupe-anamorphose.com/anam/-Alienor-exagere [5 August 2010].

Alison Weir – the Official Site of the Author (n.d.). Available from: http://alisonweir.org. uk/index.asp [26 December 2012].

Amazon.co.uk (n.d.). Available from: www.amazon.co.uk [26 December 2012].

Amazon.com (n.d.). Available from: www.amazon.com [26 December 2012].

Amazon.fr (n.d.). Available from: www.amazon.fr [26 December 2012].

Amendola, Gloria (2013), 'Eleanor of Aquitaine … and the Troubadour Dream', Return of the Troubadour. Available from: http://www.returnofthetroubadour.com/eleanor. html [15 October 2013].

Ashliman, D. L. 1998–2013, 'Snow-White and other tales of Aarne-Thompson-Uther type 709'. Available from: http://www.pitt.edu/~dash/type0709.html [26 December 2013].

BD Les Reines de sang (n.d.), Éditions Delcourt. Available from: http://www. editions-delcourt.fr/catalogue/bd/les_reines_de_sang_alienor_la_legende_noire_1 [12 December 2012].

Baldit, E. (4 April 2012). 'Toulouse : les Occitans ne veulent pas des Identitaires'. *Carré d'info*. Available from: http://carredinfo.fr/toulouse-les-occitans-ne-veulent-pas-des-identitaires-8997 [15 December 2012].

Chadwick, E. (2013), '*The Summer Queen* behind the scenes 3: On Eleanor of Aquitaine's Appearance', Elizabeth Chadwick: Living the History, 5 June 2013. Available from: http://livingthehistoryelizabethchadwick.blogspot.com/2013/06/the-summer-queen-behind-scenes-3-on.html [15 October 2013].

'Claude, Palamède, Louis Macheco de Premaux (1773–1848)', (n.d.), Assemblée Nationale. Available from: http://www.assemblee-nationale.fr/sycomore/fiche. asp?num_dept=13722 [30 December 2012].

Darrioumerle, O. (n.d.), 'Autoroute A 65: les mauvais résultats du concessionnaire inquiètent', *Aqui!* Available from: http://www.aqui.fr/economies/les-mauvais-resultats-d-alienor-concessionnaire-de-l-a65-inquietent,7535.html [20 December 2012].

Ebert, Roger. (1968), 'The Lion in Winter', *Chicago Sun-Times*, originally published 4 November 1968. Available from: http://rogerebert.suntimes.com/apps/pbcs.dll/ article?AID=/19681104/REVIEWS/811040301/102 [5 January 2013].

'EDépôt 92 2II9 – Jean Besly (1572–1644), le premier historien du Poitou', Les Archives de la Vendée. Available from: http://recherche-archives.vendee.fr/archives/fonds/ FRAD085_Edepot922ii9/view:all [5 December 2012].

La Bataille de Castillon. (n.d.) Available from: http://www.batailledecastillon.com/ Bataille_de_Castillon/animations.htm [20 December 2012].

Forrester, J. (2010), 'The lying art of historical fiction'. *The Guardian*, 6 August 2010. Available from: http://www.guardian.co.uk/books/booksblog/2010/aug/06/lying-historical-fiction [28 December 2012].

'Franz Xaver Winterhalter: Works 1836–1840' (2014), The Winterhalter Catalogue, January 2014. Available from: http://franzxaverwinterhalter.wordpress.com/franz-xaver-winterhalter-works-1836-1840 [1 January 2014].

Fricker, K. (2011), *Variety*, 17 November 2011. Available from: http://www.variety.com/ review/VE1117946611 [10 January 2013].

García, A. (n.d.), 'Mireille Calmel arrasa con el relato de los amores de Leonor de Aquitania', original source unknown, reproduced on Mireille Calmel official website. Available from: http://www.mireillecalmel.com/index.php?option=com_content and view=article and id=3%3Ale-lit-dalienor and catid=2%3Abibliographie and Itemid=4 and limitstart=1 [10 January 2013].

Garrouty, G. (21 April 2008), 'Démographie: les Anglais envahissent l'Aquitaine d'Aliénor'. *Aqui!* Available from: http://www.aqui.fr/societes/demographie-les-anglais-envahissent-l-aquitaine-d-alienor,603.html [15 December 2012].

Gillian (2013), 'The Sinister March of the Headless Women', Harlots, Harpies and Harridans, 24 February 2012. Available from: http://harlotsharpiesharridans.com/blog/2012/02/24/sinister-march-headless-women [1 October 2013].

'Jocelyne Godard' (n.d.), Éditions le Semaphore. Available from: http://www.lesemaphore.fr/biblio_histo.html [1 January 2013].

Hagopian, Kevin (n.d.), 'Film Notes: The Lion in Winter', *New York State Writers' Institute*, State University of New York – Albany. Available from: http://www.albany.edu/writers-inst/webpages4/filmnotes/fnf03n10.html [5 January 2013].

Hu, J. (2012), 'Something in The Act of Becoming: on Hilary Mantel's "Bring Up the Bodies" ', *Los Angeles Review of Books*, 11 August 2012. Available from: http://lareviewofbooks.org/article.php?id=833 [30 December 2012].

'Interviews' (n.d.), Jocelyne Godard official website. Available from: http://www.jocelynegodard.com/pages/interview.htm [30 December 2012].

Lambert, B. (1993), 'Eleanor Hibbert, Novelist Known as Victoria Holt and Jean Plaidy', obituary, *New York Times*, 21 January 1993. Available from: http://www.nytimes.com/1993/01/21/books/eleanor-hibbert-novelist-known-as-victoria-holt-and-jean-plaidy.html [2 January 2013].

Leveen, L. (2012), 'The Paradox of Pluck: How Did Historical Fiction Become the New Feminist History?', *Los Angeles Review of Books*, 12 September 2012. Available from: http://lareviewofbooks.org/article.php?id=964 [30 December 2012].

'Le Lit d'Aliénor' (n.d.), Mireille Calmel official website. Available from: http://www.mireillecalmel.com/index.php?option=com_content and view=article and id=3:le-lit-dalienor and catid=2:bibliographie and Itemid=4 [20 June 2012].

La Ligue du Midi (2012a), 'En souvenir d'Aliénor d'Aquitaine!', *facebook*, 28 March 2012. Available from: http://facebook.com/notes/la-ligue-du-midi/a-lyon-%C3%A0-la-manifestation-pour-les-libert%C3%A9s/201631503211387 [20 December 2012].

La Ligue du Midi (2012b), 'Sans commentaire...', *facebook*, 28 September 2012, Available from: https://www.facebook.com/photo.php?fbid=441580769216458 [20 December 2012]

Loge Maçonnique Aliénor d'Aquitaine. Available from: http://www.alienor-pertuis.fr/categorie-11683682.html [30 July 2012].

Lowry, B. (2004), 'The Lion in Winter'. Review, *Variety*, 16 May 2004. Available from: http://www.variety.com/review/VE1117923841/?refCatId=32 [10 January 2013].

Massie, A. (2012), 'After Hilary Mantel's second Booker triumph, will historical fiction finally get the respect it deserves?'. *The Telegraph*, 17 October 2012. Available from: http://blogs.telegraph.co.uk/culture/allanmassie/100066893/after-hilary-mantels-second-booker-triumph-will-historical-fiction-finally-get-the-respect-it-deserves [1 January 2013].

'Member Directory' (2013), Historical Novel Society. Available from: http://historicalnovelsociety.org/directory [10 October 2013].

Meslow, S. (2013), 'Interview: *The White Queen* author Philippa Gregory'. *The Week*, 9 August 2013. Available from: http://theweek.com/article/index/248099/interview-the-white-queen-writer-philippa-gregory [1 December 2013].

Penman, S. K. (n.d.a) '*Devil's Brood*: A Reader's Guide, Sharon Kay Penman official website. Available from: http://sharonkaypenman.com/pdfs/devils_brood_rg.pdf [31 December 2012].

———. (n.d.b), 'Lionheart Bibliography', Sharon Kay Penman official website. Available from: http://sharonkaypenman.com/lionheart_bibliography.htm [31 December 2012].

Philpott, Matt. 'A Novel Approaches Prelude (2): Theories of Historical Fiction', *IHR Digital*, 4 November 2011. http://ihr-history.blogspot.com/2011/11/novel-approaches-prelude-2-theories-of.html?q=philpott.

Review of *Duchess of Aquitaine: A Novel of Eleanor* (13 June 2007), Amazon.com. Available from: http://www.amazon.com/Duchess-Aquitaine-Eleanor-Margaret-Ball/dp/0312205333 [1 October 2012].

Schoenberg N. (2008), 'Off with their Heads! A Cover Art Mystery Stalks the Book World', *Chicago Tribune*, 12 March 2008. Available from: http://articles.chicagotribune.com/2008-03-12/features/0803100314_1_jane-boleyn-headless-book-choices. [1 October 2013].

Sutherland, E. (2010), 'The History and Worth of the Historical Novel': Review of Jerome de Groot, *The Historical Novel. TEXT Journal*, 14. Available from: http://www.textjournal.com.au/april10/sutherland_rev.htm [23 December 2012].

The Devil's Crown (1978) (n.d.), Zoe Wanamaker official website. Available from: http://www.zoewanamaker.com/tv.php?name=The_Devil's_Crown [10 January 2013].

The Eleanor of Aquitaine Tour (2011) (n.d.), Sharon Kay Penman official website. Available from: http://sharonkaypenman.com/blog/?page_id=270 [31 December 2012].

'The Family Tree of Guillaume de Tournemire', (n.d.), geneanet.org. Available from: http://gw.geneanet.org/pierfit?lang=en and p=claude+palamede+louis and n=de+macheco [30 December 2012].

'The Winterhalter Catalog', http://franzxaverwinterhalter.wordpress.com/franz-xaver-winterhalter-works-1836-1840/.

Tod, M. (2012), 'From the World of Historical Fiction – Readers Share their Perspectives', April 2012. Available from: http://awriterofhistory.files.wordpress.com/2012/04/hf-readers-share-their-experiences-1.pdf [30 December 2012].

'University of Rochester History: Chapter 13', (n.d.), The University of Rochester. Available from: http://www.lib.rochester.edu/index.cfm?PAGE=2319 [31 March 2009].

Van Eyck, L. (2013), 'Les couvertures historiques de Jef de Wulf', 12 May 2013. Available from: http://lenaweb.voila.net/Brantonne.htm [1 October 2013].

Wilmore, A. (2013), '*The White Queen* Writer Emma Frost on Sex, Historical Accuracy and Making 'The Real *Game of Thrones*'. *Indiewire*, 9 August 2013. Available from: http://www.indiewire.com/article/television/emma-frost-interview-the-white-queen [1 December 2013].

Music recordings

Sinfonye (1993), *The Court of Love: Music from the Time of Eleanor of Aquitaine (CD)*. London: Hyperion Records.

Index

Note: Locators followed by the letter 'n' refer to notes.

29666311R00137

Printed in Poland
by Amazon Fulfillment
Poland Sp. z o.o., Wrocław